Getting Started in Woodturning

The American Association of Woodturners Official Guide
Getting Started in Woodturning
18 Practical Projects & Expert Advice on Safety, Tools & Techniques

Selected readings from *American Woodturner*,
Journal of the American Association of Woodturners

Edited by John Kelsey
Designed by Maura J. Zimmer

© 2014 American Association of Woodturners
222 Landmark Center, 75 5th Street W, St. Paul, MN 55102-7704
www.woodturner.org

ISBN: 978-1-940611-09-9

Library of Congress Control Number: 2014943450

Printed in the United States
Second Printing: October 2017

To learn more about Spring House Press books, or to find a retailer near you, email *info@springhousepress.com* or visit us at *www.springhousepress.com*.

Getting Started in Woodturning

18 Practical Projects & Expert Advice on Safety, Tools & Techniques

Selected readings from *American Woodturner*,
journal of the American Association of Woodturners

SPRING HOUSE PRESS

Contents

Section 3: Techniques

Section 4: Practical Projects

Introduction

If you are reading this book, you have made the decision to get started in woodturning. You won't be disappointed: woodturning is a fun, engaging, and tremendously rewarding hobby that will last a lifetime. This collection from *American Woodturner* magazine will help you get off to a great start with the best safety practices, tool knowledge, fundamental techniques, and skill-building projects available. There's a lot of detailed, practical advice in this book, covering most of the problems, challenges, and questions that all beginners encounter. Alongside all this practical, skill-building information, you'll discover two additional currents running through *Getting Started in Woodturning*. First is the infectious enthusiasm and pleasure that woodturners take from their craft, which shines through every one of these articles and stories. Second is the shared understanding that none of this information would be available without the fellowship and open exchange fostered by the American Association of Woodturners. In fact, you'll find the best advice in this book right here: *join your local AAW chapter*. The many members of this respected, national association are willing to help beginners like you learn how to turn. Go find a chapter today. Visit www.woodturners.org.

Section 1: Getting Started

All glory comes from daring to begin. —Eugene Ware

The joy of woodturning is discovering and developing your own woodturning style while crafting something with your own hands. But, when it comes to safety, equipment set-up, and sharpening, there's no reason to reinvent the wheel. Others before you have learned valuable lessons the hard way so why repeat them? While this entire book is about *Getting Started*, this section covers the initial, and most critical, steps of your journey. In short, it covers some of the boring stuff you'd prefer to skip in your enthusiasm to press the "on" button and make chips fly. This is the time to heed the lessons of your fellow woodturners and learn the fundamentals of keeping yourself safe and your tools sharp. You'll be glad you did.

Advice for Beginning Woodturners

Get started with helpful hindsight from a thirty-year pro

Every advanced woodturner was once a beginner. Some of us were lucky enough to enjoy lessons or had access to books and DVDs on woodturning topics. For many turners, however, woodturning is a self-taught endeavor. Based on my thirty years as a woodturner, I offer a list of tips and suggestions that I wish I had known when first starting to turn wood.

- **Good lighting is key to producing good work.** Purchase quality task lights and utilize full-spectrum (sunlight) fluorescent bulbs in overhead lighting. Sunlight bulbs help to distinguish colors and the surface condition of turned wood better.
- **Dust is your enemy.** It is simply bad for your health. Invest in a good dust collector and dust mask. *Wear* your dust mask.
- **Sharp tools are a must.** Purchase a grinding system to quickly touch up and sharpen tools. Keep your tools sharp; you have to sharpen them more often than you think is necessary. Some woods have high silica content and will dull tools in seconds. Clean cuts on wood will not happen with dull tools. Using dull tools results in more sanding. Purchase an 8" (20cm) -diameter, slow-speed grinder and a good-quality wheel, appropriate for use with turning tools. A fine oilstone and a 600-grit diamond slip are important for honing.

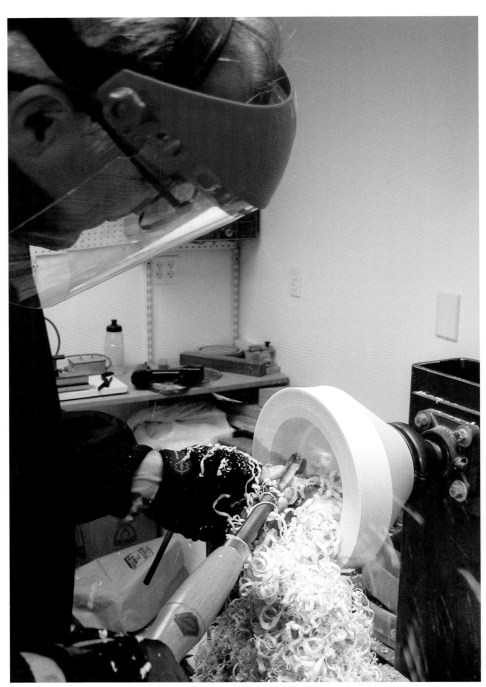

Jim Echter turns a bowl in his shop.

AW 25:3, p27

Getting Started in Woodturning

- **Learn to hone.** You don't have to hone all your woodturning tools, but some, like the skew, just work better when honed. Honing, once learned, is usually quicker than sharpening and removes less of that expensive tool steel. Many excellent DVDs are available on sharpening and honing—get one!
- **Cut sheets of abrasive paper into small pieces, use them once or twice and throw them out.** This provides 100% utilization of each full sheet. Also, using fresh sandpaper gives a better surface finish.
- **Cyanoacrylate (CA) glue is a woodturner's duct tape.** It can be used for gluing wet or dry turning blanks to waste blocks, repairing cracks, attaching HSS tool bits into handles, and for gluing a minor cut closed to stop the bleeding. Purchase quality glue, spray and aerosol accelerators, and a bottle of debonder. CA doesn't stick to wax paper, so having a roll of it to cover workbenches is a good idea. The fumes from CA, as it goes through its chemical reaction for curing, are extremely dangerous. Use an exhaust fan so that you do not inhale them.
- **Smooth your toolrests and soften the sharp edges from new turning tools.** If a toolrest

CA glue is a woodturner's duct tape. Use it for repairing cracks, attaching HSS tool bits to handles, and gluing wet (or dry) turning blanks to waste blocks.

is rusted, pitted, scratched, and/or nicked, tools cannot slide effortlessly across it. File the surface smooth, run some 600-grit sandpaper across it, and wax it. Remove the sharp corners and edges on turning chisels so they don't mess up the toolrests.
- **Remember your ABCs.** You must *anchor* the tool to the toolrest and rub the *bevel* before you start your *cut*, especially in spindle turning.
- **The pressure on the tool is down toward the floor and onto the toolrest.** Directing pressure the right way lets the wood come to the tool edge without pushing the tool into the work. Beginners tend to push the tool into the wood instead of holding the tool to the toolrest.
- **Turn small bowls first.** Many instructional DVDs play tricks with viewers' eyes: Bowls appear much larger when in reality they are often no larger than 6" (15cm) in diameter. Make a dozen little bowls to learn the basics before attempting something big.

- **It is okay to adjust the toolrest, but turn the lathe off first.** The toolrest provides the mechanical leverage needed for tool control. An expert turner will tweak the height of the toolrest as little as 1/16" (2mm) to provide better cuts. If you switch from a ⅝" (16mm) to a ⅜" (10mm) bowl gouge, adjust the height of the toolrest.
- **Round over the tips of calipers.** Calipers can be purchased inexpensively at garage sales and flea markets; however, they usually have been used for metal working so they have pointed or square tips. These tips will catch on the wood and cause the caliper to be thrown across the shop.
- **Don't invest in fancy, high-end, cryogenically cooled, powder-metal chisels.** They will not make you a better turner. Purchase HSS chisels at first. Use these tools to practice sharpening—why learn with expensive tools?

Why not tape your pocket closed?

Taping your pocket closed prevents it from filling up with shavings. This is true for pant pockets, too.

Use a file to smooth the nicks out of your toolrest. Sand the surface lightly and apply wax. Do this routinely and your turning will improve.

Round over the tips of calipers to avoid catches when measuring wood while it is spinning on the lathe.

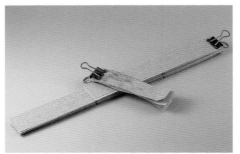

Cut sheets of abrasive paper into small pieces or strips. Use them once or twice and throw them away.

If your lathe is too short, raise its height using sturdy riser blocks. Buy a large dustpan and invest in a good-quality antifatigue mat.

Wear safety gear: respirator, ear protection, and eye protection. When turning large items, a faceshield is recommended. Wear a dust mask whenever you are in your shop and make use of a dust collector as well.

- **Join your local chapter of the AAW.** There are more than 350 chapters in the AAW, and many clubs hold sessions for beginners.
- **Take private lessons.** Two hours with an instructor will save you weeks of frustration. Or, spend a week at one of the many woodturning schools. Woodturning is fun! The sooner you learn the basics, the sooner the fun starts.
- **Learn to turn a spindle first.** I realize that beginners want to turn bowls; however, once you learn how to turn spindles, you will better understand how wood likes to be cut and will master tool usage and control. Mastering spindle turning makes transitioning to turning bowls much easier. A spindle turner can learn to turn bowls much quicker than a bowl turner can learn how to turn spindles.
- **Family and friends only need so many bowls.** Spindle turning provides many more opportunities to create useful items.
- **Find some FOG (found-on-ground) wood.** Small-diameter FOG branches are ideal for learning spindle turning. Be on the lookout for freshly trimmed trees. Green wood is a joy to practice with because it is less expensive and easy to cut.
- **Many woods are toxic.** Learn about wood toxicity and listen to your body. If you start to itch, wheeze, or your heart starts to race, stop turning that piece of rosewood, cedar, or cocobolo. Read about wood toxicity on the AAW website (woodturner.org).

- **Buy several pair of reader safety glasses.** My last pair cost $8 and I love them.
- **There really is something called the Dance of the Woodturner.** Move your body and your feet in order to effectively move your tools on the toolrest.
- **Tape your pockets closed using blue painter's tape.** It is easier than trying to remove all the chips and sawdust from inside a pocket.
- **The tannins in many woods, such as oak, react with the acids and oils in hands to turn them black.** Wash with a little lemon juice. The black will disappear.
- **Buy a big dustpan.** A big dustpan makes cleanup go faster.
- **Raise or lower the height of your lathe to achieve the correct height.** If the height is too low, your back will suffer. Here's how to measure for the correct height: Stand straight up and bend your arm so it is 90° to the floor. Measure the distance from the floor to your elbow. This is the minimum height the lathe spindle needs to be from the floor. For bowl turners, it can be 1"–2" (25mm–50mm) higher. Add risers to the lathe or build a riser to stand on to achieve the correct height. While you are at it, purchase antifatigue mats to stand on.
- **Take the time to warm up.** Begin by making a few practice cuts in scrap wood, especially if turning is a hobby and you took the summer off to play golf.
- **Stretch.** Many turners get into the "turning zone" when they are working, hovering over the lathe for long periods of time. Stop often, step away from the lathe, and stretch. Reach for the ceiling, bend over and touch the floor, twist at the waist, and/or hang from the ceiling to relax tense muscles.

- **Don't forget ear protection.** With lathes spinning, power sanders and dust collectors running, and air compressors kicking on, hearing protection is a must.
- **Listen for chainsaws in your neighborhood.** That sound means someone is trimming or removing a tree. Often it is an ornamental tree, which can yield unusual wood. Introduce yourself and ask for a couple of cutoffs. Remember to make something for the person as a thank-you.
- **The lathe is the inexpensive part of woodturning; accessories are expensive.** When the cost of chisels, chucks, calipers, a bandsaw, lighting, dust collectors, sharpening systems, air compressors, sanding systems, and finishes are factored in, the investment is significant. Select the spindle size of your first lathe so that chucks can be used on future lathes.

Turn a lot of small bowls before progressing to larger ones. The AAW has many DVDs available on turning techniques, as well as project books for beginners.

Woodturning is fun and addictive when you master the basics. I hope these tips help beginners avoid a few pitfalls. To add your tips to this list, email me! I will update the list on the AAW website to share with others.

***Jim Echter**, the founding President of the Finger Lakes Woodturners Association based in Rochester, NY, teaches, writes, and specializes in spindle work. Visit Jim at www.truecreations.biz.*

Join your local AAW chapter. Many members are willing to help beginners learn how to turn.

Shopping for Your First Lathe

Ask the right questions before you buy

Buying a lathe—especially if it's your first—can be a confusing and difficult task. However, if you take the time to answer a few questions, you'll have a much better understanding of your needs. And when you have a good focus on the type and scale of projects you want to turn, your research will narrow down the field of lathes to a manageable number of choices.

Five questions, many possible answers

Before rushing to the lathe manufacturers' websites, begin your search by answering five questions:

1. What types of things do I enjoy turning? For example, you may enjoy making bowls, hollow forms, spindles, gift items, or other projects.
2. What is the size of the pieces I'll be turning? Be specific in both diameter and length.
3. How much space will I dedicate to this machine? Don't forget to also allocate space for storage of tools and lathe accessories.
4. Will I need to move the lathe often?
5. What is my budget?

The first two questions are usually the hardest to answer, especially if you're a novice turner. If you've just caught the turning bug (or plan to become infected), it can be difficult to know what type and size pieces you will be turning now and in the future. However, the answers to these two questions will heavily influence your decision-making on the next three questions.

I encourage prospective lathe buyers to reflect on these first questions and not answer hastily. Start by considering why you became interested in turning. For example, did you admire some bowls or hollow forms at the art gallery, or do you want to make components for a rocking chair? Are you thinking of making Christmas gifts for friends and family this year? Begin a project wish list, and also note the size of finished items.

Expand your search for prospective turning ideas by going to the library, surfing the Internet, and studying the instant gallery of the works of fellow members at the next meeting of your woodturning chapter. Again, take notes about items you might like to make one day, but also identify projects that don't spark your interest. By writing down likes and dislikes (pluses and minuses), you'll establish the boundaries of your personal woodturning interests.

One size doesn't fit all

Most experienced turners agree that there is no perfect lathe. Every machine is designed to perform specific tasks, and that gives it a range of both strengths and weaknesses. In some ways, choosing a lathe is similar to shopping for a vehicle: A compact car may offer good mileage, but it won't tow a boat.

In a similar way, some lathes offer an incredibly low price while others offer top-of-the-line quality. (Bear in mind that precision machining and quality control significantly influence price.) You can easily move many small lathes, but these tools typically lack the ability to handle large or heavy

Lathe Decision-Making Chart

As you evaluate each lathe, assign it a number from 1 to 5 in each category, with a larger number reflecting a closer match with your needs.

Lathe Make/Model	Will handle projects that interest me	Has swing and length to meet my needs	Fits into available shop space	Ease of moving (if required)	Price	Total score

Illustrations: Roxanne LeMoine

AW 23:4, p52

Getting Started in Woodturning

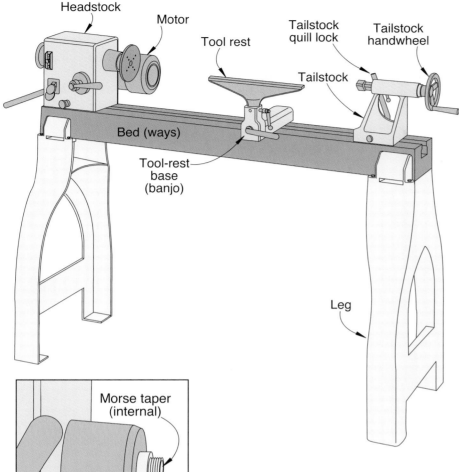

Headstock

Motor

Tool rest

Tailstock quill lock

Tailstock handwheel

Tailstock

Bed (ways)

Tool-rest base (banjo)

Leg

Morse taper (internal)

Spindle

pieces. Some lathes are purpose-designed for efficient bowl turning while others are intended for furniture parts.

What lathes are available?

Now you're ready to begin matching your needs to the lathes available in the marketplace. As you research various lathes, ask yourself how each tool's specifications meet your needs. You could even give each prospective lathe a score from 1 to 5 in each category to create an objective framework for evaluating potential lathes. See the Lathe Decision-Making Chart *opposite*.

Although the manufacturers' specifications are valuable information, you should be aware that the numbers sometimes require a reality check. For example, a lathe may physically have the capacity to hold a 20"-diameter bowl blank but lack sufficient power to move it or the mass to dampen vibrations from a large unbalanced piece of wood. If possible, check out the lathe in person at a local dealer, or discuss its capabilities with fellow chapter members.

Don't be overly influenced by which lathe got the top review in the latest publication or has a celebrity endorsement. After all, the celebrity or magazine writer won't be coming to your shop to do the turning for you. Instead, look for an opportunity to turn at the models that you're considering. Turning at a machine,

even for just a few minutes, may reveal valuable information that's impossible to get by reading or conversation. Think of it as test-driving a car: You want to make sure you and the lathe are a good fit for each other.

Learn lathe jargon

The equipment specific to each art or trade has its own specialized vocabulary, so be sure that you understand the terminology. In some cases, a single term can include several technologies, and you'll need to get further details to truly understand what the manufacturer means.Variable speed is a case in point.

Many wood lathes are listed with a variable-speed feature, yet there are several methods that manufacturers use. The least expensive and easiest method is via a **Reeve's drive**. This system uses two V-shaped pulleys and a single belt to transfer power from the motor to the spindle. A lever adjusts the width of the pulley on the spindle. (The width of the pulley on the motor is then adjusted with a spring.) When you move a lever on the headstock, the spindle pulley is either spread apart or pushed together. The belt, which travels up and down on this pulley, then interacts with the motor pulley and causes it to move inversely (widening a spindle pulley causes the motor pulley to contract).

Although this method does produce numerous speeds without the need to stop the lathe, it does have drawbacks.

First, this type of drive typically won't produce speeds below 400 rpm. Second, the lathe must be rotating to adjust the speed, and that creates a possible safety issue. Third, the system's reliance on a loose belt and a number of moving parts leads to a loss in torque as well as potential maintenance situations.

More sage advice

Michael Mocho: Become familiar with rpm

Proper rpm is a major factor in getting a good quality surface directly from the tool. The smaller the diameter, the faster it should spin. Although variable speed isn't essential, it sure makes turning more efficient.

A good range of speed should be between 500 (or slower) and 2,500 rpm, though smaller work sometimes requires up to 3,200 rpm.

Avoid the older gap-bed models. Although this design appears to offer more capacity, it really doesn't once you figure on using a faceplate or chuck. It makes it tough to get the tool rest into solid position when you are working up close to the spindle in some situations.

I also believe that an outboard handwheel is essential, and headstock spindles should also have a through-hole for the option of using vacuum chucks.

A faceplate or chuck screwed on should tighten against the spindle shoulder, with provision of tightening the grub screws onto the spindle notch (rather than the spindle threads).

The ability to reverse the rotation of the lathe is useful for some sanding operations, especially when turning bowls and when turning softer woods.

If you are turning a lot of wet wood, there are a few lathes now available with stainless-steel ways (the bed), though keeping the ways free of rust and grit is always important on any lathe.

Before you buy, make sure the tailstock doesn't slip when a workpiece is pressed between centers.

Bonnie Klein: You really need two lathes

You wouldn't buy a car without taking it on a test-drive, right? Before you buy a lathe, find someone who owns the lathe you're interested in and ask if you can turn on it. Most turners would be more than happy to invite you over to their shop.

I tell turners they need two lathes—a mini lathe and a full-size lathe. I just wish there was a really good full-size lathe on the market for about $2,000!

Mobility makes the mini lathe ideal to take to demonstrations, to take on vacation, and for small projects (up to 10" diameter) in your shop. If you are shopping for a mini lathe, put your money into a variable-speed model.

Without variable speed, you put too much load on the bearings and they get too hot, which reduces the lifetime of this important part.

There are upgrades you can make to a mini lathe. For example, Steve Sinner (ssinner@mchsi.com) makes a nice 6" machined tool rest (right; about $45). You will notice the difference!

Attach a mount on the top of the headstock for a Stay-Put Work Lamp (Craft Supplies USA; woodturnerscatalog.com). Jet makes a mini lathe stand with an accessory kit of locking casters.

Alan Lacer: Think used

1. Don't be afraid of an older lathe. Two of my favorite lathes in the shop were made pre-1940, with one of these made between 1910 and 1920. Other than bearings and inside tapers, not much can wear out if the lathe was not abused. Many items for the lathe can be found premade or custom made, such as faceplates, chuck inserts, belts, tool rests, tool-rest bases, drive centers, live centers, and the like. In addition to AAW chapter and newspaper classified ads, don't forget to search Internet sites including exfactorymachinery.com, redmond-machinery.com, Craigslist.com, and ebay.com.

In major cities, make inquiries at used machinery dealers as well as new dealers that take trade-ins or buy used machinery at auctions (especially from school settings).

2. Avoid lathes that have been abused and show any cracked castings for the bed or tailstock, severely damaged spindle threads, or a bent headstock spindle. The headstock spindle generally has the most machining of any lathe part, so replacing it can be expensive (this is not to be avoided, but be aware of the potential high costs).

3. The electrics can often be replaced, repaired, or upgraded. In the past, many who were searching for a lathe would avoid three-phase machines. This is no longer the case, as these can often be upgraded to function like most of the top-end machines today with a variable- speed

controller/inverter. Another option is to use a phase converter (dynamic versus static), available from Enco (use-enco.com). Dealers Industrial Equipment (dealerselectric.com) is a source for parts to upgrade to a variable-speed system with motor and controller or to purchase a controller/inverter. Most motors and switches can be repaired or replaced, sometimes with a little more horsepower if you intend to do bowl and vessel work. Be sure to replace the motor with a totally enclosed model.

4. Look for a machine that uses Morse tapers rather than some other system. I have had a machinist convert a Roberts taper to a Morse taper on one older machine, but most turners will want to stay with Morse tapers. Size is not so critical as adapters are inexpensive and readily available through companies like MSC (mscdirect.com). I suggest taking one of your Morse taper centers with you to make sure it seats firmly into both the headstock and tailstock sides.

5. As many of the older standard lathes had only a 12"-diameter capacity, some turners have found it easy to block up the headstock and tailstock with metal or even wood blocks to achieve more capacity. My advice is to befriend a machinist to accurately mill some aluminum blocks to achieve this increase in capacity. Depending on the lathe, you will probably need to extend the belt length and replace the tool-rest base to come out farther and go higher. Oneway (oneway.ca) and others sell replacement tool-rest bases.

6. Bearings do wear out and, depending on the quality and how well shielded from dust, may need replacing. On most lathes these are not that difficult to remove. A simple test is to turn a short cup shape from a piece of hard material like maple, mounted on a faceplate or quality scroll chuck. First turn a cylinder, then hollow to about 1", thinning the walls to around 1/8" or less thick: Is there a noticeable "thick-and-thin" appearance, or even breaking through in spots? This can be a sign of worn bearings or, the worst case, a bent spindle. Also feel the bearing smoothness when turning the spindle by hand as well as note any sound coming from the headstock.

7. If indexing is one of your intended uses, inspect the indexing wheel if possible. On some lathes, the indexing wheel is notoriously stripped of a number of holes (probably by starting the lathe with the pin locked or using it as a spindle lock to remove chucks). Sometimes these are replaceable, but you might have to resort to a homemade version that usually mounts on the outboard side of the lathe.

Reeve's Drive

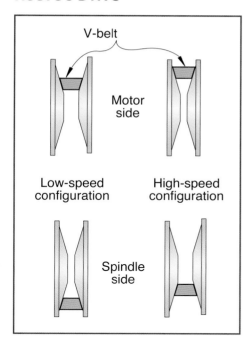

V-belt

Motor side

Low-speed configuration

High-speed configuration

Spindle side

DC variable speed combines a DC motor with a controller. The system converts your household AC power into DC power, and then adjusts the speed by varying the voltage into the motor. The operator uses a dial to easily control the speed. This type of drive can be unreliable because it may not produce the necessary torque required for turning wood.

The third system, **AC variable speed**, uses an inverter and a 3-phase motor. The inverter converts your household AC single-phase power into 3-phase power, then adjusts the motor's speed by varying the frequency delivered to the motor. This system, also dial-controlled, adjusts easily. AC variable speed can cover a wide range: from 0 to more than 3,000 rpm. (See Michael Mocho's comments.) When the drive involves only a few pulleys, this system delivers exceptional torque. Unfortunately, this convenience and capability come at a hefty price.

Additional buying points

Other considerations include what accessories are available for the lathe. Bed extensions easily increase the length capacity of small lathes and are relatively inexpensive compared to a lathe with a long one-piece bed.

The Morse taper size and spindle thread deserve consideration. The #2 Morse taper is the most common one used at woodturning lathes, and numerous accessories are available in this size. Additionally, check the headstock's threads. Common thread patterns are 1" × 8, 1¼" × 8, and M33 × 3.5. Manufacturers offer a wide variety of chucks, faceplates, and other gadgets for these spindles.

The bottom line

For most turners, price can often be the deciding factor in determining which lathe to purchase. But giving too much consideration to price can be a dicey proposition. An inexpensive lathe that meets your needs can be a wise choice. But sacrificing satisfaction to save a few dollars is no bargain. On the other hand, spending more money than necessary won't guarantee happiness. Consider the lathe as an investment toward achieving results, and you'll help maintain a good perspective.

If you are just beginning and aren't sure what your needs will be in the future, you may want to consider one of the numerous mini lathes on the market. Most of these lathes can handle pieces 10" to 12" in diameter and 12" to 48" between centers. Choosing a starter lathe like this may compromise the size of pieces you can turn, but with common spindle sizes and Morse tapers, you can purchase accessories that will fit an upgraded lathe purchased later. (See Bonnie Klein's comments.)

If an occasional project requires the use of a larger lathe, your local turning chapter can be a valuable resource. Many chapters own lathes that are available to members at minimal or no cost. There also may be chapter members who are willing to offer the use of their larger lathe.

Don't rule out the used tool market. (See Alan Lacer's comments.) You may find a high-quality lathe just waiting for a new home. Although some of these lathes may be in need of a major repair, others may require only minor maintenance before they're ready to produce fresh shavings.

So whether you decide to purchase a top-of-the-line, full-sized, fully accessorized lathe or a bargain-basement (or even garage sale) treasure, do your research and make sure it will meet your needs. Don't be concerned with the manufacturer's selling points. Instead, ask yourself whether you will need each of its features and if they are worth their cost to you.

*A resident of Des Moines, IA, **Brian Simmons** is a writer, teacher, and has demonstrated at local and National AAW Symposiums.*

Are You Wearing the Right Faceshield?

Don't skimp on this critical piece of equipment

For woodturners, faceshields are important safety equipment, so much so the AAW requires demonstrators to wear one while demonstrating at the annual symposium. That is not the case everywhere. Last November, I was invited to do a demonstration at the Taiwan Association of Woodturners in Taipei, one of the newest AAW chapters. I was not able to bring a faceshield, and I requested one. I was disturbed when they handed me the "faceshield." Similar to the one in Photo 1, it had a thin clear plastic shield reinforced with an aluminum rim—not the adequate protection I was used to. Fortunately, though, I was turning a goblet out of 2"- (5cm-) square wood and the flying debris would probably not cause the shield to fail. I thought this was a good opportunity to educate the audience, primarily consisting of new turners. It also made me wonder how many AAW members were cognizant of various types of faceshields.

Different types of shields

There are many different types of faceshields designed for various purposes. All turners probably know not to use a welder's faceshield or the type a dental hygienist wears, but do you know what kind of faceshield is good for your protection while turning? The type I used in Taiwan is a splash shield designed for chemical (liquid) splashes. Its thin plastic shield is not strong enough to protect, even from medium-sized flying wood objects. The aluminum rim merely supports the flimsy plastic to help hold its shape. The metal rim

actually presents a greater hazard because if the plastic is shattered, or simply deflected by a flying object, the aluminum can be forced into your face, which is exactly what happened to a couple of members of our club a number of years ago—the aluminum ended up in their cheeks causing severe lacerations and a trip to the emergency room. Even so, some stores that cater to woodturners and woodworkers carry this type of faceshield. If I had not known about the injuries suffered by my fellow turners, I might have bought one.

Correct faceshield

The correct type of faceshield woodturners should wear is the thick polycarbonate (PC) shield without the metal rim (*Photo 2*). Testimony to that came from another member of our club who is known for turning large projects (20-plus inches [50cm] in diameter). These massive mesquite root balls have defects and bark inclusions, and at last December's meeting, he reported that a large chunk of bark inclusion flew off a mesquite turning and broke his faceshield. Fortunately he came

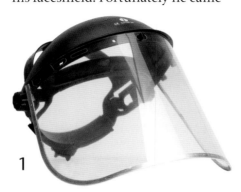

1

A splashguard-type faceshield is not suitable for woodturning protection.

through unscathed physically—he was wearing a thick polycarbonate faceshield. The faceshield was a loss, but it did its job.

These thick PC faceshields are widely available for about $15. When purchasing a faceshield, make sure it is rated Z87+ (*Photo 2, insets*) as opposed to just Z87. Although it is an improper way of labeling, sometimes you will find Z87.1 instead of Z87+. These ANSI (American National Standards Institute) ratings are primarily designed for eye protection.

Although the standards were revised in 2010, standards for faceshields did not receive substantive revision from the 2003 guidelines, which basically stipulate that lenses will be divided into two protective levels, basic impact and high impact, as dictated by test criteria. Basic-impact lenses must pass a "drop ball" test: a 1"-diameter steel ball being dropped on the lens from 50 inches (127cm). High-impact lenses must pass a "high velocity" test where ¼"s (6mm) steel balls are shot at different velocities. For faceshields, that's 300 ft/s (~205 mph, 329 km/h). Thus, the high-impact (Z87+) standard requires the faceshield to withstand more than five times the kinetic energy of the basic-impact standard (Z87) (4.41 joules vs. 0.84 joules).

Powered respirator

Instead of a simple faceshield, some turners prefer a powered air-purifying respirator (PAPR), such as the 3M Airstream (*Photo 3*) or Trend Airshield (Photo 4, Pro model shown). In addition to protection from flying debris, these PAPRs provide lung

AW 28:2, p14

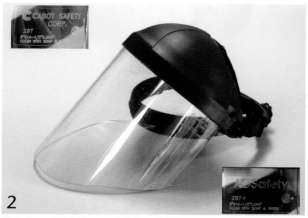

2

This faceshield has a thick polycarbonate shield. Note the impact rating in the inset images, basic impact, Z87 (upper left) and high impact, Z87+ (lower right).

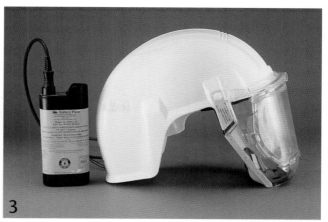

3

The 3M Airstream powered air-purifying respirator. Photo: Paul Millo

4

The Trend Pro model powered air-purifying respirator. Note the ANSI Z87.1 label, inset image.

5

Even though this faceshield is rated Z87+, it may not offer as much impact protection as one with a thicker shield.

protection by filtering out wood dust. A PAPR is my personal favorite because the filtered airstream also prevents condensation on my glasses and on the faceshield from my breath.

A word of caution: Although the Airstream and Airshield are rated high impact, the window (visor) on these faceshields is only about half as thick as the Z87+ non-PAPR faceshields (0.04" [1mm] to 0.045" [1.1mm] vs. 0.08" [2mm]). You can actually deflect the thin plastic window by applying moderate pressure with your finger. On the Airstream and the Airshield (original), this window is reinforced with a frame made of a type of plastic other than PC. The Airshield Pro has just a steel wire at the bottom for reinforcement. Knowing of possible failure of thinner shields with reinforcement, one should be leery of PAPRs.

Some faceshields, like the one shown in Photo 5, also have a thin visor mounted in a frame. Even though it has the Z87+ rating, it may not provide the same level of protection as the thick PC faceshields.

Faceshield standards caution

There are two disturbing facts about the Z87.1-2003 standard. First, it eliminated the previous requirement of a minimum thickness of 2mm (0.08") on the protective lenses. Second, in the United States, compliance with the standard is self-certified, based on test results generated by the manufacturer as part of its initial design and ongoing quality-control procedures. No independent certification is required. Therefore, although I wear a PAPR personally, I would caution their use.

This is not an exhaustive review of all faceshields. It simply points out the danger of using the wrong type and provides the basics for selecting a proper faceshield. And, while faceshields provide protection, they can be overwhelmed by a shattering explosion of a large turning. It is essential to practice the basic safety precaution of staying out of the plane of rotation. Also, when restarting the lathe with a turning that was previously chucked, always recheck it. Make sure the chuck jaws still secure the wood, or check the screws if you use a faceplate. And, always start at a lower speed when turning large, unstable wood.

Andrew Chen, founder of the Brazos Valley Turners in Texas, is a segmented turner and national demonstrator who enjoys turning all materials, including Corian.

Collect Dust at the Lathe

Learn the basics and your lungs will love you

Peter Fedrigon knows dust. For more than 20 years, he's hopscotched across the country as a consulting engineer on dust collection, air filtration, and system design.

For the 650 employees at the L. & J. G. Stickley factory, he designed a monster system with three 150-hp fans that suck wood dust from the plant and blow it into a towering filter dubbed the "baghouse."

He watches over 40-plus systems. At a Wrigley Brothers plant in Gainesville, Georgia, the system protects the lungs of 850 employees from sugar dust.

Variety? Peter has designed systems for rock crushers, tobacco, clay, and peanut shells. And of course, plenty of wood dust.

In the mid-1990s, he started Oneida Air, which his daughter and son-in-law now run.

In sprawling factories, there are rigid OSHA standards for dust levels, which could get out of compliance from poor dust collection and improperly maintained return air from bag-room filters.

Of course there are EPA standards for the air vented outdoors. And the explosive dust must meet National Fire Protection Act requirements.

"All the factors that apply to industry also apply to our home shops," Peter says. "Think about this: The EPA doesn't allow dust masks in factories—the dust collectors have to do all the work. That's the way it should be in your shop, too."

Peter can quote dust statistics until your eyeballs roll into the next ZIP code. But his bottom line message is simple: "If you like to turn, you'd better get yourself a dust collector."

Peter is just as strident about the importance of dust collection for the AAW turners as he is about his consulting jobs. When he's home, Peter relaxes at his lathe.

Members of the Central New York Woodturners are fortunate to have him as an active member. Peter estimates that he's set up or upgraded dust systems for more than 50 members. And of course, he's always eager to talk about his favorite topic—dust.

Microns and your lungs

If you're considering adding a dust collector to your shop (and you should), you could easily get lost in a sea of technical jargon. You'll find more explanations in the sidebar "Dust Terminology."

Most of the advertising material speaks about the ability to gather dust whose particle size is measured as micrometers, or microns.

Here's what you need to know about microns:

- There are 25,400 microns in an inch. The period at the end of this sentence is about 320 microns in diameter.
- It is the tiny particles which you breathe in that damage your lungs. The dust from 1 to 10 microns in diameter is the nasty stuff that is harmful to lung cells and causes respiratory problems—coughing, nosebleeds, sinus problems, emphysema, and bronchitis. That may explain why you develop a cold after you spend a lot of time sanding. The finer you sand, the finer the dust particles.

By comparison, wisps of tobacco smoke fit in the range of 0.01 to 1.0 microns. Of course, you know what damage tobacco smoke does to healthy lungs.

In your shop, you can sweep up the nuisance chips too big to enter your lungs. It's the tiny particles and sanding dust that should be your biggest concern.

I turned for four or five years and only occasionally wore a mask. Now, I have asthma from breathing wood dust. Bad situation—I pay for three days if I get even a puff of sawdust in the nose.

I recommend moving as much air as you can when you sand. Take good care of your lungs!

—David Ramsey, Phoenix-area segmented turner and retired hospital executive

AW 21:4, p56

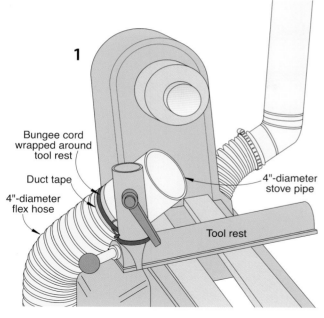

1

Bungee cord
wrapped around
tool rest

Duct tape

4"-diameter
flex hose

4"-diameter
stove pipe

Tool rest

Get after dust!

1. A method to gather dust while turning.
2. When sanding, add a second
4"-diameter hose fitted with a hood.

5 x 8" hood

6"-diameter
flex hose

2 x 2 x 4"
spacer

$1^3/_8$ x 2 x 7"
base

Tool rest

$^5/_8$" dowel slips into
lamp arm

Adjustable lamp assembly
bolted to lathe

2

Collect dust at the source

Peter has a simple solution for gathering chips, shavings, and dust when he turns: He attaches a 4"-diameter flexible duct to his tool rest with a bungee cord, as shown in **Drawing 1**. "I don't even start up my lathe without turning on the dust collector," Peter says. "This duct is never in the way while I turn. The thin flex hose lets me move the tool rest around with ease."

When it's time to sand, Peter opens a blast gate to a second 4"-diameter duct fitted with a hood, as shown in **Drawing 2**. With two ducts running, he gets 600 to 800 cfm through his 2-hp cyclone system.

"I keep the hood opening small so the air can reach out to capture the dust. I'm getting about 99.9 percent of the dust collected right at the source.

"Remember that dust is a fire and explosion hazard, too." The dust-gathering solutions *above* are typical of what he has set up for the home shops of Central New York chapter members and nearby AAW chapters (word of Peter's knowledge spreads faster than dust).

The filter factor

"Dust filtration is critical," Peter says. "If you can see dust migrate through the bags when you turn on your collector, your system needs immediate attention.

"It is important to understand the filter media and the efficiency of the media. Spun-bond polyester filter media in pleated filters is the best for your shop.

"The woven or felted polyester doesn't do as good a job because it can't hold back the high dust-loading that occurs in home shops. In addition, woven filters must be cleaned often."

When you choose filters, Peter suggests you select wide-pleated cartridges. Today's top-performing cartridges can filter 99.9 percent of the dust down to .02 micron.

A better two-bag collector

Peter has helped several chapter members upgrade a two-bag collector. Among his solutions:

- Replace the 30-micron bag (standard with many collectors) with a more efficient 1- or 5-micron bag. (The replacement bag will be larger.) American Fabric Filter (americanfabricfilter.com, 800-367-3591) provides technical support for aftermarket bags.
- Replace the top bag with a pleated canister filter, which provides at least four times the media surface over a cloth bag. For details, check with your original manufacturer. Donaldson Company (airfilterusa.com, 800-667-8563) is one online source.

A system for your shop

There's not one perfect system for every shop, but Peter's design looks something like **Drawing 4**.

Whatever choice you make for a dust collector, Peter urges you to keep it running in top form. To check his shop system's efficiency, he spent less than $5 in a U-tube manometer assembled from plastic and copper tubing and colored water. This device, shown in Drawing 3, measures the static pressure required to push air through the filter.

On his system, Peter knows that if the pressure jumps by +1.5", it's time to clean his filter. For best results, Peter recommends that you install the manometer between the fan and the filter, as shown in Drawing 4. "You can even install this on your two-bag system. Poke a hole in the flex hose right before the bags. You'll see an amazing improvement if you monitor this."

You also can buy an 8" flex U-tube manometer for about $20 (dwyer-inst.com).

Understand fan curves

Okay, this is getting a little technical. But your lungs will love you if you just stick with this.

If you've gone to the trouble of checking your systems and efficiency, you'd better at least have a pedestrian knowledge of a fan curve. When adding a manometer to check on your system, the fan curve, as shown in Drawing 5, takes on new meaning.

In Peter's shop, he knows that with 8" SP (static pressure), he's getting about 880 cfm in his shop. See how an additional 1" of static pressure (resistance from clogged filters) drops his system from 880 cfm (blue line) to down to 600 cfm (red line). Result: much less suction to grab up all that sanding dust.

You may have noticed that your shop-vacuum barrel doesn't have to be full to lose its efficiency. The same story is being repeated in shops all across the country.

Be sure you know the true capacity of the system you're considering installing. Some companies advertise a fan of 1,200 cfm or greater. Sounds impressive, right? But add your duct work, as Drawing 5 shows, and the cfm drops dramatically.

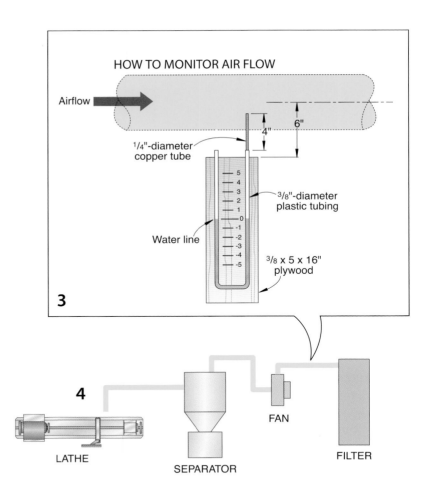

Separate grinder system

Don't forget to connect your grinder to a separate dust collection system. Because grinding involves sparks, you don't want this machine to share the same lines as your wood dust system.

Peter recommends a shop vacuum (at least 70 cfm) connected to your grinder dust port, as shown in Drawing 6.

"You can easily set up your collector so it automatically turns on every time you switch on the grinder," Peter advises. "It's real easy to switch the hose from one side of the grinder to the other.

"Aluminum oxide and ceramic dust from grinder wheels are really nasty stuff. You're especially throwing off a lot of dust when you dress your grinding wheel."

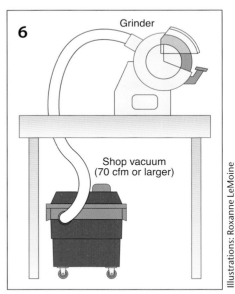

A simple dust collection system at your grinder will trap aluminum oxide and other harmful dust from your wheels.

Illustrations: Roxanne LeMoine

Dust terminology

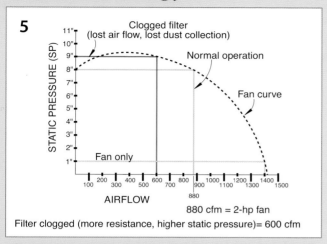

5

Graph axes: STATIC PRESSURE (SP) (vertical, 1" to 11") vs AIRFLOW (horizontal, 100 to 1500)

- Clogged filter (lost air flow, lost dust collection)
- Normal operation
- Fan curve
- Fan only

880

880 cfm = 2-hp fan

Filter clogged (more resistance, higher static pressure)= 600 cfm

Okay. You've decided to make the investment in your respiratory system by reducing your sawdust. Now what?

Your dust collector fan creates the criteria that follow. If your fan can meet these requirements and collect dust, you have a good system.

If you're not a dust engineer, you could easily get sucked up in a dust storm of numbers and acronyms. Here are some key definitions:

Air Volume. The amount of air that is moved through the duct in a prescribed amount of time. Air volume is measured in cubic feet per minute, expressed as cfm. A roll-around shop vacuum may have a rating of 70 cfm; a complete system for a home shop (with blast gates, hoods, and ductwork) should be in the range of 600 to 800 cfm.

Static Pressure (SP). Moving air through a pipe, cyclone, or filter involves resistance. Stick your hand out of the car window and drive down the road at 5 mph—that's static pressure you feel. When the resistance from each of your machines is added together, the total is the amount of static pressure the fan needs to produce.

The above are all the things created by the fan and these are the necessary requirements your fan should overcome to perform as a reliable dust collection system.

Want to learn more?

Here's a website you can learn more about dust collection: allwoodwork.com/article/woodwork/gettingtoughondust.htm

Control noise

Woodturners who do battle with dust wrestle another nemesis: irritating noise from the collector. The noise comes from the exhaust side of the fan; the higher the velocity, the greater the noise.

Many dust collectors now include a silencer or have silencer accessories (something like a muffler on an auto).

To the turners who use "too much noise" as a reason to avoid installing or running a dust collector in the shop, you need a better plan.

One strategy is to locate the collector beyond the shop (either outside or in an adjoining room). Morton Kasdan, a member of the Louisville Woodworkers Association, chose to locate his 3-hp cyclone collector in the center of his shop, which reduced the length of his duct runs.

Mortie dampened the noise in his shop, a converted three-car garage, by constructing a 3×2' closet framed by 2×4s and covered with 3/4"-thick plywood. (The top sections surrounding the external filters are larger.) Each side is lined with insulation panels, as shown at right. A hinged door makes it easy to empty  the dust barrel; he can easily remove four clamps on one side for filter maintenance.

Mortie also added an insulated top over the closet that has 4"- to 6"-wide slots for air exchange. Perforated hardboard over the plywood panels expands his tool hanging storage.

Although the center location in his shop reduced the length of duct lines, Mortie lamented that "If I had it to do over, I would put the collector in the corner. I could control the noise better there. Regardless, the insulation has reduced the noise level significantly."

A Checklist for Safe Woodturning

Take safety seriously with this easy-to-follow list

Woodturning is safe, until something goes wrong. Accidents at the lathe happen incredibly quickly, and woodturning accidents can be lethal. Yes, lethal.

That's tough talk, but think for a moment—you would be hurt and you could be killed if a heavy chunk of rotating wood were to fly off the lathe and smash into your face. It has happened to others and it could happen to you. That's why good woodturners take responsibility for their own safety by internalizing a safety point of view. Your attitude is your first line of defense, with faceshields and other protective gear the backup system.

And that's why safe turners, like airplane pilots, run down a checklist before hitting the "ON" switch, and they pay close attention to working safely while the chips are flying.

The risks include:

- Body parts battered by airborne wood flying off the lathe. Most dangerous: irregular and unsound wood.
- Nasty cuts from dropping sharp turning tools on unprotected feet.
- Violent injury if loose hair, jewelry, or clothing were to catch on the spinning chuck or workpiece.
- Fingers crushed under dropped wood, made worse if you're wearing rings.
- General mayhem if the turning tool was wrenched out of your hands because it tangled with the workpiece before you got it firmly planted on the toolrest.
- Nose and lung damage from inhaling fine dust. Wood dust, sandpaper detritus, grinder debris—all bad.

Woodturners are at risk when using bandsaws, chainsaws, and power carving tools, so it's essential to learn and follow safe practices for that equipment too. But that's another story—this one's about how to prepare and protect yourself at the lathe and how to avoid turning mishaps.

Attitude checklist: your sharpness

1. Stay alert.
Understand the Danger Zone. Pay attention to unusual sounds or vibrations; stop the lathe to investigate the cause. And yes, it is dumb to operate machines when you are tired or under the influence of drugs or alcohol.

2. Workshop.
Plug your lathe into a grounded outlet, no extension cords. Keep your work area well lit. Don't set up in wet locations. Mount a fire extinguisher beside the exit door.

3. Lathe.
Keep your lathe in good repair and develop the habit of scanning it for damaged parts, misalignment, or binding parts. Listen for unusual sounds. If you detect something amiss, deal with it immediately, before continuing your project.

4. Stance.
Stand like a soldier, easy but firm with your feet comfortably apart, shift your feet to maintain solid footing and keep your balance. Your stance powers all turning cuts. If you use an anti-fatigue mat, make it big so you can't trip on its edge.

5. Tools.
Learn what tools to use for each task, and keep tools sharp and clean. Forcing a dull tool invites a mishap, so pause often to touch up the cutting edge.

6. Know thyself.
Know your capabilities and limitations. An experienced woodturner can handle lathe speeds, techniques, and procedures that are not so smart for beginners to attempt.

Personal protection checklist: every time you turn

1. Eyes and face.
Wear a full faceshield all the time. If you also wear eyeglasses, get shatterproof lenses with side shields.

2. Body.
Wear a turning smock with short sleeves or tight cuffs. Tie back long hair, and avoid loose clothing, dangling jewelry, or ear-bud wires that could catch on the lathe, chuck, or workpiece.

3. Lungs.
Wood dust, sandpaper debris, and fine particles from a grinder will harm your respiratory

AW 28:1, p20

system. Ventilate your workshop and wear a dust mask or air filtration helmet, or install a dust collection system.

4. Ears.
Wear hearing protection during extended periods of turning.

5. Feet.
Wear closed-toe shoes or work boots, never sandals, to protect your feet from dropped tools and chunks of wood.

Lathe checklist

1. Lathe bed.
Clear turning tools, setup tools, materials, and coffee cups from the lathe bed.

2. Headstock and chuck.
Remove and stow chuck keys, adjusting wrenches, and knockout bars. Form a habit of checking for these before switching ON. Also check to be sure the belt guard or cover is in place.

3. Tailstock and toolrest.
Use the tailstock to support the workpiece whenever possible. Check that all locking devices on the tailstock and toolrest assembly (rest and base) are tight.

4 . Sanding and finishing.
To protect your fingers, always remove the toolrest before sanding, finishing, or polishing operations on the lathe. Apply finish with small scraps of cloth or paper towel, not large rags, and stand aside to avoid flying droplets.

5. Full stop.
Never leave the lathe running unattended. Turn the power OFF. Don't leave lathe until it comes to a complete stop.

Workpiece checklist

1. Clearance.
Rotate the workpiece a full turn by hand to be certain that it clears the toolrest and bed before turning the lathe ON. If it's

The Danger Zone

The Danger Zone is the space directly behind and in front of the workpiece. This is the red zone or firing zone, where the workpiece would be most likely to travel if it were to fly off the lathe.

Don't be in the Danger Zone when you first turn the lathe on, and keep your hand on the switch while the motor revs up, in case you need to turn it off fast. When observing someone else turn, stay out of this zone. When turning irregular, unbalanced, and unsound wood, train yourself to keep your head out of the Danger Zone.

possible to use the tailstock for support, do it.

2. Chuck and faceplate.
Grab and push the workpiece to be sure it's firmly seated in the chuck jaws. When using a faceplate, be certain the workpiece is solidly mounted with stout steel screws (#10 minimum).

3. Reversing.
When running a lathe in reverse, securely tighten or lock the chuck or faceplate on the lathe spindle so it can't unscrew and fly off.

4 . Speed.
Always check the speed of the lathe before you turn it on. Use slower speeds for larger diameters and rough pieces, and higher speeds for smaller diameters and balanced pieces. When the workpiece is unbalanced, start slow. If the lathe shakes or vibrates, slow it down. If the workpiece vibrates, stop the machine to find out why.

5. Unusual wood.
Wood with cracks, splits, checks, bark pockets, knots, irregular shapes, or protuberances could fly apart on the lathe. Beginners should stick with sound wood.

Start slow and keep your head out of the danger zone until you balance the piece and assess its soundness.

6 . Toolrest.
Hold turning tools securely on the toolrest, gripping the tool in a controlled but comfortable manner. Always plant the tool on the rest before you allow it to contact the workpiece. Turn the lathe OFF before you adjust the toolrest or toolrest base.

7. Have fun!
You'll enjoy turning the most when you're confidently on top of safety.

John Kelsey is a retired journalist and amateur woodturner living in East Lampeter, PA. He is a member of the Lancaster Area Woodturners.

Learn to Sharpen All Your Turning Tools

Sharper tools make for sharper work

Were these your first experiences in sharpening turning tools?

- You believed the tools came ready to use?
- You thought because the ad said you could turn 4,822 bowls without sharpening, they weren't kidding?
- When you did try grinding, the surfaces looked like a flint-chipped arrowhead?
- In frustration, you went out and spent several hundred dollars for every grinding jig on the market, only to discover they had not reached the level of a pencil sharpener?
- You sent your tools to a sharpening service only to have them sharpened like a saw blade?

Sharpening takes some knocks because some turners see it as a task or chore to be endured and not as a skill—just like turning—that will take time to learn. The good news is that sharpening is closely related to the skill of woodturning.

At one time every conceivable woodworker learned sharpening skills as part of their activity—whether it be sharpening saw blades, axes, spokeshaves, chisels, or plane irons. Today however, few cabinet or furnituremakers sharpen circular or bandsaw blades, planer and joiner knives, router bits or

Don't be too bashful in grinding tools. You really can't hurt them—you only shorten them.

shaper cutters—either these are throwaways or cutting tools sent to specialty shops. Even the other domain where sharpening was essential to learn—that of carving—has often been replaced by spinning bits and cutters that require no sharpening, just replacement. Alas, the poor woodturner still must learn to sharpen. However, there are numerous benefits from learning this skill.

AW 18:3, p52, AW 18:4, p56

Here's how sharpening skills mimic woodturning: You take a turning tool and place it on a tool rest, it meets a round object approaching the edge, and you manipulate the cutting edge. Sounds like what we do as turners, right? Learn the skill to sharpen and you are learning turning—and vice versa.

If sharpening frustrates you, you may need to adopt a tried and true learning strategy: a progression from simple and relatively easy activities to something difficult and more complex. If you think about it, this is how most skills are acquired. If you take up playing the fiddle, you don't start with the Brahm's violin concerto as your first task. You probably start with playing notes, then scales, *Yankee Doodle*, and finally progress in difficulty at the rate of your learning. The same path that works for learning math, cooking, computers, golf, drawing, driving, and sailing holds true of sharpening turning tools.

The good news to all of this is that learning those simple tasks first has several benefits: Most of those tasks are also foundational—not just easy—and will be the basis for learning the more difficult maneuvers.

I wonder how many folks have quit woodturning over the years because they either could not sharpen the tools or found they spent more time sanding than turning? So, if you are early on in your career as a turner or you are still frustrated about this sharpening thing, join me and try this progressive order of learning to sharpening your tools.

To begin with, you can't shape and sharpen your tools by hand. We can certainly hone the tools by hand—but honing only keeps a sharp tool sharp or regains a small loss of keenness on a cutting-type turning tool.

Working with dull tools is like trying to drive your car with flat tires—it just isn't very satisfying.

No, power equipment is the order of the day for a host of reasons, not the least of which is the type of tool steels used today. Most turning tools currently being sold are not just higher heat-working steels but also higher wear-resistant steels. Your grandpappy's Arkansas oil stone is going to have a tough go on a Glaser V-15 tool or on most of the English, Canadian, and Australian tools now on the market. And the fact that too many tools need major reshaping from their new condition, we will need some power assistance to do the job.

Buying your grinder and wheels

I find that it is not as simple as "anything will work" for a grinder. If you have a 3600 rpm grinder with a 120-grit gray wheel, 1/2" wide and worn down to 4" in diameter—it will be tough sledding. Nor do I find the slow speed water grinders to be my first choice for a grinder. Ditto for a belt or disc sander either. At least 90 percent of the turners I know worldwide use a wheel grinder—and for good reason.

Here's my grinder preference: an 8" dry wheel grinder, with either variable speed or a fixed rate of 1725 (or 1800), a rock-solid tool rest system, and at least one decent wheel. The 8" wheel offers a lot over smaller and larger wheels: the 8" has 25 percent more surface area than a 6" wheel per revolution. This translates to greater efficiency, cooler grinding, and a much longer wear period before replacement. The 10" and greater diameter wheels leave too little of a hollow-grind for me—and I use the concave surface as a two-point honing jig (see Spring 2002 article).

I prefer the dry wheel as the action is towards me—this allows me to determine a lot of things from the spark trail: where I am grinding, the degree of grinding, and when to stop grinding (sparks just trail over the top of the tool). With a water-type grinder, the action is away from

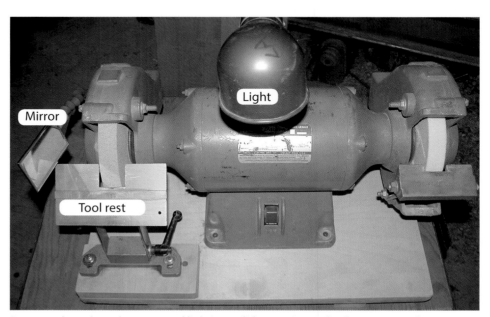

Strong and sturdy tools rests, good lighting, solid mounting and at least one good wheel are minimal requirements for a reliable grinder. The tool rest on the left is an after-market rest. A supporting strap was added to the right rest for increased rigidity.

me and there is no longer a spark trail. Those grinders are fantastic for carbon-steel tools like plane irons, cabinet makers chisels, scissors and the like—but not a first choice with most turners. I like the slower 1725 speed for a grinder. As I aim to remove minimal material, the 1725 speed grinder has a cooler action, and I just find it a more gentle action than a 3600 rpm screamer (those seem to double my mistakes!). We are now seeing two-speed grinders and infinitely adjustable grinders on the market, which will probably be common with most grinders at some point.

If the tool rest assembly is flimsy, I cannot consistently grind my tools nor is it really safe to do so. Place your thumb in the center of the tool rest of your grinder and push down. You should feel virtually zero give—if it feels springy, improve or replace. You can add extra support strapping, build a wooden rest, or purchase one of several after-market accessory rests. Also, the rest should be adjustable both in angle and the ability to slide towards the stone to accommodate for wear as well as keeping the rest close to the stone for safety purposes. Finally, a light is a worthwhile accessory to the grinder if one did not come attached to it.

Thoughts on grinding wheels and dressers

First, work with the widest wheel you can fit to your grinder. In most cases this is 3/4" or 1"—but the wider the better. Next, throw away your gray wheels. Spend a lot or spend a little, but acquire at least one decent grinding wheel to sharpen with.

The wheels I would suggest are friable aluminum oxide—now in patriotic colors of red (okay, often pink), white, and blue. The word "friable" refers to the ability of the stone to fracture, exposing fresh grinding surfaces as you use it. Gray wheels usually are not very friable, the cutting particles round over, thus reducing grinding ability and often glazing and generating considerable heat. The color code of these wheels makes them easy to spot. However, there really is a difference between a $10 wheel and $100 wheel.

My advice: If you have an 8" grinder look for wheels that sell for between $25 and $55 and you'll be fine. Two other critical aspects of the wheels: grit size and hardness. I like to work with two different grits on my grinder. For initial shaping of a tool or any other heavy grinding operation, I rely on a 36- or 46-grit wheel. For the actual process of sharpening an edge, I prefer either a 60- (the new 54-grits are close

enough) or 80-grit. My ideal setup is a 60-grit on the left side of my grinder (I am right handed; reverse this if you are a lefty) and a 36-grit on the other side.

And finally, how hard should the stone be? Most stones—but not some of the real cheapies—indicate the hardness as shown in the photo. This makes a difference in its friable quality and how well it performs on tougher steels. Stone hardness follows the alphabet scale from soft to hard as you go down the alphabet. Most of the stones commonly found range from H through K. My first choice is a J followed by the K.

Almost as critical as a good stone is a dresser. These are tools that perform a number of functions: true the wheel to the axis of your grinder, flatten the face of the wheel, remove the buildup of metal particles, and expose or sharpen the abrasive particles. There are several choices: star-wheel, gray dressing stick, boron carbide stick, and diamond. I prefer the multiple diamond dresser (not a single point) in a round or tee shape. Keep it by the grinder, and use it lightly but frequently.

Finally, deal with the hazards associated with tool grinding. One of the greatest hazards is to protect yourself from flying particles, whether they are grit from the

Wheel dresser examples left to right: gray dressing stick, tee diamond, round diamond, star-wheel. In the foreground is a boron carbide stick.

It is challenging to look at a wheel and guess its grit size and hardness. Most stones have a code—in this case, the bottom row of numbers. The most important codes to a turner are circled. The "54" designates grit size; "J" indicates the hardness designation.

wheel or pieces of steel removed in the grinding process. The plastic shields on most grinders are worthless to see through after a short time—a full face shield is my first choice followed by goggles. Only use a grinder with metal shrouds to contain the wheel just in case it shatters into pieces.

Another serious hazard is the dust produced from grinding. I like to think of it as ground up glass. I know of no turners who use a wet dust collecting system to direct the grinding dust into—but this is more common with jewelers and other metal workers. And, of course, don't direct the dust into your normal wood dust collecting system—think of the drama of sparks and wood dust meeting!

What is most common is to wear a quality respirator, one rated for small particulate matter. And finally, keep the pinch and crush factor to a minimum by always working with the tool rest as close to the wheel as possible.

Order of learning

From my own learning and watching hundreds of students try to learn the sharpening process, I recommend learning the turning tools in this order:

1. **Scrapers** (all shapes, but not including profile scrapers)
2. **Parting Tools**
3. **Skew Chisels** We'll cover the above tools in this issue.
4. **Roughing Gouges**
5. **Detail Gouges**
6. **Bowl Gouges**

1. Sharpening scrapers

These are tools, of almost any shape, that are intended primarily to cut with a burr and not rub the bevel on the wood. Yes, I know we violate both of those guidelines from time to time, but that does not help someone who is starting out. Of all the turning tools, scrapers are

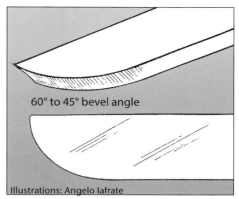

60° to 45° bevel angle

Illustrations: Angelo Iafrate

One version of a side-cutting scraper

some of the most straightforward to sharpen. Few turners struggle with these tools in getting the basic process, and we don't have to be too fussy about shapes, angles, and multi facets on the ground face.

The first rule of sharpening turning tools: Profile the tool first, then pull a bevel up to meet that profile. For a scraper, personal preference determines the shape. You will probably discover that the slight dome on a new "round nose" scraper you just bought isn't very rounded. You may even find you don't use one side of the rounded end, so it may take on the shape of

Woodturning scraping tools are quite similar to the cabinetmaker's scrapers (background, shown with a burnisher). Both types of scrapers usually cut with a burr and both can make use of a burnisher to raise that burr. Turning scrapers are thicker and heavier in weight and come (or can be made into) in an array of shapes for specific purposes.

a side-ground scraper. Whatever the specific need or your style of turning, shape the tool first.

Next, rough in the bevel angle. When most of these tools are new, I find the bevel to be 80 to even 90 degrees below the cutting edge. I believe manufacturers started with the notion that a scraper needs a lot of support under the edge since you don't have the secondary fulcrum of a bevel-rubbing tool to add extra support (your tool rest is the primary fulcrum). Unless your scrapers are 1/8" thick, this is a bad notion.

As a matter of fact, if I am using the tool at a scraping angle (with no bevel support) and the bevel inadvertently touches the wood, I can get a catch. I treat the bevels on scrapers as clearance angles, so mine are ground between 45 to 60 degrees. I also don't have to worry about single facets and a hollow grind on the ground bevel: I don't hone the bevel on these tools so it is not as critical as it is with other turning tools. However, grinding uniform bevels on these tools is great practice for all the tools to follow.

The process for sharpening is straightforward. After profiling, proceed to grind the bevel to match the profile. If you need some assistance early on in sharpening, set the tool rest angle to that 45- to 60-degree window. Start at the back of the bevel, keeping the tool flat on the rest, and progress along the cutting edge until sparks just come over the top. I don't look for a heavy stream of sparks, but consistent "tracer bullets" that tell me I have reached the cutting surface.

Being a scraper, the raised burr will be my cutting edge at least 90 percent of the time. I can use the burr right off of the grinder (useful if heavy stock removal is called for) or remove that burr with a flat stone and pull up a new burr with

a cabinetmaker's burnisher or the honing stone.

By using one of the other methods, I find it easier to produce different types of burrs—some for heavy work, some for fine finishing work. In those cases where the burr is too aggressive for a particular piece of wood (you may feel it "picking" at the wood rather than a smooth leveling action), try scraping with a sharp edge—produced by grinding—then removing the burr on top with a flat honing stone. This is similar to the action of scraping with the edge of a knife or the furnituremaker scraping the top of a table with a large piece of broken glass. When you work a sharp edge in a scraping action, it may quickly dull the edge. However for that window of doing fine scraping, it may be just the ticket.

2. Parting tools

There are several variations of this tool, but the most common is a rectangular section of steel with the cutting edge in the middle that's ground on both sides. This is a great tool to learn cutting tool sharpening as it has a relatively small area to grind (the edge is usually no greater than 1/4") and the edge is in a flat plane.

For profiling, make sure the edge is ground straight across, and the included angles of the ground bevels are around 25 degrees. Fortunately, new parting tools most often arrive profiled in an acceptable manner—not sharp mind you, but routinely shaped fine. To sharpen, either set the tool rest at the approximate angle desired, use the edge of the rest as a steady, or use your fingers to adjust the angle.

Start at the back of the bevel (called the "heel"), keep the edge horizontal, and lap from side to side on the wheel until you just see sparks trailing over the top of

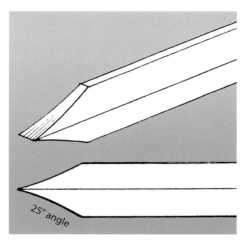

Diamond-section parting tool (profile and angles same as rectangular tool)

the cutting edge. Flip over the tool and repeat the same procedure on the other side. The objective is to produce a single facet with a slight hollow grind. If your movements are controlled and steady, this all happens. If jerky, uneven, inconsistent, too much pressure, "grind and look" and "grind and look," then things probably won't be so good.

Go slow, be deliberate, leave the tool on the wheel, and use only enough pressure as it takes to keep the tool from bouncing on the rest. I am always surprised how much of grinding and turning is really about feeling your way along rather than seeing.

In grinding, most of the action is on the other side of what you can see. We can help the looking part along—especially when learning the process—by placing our head to the side of the grinder or by the use of a mirror (attributed to a North Carolina turner). In time, most of your grinding will be by feel and watching the spark trail to give the additional feedback.

3. Skew chisels

Fortunately, the sharpening of a skew chisel is similar to the parting tool: two ground flat planes that meet to form a cutting edge. The only real difference is in the skewed angle of the cutting end—essentially a clearing and viewing advantage over a square-across chisel.

Again, profile the tool first. For a "traditional" straight-edged skew, I recommend 70 degrees from point to point. Rather than measuring included angles to measure the steepness of the two ground bevels, I use the thickness of the steel as the reference. Using this method, grind the bevels back to approximately 1.5 times the thickness of the blade.

For the sharpening process, follow these steps: Keep the edge horizontal and parallel to the face of the wheel, start at the heel and lap back and forth. Continue this process until sparks just trail over the edge. Flip over the tool and repeat the same procedure.

If you have an "oval style" skew (my last choice for a skew) you will find it wants to wobble rather than remain in a flat plane. In that case, maintain pressure in the center of the tool with a thumb to essentially lock it into a fixed plane. As an alternative, investigate a grinding jig that locks the darn thing in place.

If you are grinding a curved-edged skew, simply grind the edge while it is generally parallel to the face of the wheel. This will require a rotational motion that follows the curve of the edge. If the skew plagues you with multiple facets, go ahead and set the tool rest to the suggested bevel angle. Keep the tool flat on the rest and follow the above strategies. I have had good success just using the front or back edge of the tool rest as a point to slide along for a straight skew or to pivot on while grinding a curved edge.

Until you have a sense of where you are grinding on the tool, it's helpful to either place your head to the side of the wheel or make use of a small mirror. The mirror, shown above, allows you to see your placement of the tool on the wheel.

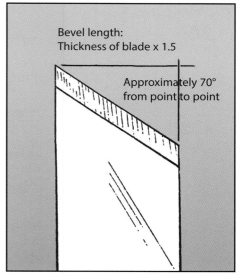

Bevel length:
Thickness of blade x 1.5

Approximately 70° from point to point

Typical grinding of a skew chisel

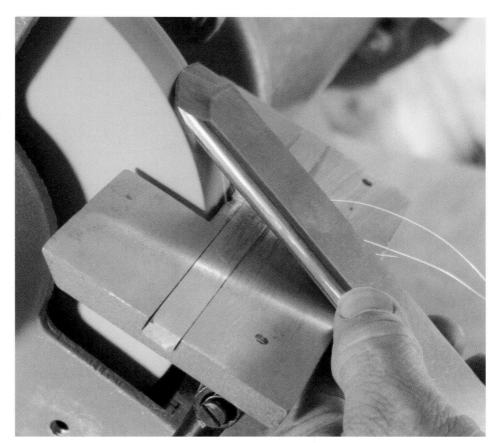

Using the back edge of the tool rest, pivot the curved skew to grind the edge. Using a rotational movement, grind in the area that is roughly parallel to the face of the wheel.

Tests for sharpness of cutting tools

If you can see the edge, there is no edge. Short of turning, this is the best test I know. Use an incandescent light to check for any reflection along the edge; a sharp edge disappears into a black line. Dull spots will reflect light.

What comes off the tool, dust or curls? Even in dry material, a sharp tool forms a longer chip or ribbon, dull tools produce dust or very short chips.

How much effort does it require to remove the material? Unless you are roughing out a large piece, a sharp tool presented at the right angle is almost effortless; a dull tool requires more force.

What does the cutting action sound like? A sharp tool makes a sound reminiscent of a sharp hand

If you can see the edge, there is no edge.

plane; the dull tool sounds flat or makes a scraping sound.

How clean is the surface when you stop the lathe for inspection? Sometimes it is a difficult piece of wood, but generally a sharp tool gives far superior results to the surface of the wood.

4. Spindle roughing gouge

The spindle roughing gouge is perhaps the friendliest gouge to use and one of the easiest to sharpen. It differs from all the previous tools (Fall 2003 issue) as we are now into curved edges. Traditionally, the tool is a deep U-shape with a straight across cutting edge.

Profiling is fairly straight forward. Make sure the tool is straight across when viewed from the top and viewed from the side. You can have the top corners canted back a few degrees, but not canted forward (a forward cant will make a more aggressive tool). The bevel angle should be approximately 45 degrees.

Sharpening begins at one corner, with the heel of the bevel touching the wheel and the cutting edge parallel to the face of the wheel. Rotate the tool in the same curved plane until you reach the other corner, then return to the point where you began by rotating backwards (but still grinding) to your original motion. I tend to repeat these motions until I have lapped all the way to the cutting edge. Stop when the sparks just trail over the top of the edge.

Notes on overheating the tool

By now you may have come up against the problem of bluing the grinding surface of the tool. If you have high-carbon steel tools, you have a problem: the steel has now been re-tempered to a hardness that is too soft to hold an edge for woodturning. If you have high-speed or high-heat-working tool steel—no problem. But how do you know what kind of steel?

Generally the high-carbon tool steels produce a complex, white, bursting spark when placed on the grinding wheel. The high-speed steels tend to have individual, orange sparks. Often the manufacturer stamps the handle or steel itself with "HSS" or "High Speed Steel." I have found some inexpensive imported tools stamped with those designations, but sparked like high carbon tools—so be careful.

Here are some suggestions regarding overheating. First, learn to grind with a lightness of hand and movement of tool that does not overwork an area, thereby reducing heat. Second, use friable wheels that grind cooler, and dress the wheel often. If you have

carbon steel tools—and some of my old favorites are of that steel—quench in water frequently for heavy grinding or delicate points of skew chisels.

If you have high-speed tools, don't quench in water: the effect may be too shocking for the steel and possibly produce small fractures at the cutting edge. The high-speed steels easily handle temperatures of 700 to 1000 degrees F with no loss of hardness (bluing is around 580 degrees F). If the high-speed tools get too hot to handle (during heavy grinding), I just place them on a large metal heat sink like a lathe bed and take a short break. The best rule for all steels is learn to work without generating a lot of excessive heat and eliminate the need for quenching.

Gride the bevel and not the edge.

Grind the bevel and not the edge.

On the larger roughing gouges, some turners like to work about one third of the edge at a time until that section is fully sharpened. They make one final pass along the entire length of the bevel to blend it all together. The biggest problem turners seem to have is moving the tool edge in and out when trying to rotate the tool through that large curved plane. Use your fingers to create an artificial plane to lock the tool in. If you have trouble staying in that 45 degree bevel zone, set the angle of the tool rest and maintain downward pressure to keep the tool flat and thereby in the correct orientation.

If by chance you have a large shallow gouge (3/4" or larger) that was packaged in your tool set as a roughing gouge, here are my suggestions. Odds are pretty good it has a domed edge (maybe almost looks like your thumbnail). You might consider simply grinding it straight across and sharpening as suggested for the deep-fluted roughing gouge.

If you decide to leave it with that "fingernail" look—in order to do some detailing work such as large coves or beads— then approach it the way you would the detail gouge.

At right are improperly ground gouges:

A: A detail gouge ground too pointy. This is caused by either rotating the entire tool parallel to the face of the grinding wheel (as with a roughing gouge), or over grinding the sides.

B: A bowl gouge ground on the side with a concave profile. This makes an aggressive tool and one that does a poor job of leveling if used to shear scrape.

C: A roughing gouge overground along the edge. This most often shows up as a jagged or saw-toothed edge.

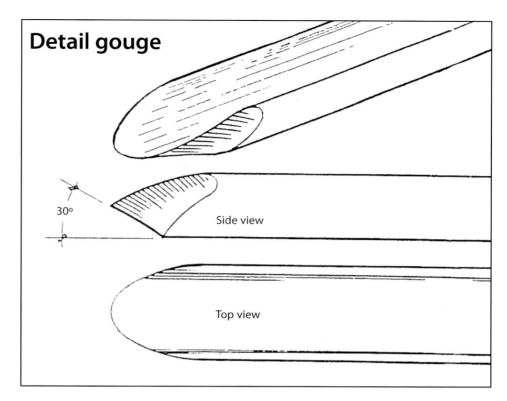

Detail gouge

30°

Side view

Top view

5. Detail gouge

What's in a name? A shallow fluted gouge with a fingernail shape--primarily designed for spindle work and used for detailing work--will be the same tool no matter what we call it. I wish we could some day standardize a few names for turning tools, but that's a lot to ask for. This tool goes by at least four names: detail gouge, spindle gouge, shallow gouge, and fingernail gouge. All of these names point to some truth about it, but still leads to much confusion. For this article, it's a detail gouge.

This detail gouge is probably the first tool to get your goat. (It

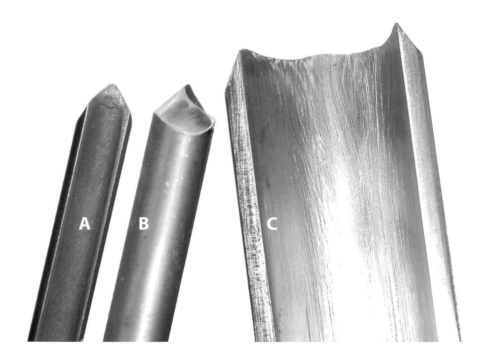

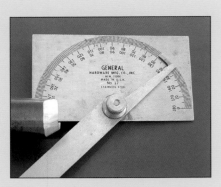

Give a protractor a try

We got a few letters after last issue's grinding article about grinding the correct angle. This metal protractor—available for about $12—is one inexpensive and reliable solution.

was the first tool I'm aware of that a grinding jig was developed to do the sharpening.) No tricks of setting the tool rest at the right angle will help, nor will simply rotating the tool back and forth. Nope, we now have a tool that is in an oval plane with the steel below the edge in varying thicknesses.

Let me explain. If I shape the tool into a fingernail shape, orient the tool with the flute facing the grinding wheel, and rotate it along a circular path that is parallel to the face of the wheel, I will probably produce a pointy or "spear-pointed" cutting edge that is not very versatile nor friendly to the user.

Profiling is essential to the detail tool. It performs astutely in forming concave and convex forms in between center work or details on feet, bases and rims of bowl and vessel work. The shallow draft of its flute (a low "sweep" if we are talking to carvers) allows the tool to sneak in between details, often on its side and do its fine work.

The deep fluted roughing gouges and bowl gouges have

trouble detailing elements that are close together. So, the detail profile should reflect its intended activities. Establish a fingernail shape to the cutting edge—thus making the detail gouge more of a side-cutting tool, especially when rotated on its side.

Just as your fingernail would not grow to a point, so must the end of the tool not be too pointy. The analogy with the fingernail is a good one: the smaller the gouge the more it is like a little fingernail; the larger the gouge the more it is domed like a thumbnail. I like to profile by holding the tool nearly flat on a tool rest set to about 90 degrees to the wheel. Gauge your progress by the view from above—striving to get a balanced radius on both sides of the tool (see illustration). Next, rough in an approximate bevel angle of 30 degrees. This flatter angle reflects the need of the tool to fit between details while in use.

There are several strategies for matching the edge to the profile, but I will give you the easiest one for me. Treat the bevel of the tool as having three parts: a middle section, and a right and left side. Start by holding the tool with the flute pointed up, contacting the bevel heel in the middle section. This will be the basis for all detail grinding, and the reference point for grinding of the bevel middle area or sides.

With a push up and rotation to the right, move the tool to the left side of the wheel. Grind as you reverse this action and return to the original starting point. When both sides show sharpness from the spark trail, blend the center section into each side.

6. Bowl gouges

I recommend tackling bowl gouges last, but not because they're extraordinarily difficult. In major reshaping, you'll remove

A sharp tool at the right cutting angle is virtually effortless.

considerable amounts of steel. Plus, bowl gouges have at least one tricky grind that causes some problems.

The preferred profile is one of personal choice. Most turners use one of three common grinds. What I term "traditional" is shaped exactly like a roughing gouge— and the sharpening is attended to in the same manner, only easier because of the reduced size. The "transitional" is one favored by many bowl turners, and may be the only profile you require on a bowl gouge. Careful study of the diagram shows it to be close to the fingernail shape we put on the detailing gouge. The side profile should be straight or a bit convex— just avoid concave. Once profiled, I sharpen in the same manner as the detail gouge.

The bowl grind that has launched more than a few commercial and shop-made jigs is the Irish grind. Although it looks formidable with such a long edge, it is in truth quite tame—if you have a strategy. Get the profile correct from above, the side, and rough in the steep bevel angle on the nose. Then divide the tool into three sections: the two long sides and the front nose. Grind the sides nearly parallel to the face of the stone. Finally, grind the small front section with the same technique for the detail gouge. I finish with a little blending of the nose into the sides.

Tests for sharpness of cutting tools

- If you can see the edge there is no edge. Short of actually turning, this is the best test I know. Use an incandescent light to check for any reflection along the edge. A sharp edge disappears into a black line; dull spots reflect light.
- What comes off the tool—dust or curls? Even in dry material, a sharp tool forms a longer chip or ribbon while dull tools produce dust or short chips.
- How much effort does it require to remove the material? Unless you are roughing out a large piece, a sharp tool presented at the right angle is almost effortless; a dull tool requires more force.

- How does the cutting action sound? A sharp tool makes a sound reminiscent of a sharp hand plane; the dull tool sounds flat or makes a scraping sound.
- How clean is the surface when you stop the lathe for inspection? Generally a sharp tool gives far superior results to the surface of the wood.

A traditional (fingernail) grind has some sound applications: the outside of a face grain bowl when mounted backwards (base is at tailstock side) or for opening the interior of a bowl (opening is now facing tailstock side).

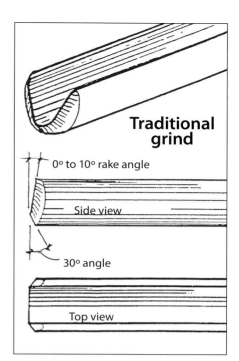

Traditional grind

0° to 10° rake angle

Side view

30° angle

Top view

Two ways to sharpen a bowl gouge

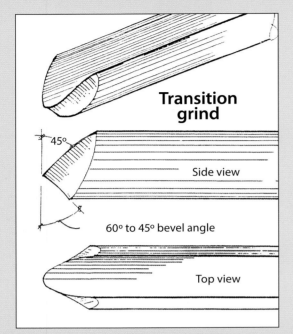

Transition grind

45°

Side view

60° to 45° bevel angle

Top view

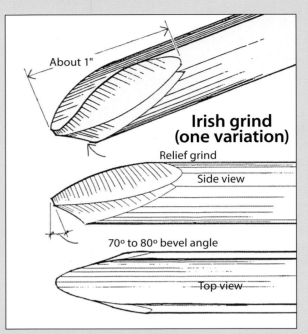

About 1"

Irish grind (one variation)

Relief grind

Side view

70° to 80° bevel angle

Top view

I recommend the transition grind for new bowl turners. You work the outside of a face grain bowl regardless of the orientation. The ground sides provide the opportunity to do a little shear scraping.

Experienced turners may prefer the more-complicated Irish grind. It's a good roughing tool for bowls, a detailing tool with the elliptical front, a shear-scraping tool, and a tool to make a smoother transition from sides to bottom.

Grinding jigs

This is perhaps sacrilegious, but I am not a big fan of the grinding jigs. I still find most individuals learn sharpening with no other "jig" than their tool rest and hands—at least for most tools.

But is there a place for the grinding jigs? Yes! For those folks who cannot seem to learn freehand grinding, those with physical limitations, those who need a crutch to get started (like training wheels on your first bike), those sharpening a large number of tools for others (some classroom or manufacturing situations), or those one or two difficult tools you just can't seem to get at all or consistently. If you fall into one of these camps, get a jig—but at least learn to resharpen your tools by hand when all that is needed is a light refreshing. The information in this article applies to most aspects of sharpening whether you do it freehand or with a grinding jig. Be forewarned though, jigs still require considerable judgment and they can also "shorten" your tools.

A past President of the AAW and an Honorary Lifetime Member, **Alan Lacer** *has spent four decades as a turner, instructor, and contributing editor to* American Woodturner. *Visit Alan at www.woodturninglearn.net.*

A jig may be helpful in some situations of learning to grind.

Sharpening Jigs

Be sharp and stay safe when using these handy devices

As the use of sharpening jigs increases, so, too, do the instances of sharpening accidents. Injuries that result from fragmented grinding wheels and tools and holders that have slipped have sent woodturners to the hospital with serious injuries to hands and/or eyes.

Sharpening jigs were developed so that we could quickly and repeatedly produce a tool shape, bevel, and edge. When using these jigs, however, woodworkers need to be aware of some potential dangers. Tools can slide off the face of the grinding wheels and wedge between the wheel and the frame of the grinder; the arms of sharpening jigs can slip outward away from the wheel, causing the tip of the tool to move down the surface of the grinding wheel until the tool grabs at the wheel's equator and instantly wedges itself, fracturing the wheel and potentially injuring the operator's hand; tools can slip forward in the tool holder itself causing similar problems.

While mechanical failure of sharpening jigs contributes to some injuries, human error is usually the cause. Here's why:
- The person sharpening the tool is distracted and the tool no longer rides on the wheel. A quick turn of a person's head can easily cause the movement of a tool off a 1"-wide grinding wheel, jamming it between the wheel and the body of the grinder.
- An improper handhold on the jig can cause fingers to be driven into the still-running grinding wheel.
- Too much pressure is applied to the tool causing mechanical slippage of the jig's arm.
- Improper grinding-jig geometry is set, placing the tip of the tool too close to the maximum diameter of the wheel (the equator).
- The process of sharpening tools is hurried.
- Small-diameter tools are improperly placed in jigs not meant to handle their smaller size.

Proper use of grinding jigs
- Firmly lock the jig's extension arm and recheck it by pushing or pulling on it.
- Establish a more acute bevel angle on your turning tool. Placing the tool high on the sharpening wheel's surface reduces the possibility of an accident.
- Reduce the amount of downward pressure applied during sharpening; this will save tool steel and reduce heat buildup.

Wear safety gear
A faceshield or safety glasses should be worn while at the sharpening station. Eye injury is possible while sharpening as a result of flying

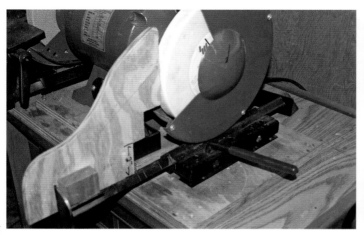

Using a simple shopmade template to set up your sharpening jig for repeatable distances saves time and tool wear.

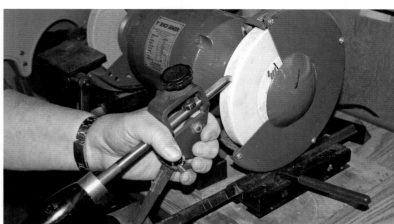

Wrong way! If the sharpening jig slips, fingers will contact the rotating wheel before the jig does.

A safer way to hold the jig is on the top. If a slip occurs, the hand is protected.

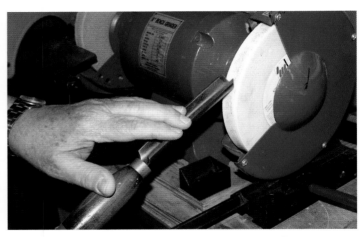

Potential danger: Using a long fixture arm and a blunt sharpening angle brings the tip of the tool too close to the wheel's equator. If the arm of the jig slips or too much pressure is exerted, it could cause the tool to jam against the wheel.

debris. When dressing a wheel for cleaning or reshaping, wear a dust mask. The aluminum oxide dust from a grinding wheel is potentially damaging to lungs.

Proper hold

When holding the sharpening jig, never place your hand between the jig and the grinding wheel. Place one hand on the handle of the tool and the other on top of the jig. Accidents occur when the hand hits the rotating wheel during a slippage.

Light touch

Sharpening should be done with a light touch; this reduces the amount of metal being removed and the heat buildup during the sharpening. A light touch also allows the operator to react quickly when a slippage occurs, perhaps saving a finger.

New sharpening jigs

Until recently, most sharpening jigs managed the sharpening geometry well, but still allowed for uncontrolled side movements that contributed to most accidents. Currently two manufactures,

Sharp Fast and Oneway, have introduced jigs that eliminate the accidental sideways movement while maintaining the proper sharpening geometry. As a teacher of woodturning at both high school and adult levels, I would not be without such a jig!

Jim Rodgers, author of A Lesson Plan for Woodturning *and past President of the Bay Area Woodturners Club, is the Director of turning programs for Mt. Diablo Unified School District. Visit Jim at www.jlrodgers.com.*

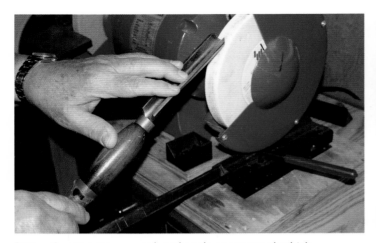

Better: Create a more acute bevel angle on your tool, which will place it higher up on the wheel in a safer position when sharpening.

Consider learning how to hand sharpen turning tools. This allows you to place a toolrest close to the grinding wheel, eliminating many potential dangers.

Tuning and Aligning Your Lathe

Five easy checkpoints to get your turning in line

Oval pens driving you nuts?
Can't align two halves of a segmented bowl for glue-up?
Join the crowd. If your lathe—or your turning work—suffers from poor alignment, call a time-out and review these five alignment checkpoints.

1. Tailstock does not align with the headstock

To check the alignment of your headstock and tailstock, insert a live center into the tailstock and a spur drive into the headstock. Make sure that the points are not dulled or bent in either the spur or the live center—this will mislead you in your measurement.

Bring up the tailstock to within 1/4" to 1/2" from the spur center, then tighten down the tailstock and quill. Now, observe the alignment of the two points. If the points are misaligned, you can compensate by placing a shim under the appropriate corner(s) of the tailstock to adjust the alignment. Often a sheet or two of paper will be adequate to shim the tailstock.

For more exaggerated errors, contact the lathe manufacturer for repair or replacement of the tailstock or tailstock quill. An extreme case may require reboring of the Morse taper on the tailstock quill.

If the lathe headstock is bolted to the frame or ways as with the Jet mini-lathe and Delta Midi, you can realign it with the addition of a permanent shim under the appropriate corner. On other lathes such as the Oneway, for example, you can align the headstock by adjusting the jack screws provided for that purpose.

If you own a Nova 3000/DVR, you can reposition the lathe ways themselves, as they are screwed to the headstock unit. Be sure to follow the instructions in your owner's manual for all adjustments noted above.

On lathes with a rotating headstock, the click stop positioning may not be accurate enough to return to perfect alignment. A double-ended Morse taper will aid in regularly realigning the headstock each time it is moved.

AW 20:2, p16

2. Live center does not run true

Inexpensive live centers, centers with worn out bearings, or poorly designed live centers like the examples shown cause problems. If the live center was inexpensive, just discard it and upgrade.

One of the causes of a live center becoming out of true is excessive wear of the bearings due to operating the lathe with a headstock/tailstock misalignment. Angular pressure on the live center will rapidly increase the radial runout to an unacceptable point. (Oneway advertises that the radial runout of its live center system is less than .001 inches.)

If you have a reliable live center that's repairable, consider replacing the bearings. For a minimal fee, you can return many live centers for bearing replacement.

3. Too much pressure applied to the mandrel in penturning

If your pen barrels are oval and you've checked the first two solutions, applying too much pressure to the tailstock when tightening on the mandrel may be the culprit. The amount of pressure applied should be just enough to stabilize the mandrel shaft and minimize vibration from the turning activity. Too much pressure bends the shaft as shown.

A crooked live center point will also cause the mandrel to operate eccentrically and will enlarge and distort the alignment dimple in the tailstock end of the mandrel shaft. The better designed mandrels allow the user to replace the shaft when it becomes bent or the dimple has excessive wear.

4. Poor centering with vacuum chucks

If you align a bowl or vessel in your vacuum chuck and it slips or won't

Tips to improve your accuracy

- Always clean the female Morse tapers before inserting any accessory.

- Remove all defects or burrs from the surface of male Morse tapers.

- Store and protect spur drives and live centers from scratches and dings. Find a place near your lathe where these valuable attachments won't get beat about by lathe tools, hammers, and accessories.

hold the desired alignment, the cause may be related to the material used to seal the vessel to the chuck. Foam rubber and other soft, flexible seals may vary in density throughout the material, thus not compressing equally everywhere, causing the vessel to be forced out of alignment.

Vacuum chuck design and the shape of the vessel also tend to exaggerate this problem. A round vessel held against a rounded chuck surface may exhibit this problem more readily.

To improve centering, try each of these solutions: Replace the material, readjust the material, or buy thicker (or thinner) stock.

Silicon rubber works well but is difficult to attach to the chuck because there's no known effective adhesive for this material.

On a finished edge bowl, consider using a flat plate as a vacuum chuck, thus spreading out the hold over a large area and minimizing the problem.

5. Hole-drilling errors

Improperly mounting a Jacobs chuck on a Morse taper may cause centering problems when drilling holes in the end of a project. To avoid this problem, be sure that you properly seat the Morse taper in your tailstock, then run the quill out far enough that the drill chuck completely seats—no further. Bring the tailstock up into close proximity of the work and lock down the tailstock before drilling.

Other drilling issues may not be related to the alignment but be caused by the drill wandering from hard, winter-growth grain and into softer summer growth. Solve this issue by creating a small pilot hole for the drill point. Brad-point or Forstner bits also reduce this drifting problem. Always be sure that the bit you select is sharp.

Jim Rodgers, *author of* A Lesson Plan for Woodturning *and past President of the Bay Area Woodturners Club, is the Director of turning programs for Mt. Diablo Unified School District. Visit Jim at www.jlrodgers.com.*

Section 2: Tools

A determined soul will do more with a rusty monkey wrench than a loafer will accomplish with all the tools in a machine shop. —Robert Hughes

Turning wood is a lot more fun when you've got the right tools for the job. But, the world of turning tools can be bewildering and confusing. At first glance, there's not much difference between spindle gouges, detail gouges, roughing gouges and bowl gouges, but the small, subtle differences in each tool are hugely important to the tasks they perform. The same goes for parting tools, skew chisels, and scrapers. And, you might ask, what's the best tool for keeping the wood secured to the lathe? Don't let the tool talk intimidate you. As you develop your woodturning skills, you'll quickly discover how each tool works and how to master each one. Be patient. And, while there's a ton of expensive stuff out there, you can get started turning using simple, inexpensive equipment and the time-tested strategies described in this section.

Get a Good Start with Your Lathe and Turning Tools

Expert answers to the most asked woodturning questions

People just getting started in turning usually have as many questions as a new runner hoping to finish a 5k race:
• What's the best chuck on the market?
• What kind of tools should I buy?
• What grit is best for sharpening?
• Should I buy a sharpening jig?
• What's the best way to sand?
• If you teach or demonstrate frequently, you've heard all these questions many times over.

Sharpening

1 What grit do you recommend for sharpening tools?
Pitch the gray wheels that accompany most grinders and sharpen with a 60- or 80-grit aluminum oxide wheel. Although others advocate honing, I find it unnecessary for most woods and projects I turn. I go directly from the sharpening wheel to the lathe.

Over the years, I've discovered that a Oneway diamond-tip wheel dresser tears up the wheel less than a star wheel dresser. If used properly, the diamond-tip dresser prepares a true wheel and your lathe tool will not bounce (a problem with handheld dressers).

2 What speed grinder do you recommend?
Instead of the better-known 3,500-rpm grinder for general woodworking, I prefer to sharpen lathe tools with a 1,725-rpm grinder, sometimes referred to as a slow-speed grinder. The slow-speed grinder removes metal at a slower rate and allows me to work with the edge of the tool a bit (it's also more forgiving of errors). When I first started turning, I shortened the life of many tools by attempting to sharpen at 3,500 rpm. Don't make the same mistake.

3 Should I buy a sharpening jig or should I learn freehand sharpening?
I often repeat Bonnie Klein's answer: "If you turn a lot, you probably don't need a grinding jig. But if you only turn a couple of days a week, it's well worth it."

I'll go one step further: Even though I learned freehand sharpening first (jigs weren't commonly available then), I now use a sharpening jig all the time.

If you use a jig for sharpening, keep in mind that it will not sharpen the tool for you and you still need to know what you want the grind to look like.

4 I just want to turn. Why is sharpening so important?
John Jordan has popularized this saying: "If you can't sharpen, you can't turn." I think that John is absolutely right. You'll never become a proficient turner without first learning to sharpen your tools. And it's not only about speed and proficiency: A dull tool is far more dangerous than a sharp tool.

Before you get too excited about turning, I suggest investing a few hours of time (and money, if necessary) standing shoulder to shoulder with an expert sharpener.

Regular use of a wheel dresser will true your wheel and expose fresh grinding surfaces.

If you don't turn frequently, a sharpening jig may become your best friend.

AW 23:3, p50

Buying tools

5 **What set of tools should I buy?**
My answer is don't buy a set. Every set I've seen seems to include one or two tools that you don't need. It's better to buy individual tools and learn how to use them.

When you shop for tools, make sure you buy high-speed steel (HSS) tools. They hold an edge better than the carbon-steel tools that used to be popular. If you stumble across some garage-sale bargains or inherit a set from a relative's estate, chances are those are carbon steel. (Some deceptive marketers actually pass off new carbon steel as HSS. If the price seems too good to be true, be careful.)

There is nothing wrong with carbon steel, but if you are just starting out and have difficulties sharpening, you will probably blue the steel, removing the temper. The great thing about HSS is that you can blue the edge and the tool will still stay sharp. (The blued edge dulls instantly.)

I've also had people tell me that they purchased yard-sale tools (old, worn-out carbon-steel tools) to practice on until they got better at turning. The problem with this is that as a novice turner, you're compounding your problems: Now you have some inferior tools that you're not sure how to use.

Buy the best tools you can afford, even if you buy only one tool at a time.

Another reason I dislike tool sets is the uniformity of handles. A matched set of tools looks great hanging on your wall, but when you are turning and the chips cover the bed of your lathe, it's difficult to identify each tool. Virtually all of my tools have different handles, and I can identify each one amid the chips when I am hard at work.

6 **What tools should I start with?**
I'd suggest a 3/4" spindle roughing gouge, a 3/8" spindle gouge, a 1/2" skew, and a diamond parting tool. If you want to turn bowls, select a 3/8" or 1/2" bowl gouge, although my personal favorite is a 3/8" bowl gouge. The next tools I would add are a 1/2" roundnose and 1/2" squarenose scraper.

Setting up a turning area

7 **What's the best lathe height?**
Your lathe may be set to the proper height, but I doubt it. Measure the distance from the floor to your elbow. That should be the same as the distance from the floor to the centerline of the headstock. If you have to raise your lathe, fabricate a solid base for your lathe so that it doesn't walk around the shop when you are turning. If your lathe is too high, build a stable platform that you can stand on and not trip over.

8 **How much light do I need?**
I've done countless demonstrations in shops with pitiful lighting. I don't recommend traditional fluorescent lighting because of the strobe effect it causes. (This is less noticeable with newer ballasts.) I prefer incandescent light. At my small lathe, I have three 100-watt bulbs overhead and one swing-arm lamp that I can focus on my work.

6

From left: 1/2" bowl gouge, 3/8" bowl gouge, diamond parting tool, 3/8" spindle gouge, 1/2" skew, 3/4" spindle roughing gouge, 1/2" squarenose scraper, 1/2" round-nose scraper.

5

With distinctive handles, you'll quickly locate the next tool for your turning task.

9 What's the big deal about safety glasses?

Always wear safety glasses and a faceshield! When I first started turning, I did not wear safety glasses or glasses of any kind. What a fool. After scratching my cornea numerous times and stopping to flush chips out of my eyes on many occasions, I won't even turn on the lathe today without a pair of safety glasses. Safety glasses and faceshields are necessary, not optional.

10 How much upkeep does a lathe require?

Every day, spend a few minutes doing some lathe maintenance. Feel around the bed of the lathe for rough spots and file them off. If the tool rest is new, file it and round over the edges. If the rest is old, file out the nicks and dings, and then smooth with 220-grit sandpaper. Rub a little paraffin (canning wax) on the surface of the tool rest. You'll be amazed at how it helps the tools slide.

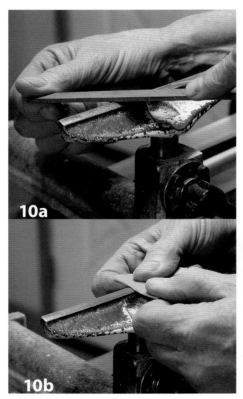

Tune up your tool rest by regularly filing (top) and then sanding (bottom) the surface.

Turning

11 How high should the tool rest be?

I cut right at the centerline. So when I'm using a cutting tool, the handle needs to be down in relation to the tool rest. That means that the tool rest needs to be a little below the centerline of the lathe. If it is set just at the centerline, you will have to lift up on the handle to complete the cut because you always complete the cut at the centerline. If you switch to a smaller tool, you will need to raise the tool rest a little.

With a little experience, tool-rest height becomes intuitive and you find yourself making only slight adjustments as you are turning. If you have to raise the tool handle every time you finish a cut, you probably need to lower the tool rest.

If you are using a scraper, the handle needs to be up in relation to the tool rest. Scrapers are almost always used this way. Using a scraper with the tool handle down is asking for a big catch.

12 How close should I put the tool rest to the wood?

Keep the tool rest as close to the work as you can. Turning is a bit of a leverage game, and if you extend the tool too far over the tool rest, you are asking for trouble. If you are roughing a square block into a cylinder, bring the tool rest as close to the work as you can and rotate the piece to see that it does not bind.

Set your tool-rest height slightly below center with the tool on center.

Start the lathe, rough the block partially, then shut off the lathe and move the tool rest closer to the work and repeat.

Moving the tool rest while the lathe is running can result in broken tool rests and possible injury.

13 At what speed should I turn?

I doubt you'll find any turning instructors who will offer up a firm answer to this question.

Variables include your skill level, what wood you are turning, even the kind of lathe you own. But if you have to ask that question, you should slow down a bit. On the other hand, it's possible to turn too slow, but that's far less dangerous than turning too fast. A good rule of practice is to reduce the speed, turn on the lathe, increase the speed gradually just to the point of vibration, and then back off a bit. (This is easy with a variable-speed lathe.) As the piece comes into round, slowly increase the speed. Your comfort level will change with time and experience. Finally, it's safest to stand to the side of the lathe when you turn it on.

14 When am I ready to turn big bowls and platters?

I often get this question at hands-on workshops. I have no problem with bigger bowls, but the techniques to turn a 6" bowl are the same as the techniques to turn a 24" bowl. If you are just learning and blow up a small bowl with an oops, you have far less time, energy, and money invested in the small bowl than you would in the large bowl. Plus, it's a lot safer turning smaller pieces

Start small and work your way up. Some people have made a career of turning small items.

15 What is the best chuck?

Pull back on those reins; there will be plenty of chances to plunk down money on a 4-jaw scroll chuck after you get your chops. After you've turned for a bit, you'll know exactly what kind of chuck you need.

Don't buy any chuck until you know what kind of turning you like to do. If you want to turn small items (up to 10"), a chuck such as the Oneway Talon or Penn State Barracuda 2N is ideal. But until you settle on what you like to turn, use a faceplate. It's a lot less expensive and you can do almost everything with a faceplate that you can do with a chuck.

For example, if you want to turn a weed pot, you can use a small chuck with #2 jaws, turn a shoulder on your turning stock, and grasp the weed-pot stock with the jaws.

You can turn the same project with a faceplate. After attaching a wasteblock to the faceplate with screws, use cyanoacrylate (CA) glue to adhere the turning stock to the wasteblock.

Sanding and finishing

16 What grit sandpaper is that? I wish I had a dollar for each time I've been asked this question during a demonstration. How I sand depends upon what I am turning.

If I'm turning a weed pot or a ring holder, I might start with 120- or 150- grit sandpaper and work up to 600 grit. On a good day, I might start with 180 or 220 grit. However, when I first started turning I generally started with 80 grit or even 60 grit. But now that my skills are better, I can cut better and I have less tear-out, so I can start turning with a higher grit. I do like to use a good quality sandpaper. I'm particularly fond of the gold sandpaper from Klingspor (800-645-5555; klingspor.com), but I also use a blue zirconia paper from Red Hill Corp. (800-822-4003; Supergrit.com). Norton and 3M also make outstanding sandpapers for efficient removal.

If I am sanding something like a bowl or a platter, I sand a little differently. I generally start by hand-sanding with 120 or 150 grit with the lathe running (slowly) to about 220 or 320 grit. I then shut off the lathe, drop down to 180 or 220 grit, and use 3" sanding discs in a drill to finish the piece at least to 600 grit.

As a general rule, I like to slow the lathe down a bit when I am sanding, because it generates less heat. For protection, I often use a foam pad between the sandpaper and my fingers. I sand at the highest grit possible, but won't hesitate to drop down to a lower grit if necessary. The problem with sanding with lower grits is that you can easily sand away those fine details in your turning.

Finally, don't be stingy by trying to reuse sandpaper. If it's still cutting okay, fine, but if it's loaded up or clogged, throw it away and use fresh sandpaper.

17 What's the best finish to apply? New woodturners shouldn't worry about a finished project! I know that sounds odd, but when you're just starting, your job is to have fun at woodturning. You need to get used to the tools, how they work, and what they will do. When you have mastered the tools, then you can start looking at finished projects.

I like the feel and look of an oil finish such as Waterlox. If I am in a rush, I may resort to a spray lacquer, let the piece dry, and then buff it. For things like my Christmas ornaments, I hang them in a row and spray them with a Deft satin lacquer.

*A previous member of the AAW Board of Directors, **Robert Rosand** is an instructor and frequent contributor to American Woodturner. Visit Robert at www.rrosand.com.*

Start easy

When I lead hands-on workshops, I limit students to small projects and usually bring sufficient material to complete three of the same projects (three birdhouses, three ornaments). I always tell the students not to worry about finishing the first project, but to go through the process, learn from their mistakes, and improve the next project. Most people are determined to complete their first project, but those who learn from their mistakes and get on to the next project are usually happiest with their results.

Finally, don't use valuable wood for practice sessions. Go out to the firewood pile and turn that wood until you are competent with the tools. Years ago, at one of the early symposiums, another turner and I purchased some beautiful redwood burl slabs. When we saw David Ellsworth, we asked him what we should do with it. His response was, "Put it away until you know the answer to that question."

What Speed is Best?

The one that makes you feel safe, comfortable, and in control

What speed do I turn at? A number of years ago in an Arrowmont class, someone asked the instructor that question. After some thought, he responded, "Well I guess it should go around."

What an insight!

On one level you might think the instructor was being a wise guy, but on another, he was close to the answer. You really can turn at a wide range of speeds and produce excellent work. However, there are a number of factors that a turner balances in choosing a speed, and this is why I have never been a fan of the speed-selection charts packaged with many lathes.

Diameters and rim speed

The rpm of the spindle is sometimes the least important number for me. No, the speed of the outside edge or surface may be far more telling in determining speed. (Comparison: the outer edge of a 10" table saw blade at 4,000 rpm is traveling at 119 mph, while the 1/2" router bit at 25,000 rpm is only travelling at 37 mph).

Look at the accompanying chart of rim speeds at different diameters and see the dramatic differences. A miniature running at 1,200 rpm may look like it is hardly moving, while a large bowl may overpower you and your lathe—which may place you in a danger zone.

When working small diameter miniatures, you really can raise the speed to fairly high levels. However, I was getting clean cuts on this 3/8" piece at speeds easily below 1,000 rpm.

Mass of the object

The real force of an object on the lathe is its velocity times its mass. So, a pen blank won't have a lot of force at 1,800 rpm—even if it flew off the lathe—while the 14-pound wet bowl blank at 1,800 rpm can be lethal. The higher the speed, the greater the force. At some very high rpm even the pen blank has real force.

Balance of the object

Look at what a few ounces of lead in the wrong spot on a front wheel of your car can do: A misplaced wheel weight causes your 2-ton monster to shake and rattle at certain speeds. We have the same problem in wood-turning: Out of round, inconsistent densities of the material, or pieces with voids all lead to excessive vibration at certain speeds. In reality, we may have some pieces that never balance—forcing us to work at slower speeds than we wish.

Stability of the lathe

This is related to everything I have already mentioned: Some lathes simply start shaking with almost anything mounted on them. Vibration is a curse to the machinist and the woodturner alike: We will have a rough ride, quality suffers, and safety issues abound if we don't have some degree of stability of the lathe itself. Also, some lathes have awful stands/legs, flimsy headstock spindles, headstock bearings that are too few, underbuilt or just too close together—all of these factors impact lathe stability and therefore the turning speed.

And one more factor: The low end speed of some lathes are simply not slow enough to do much bowl turning—they simply run too fast and are underbuilt. These are serious considerations in choosing a lathe if your interests are with bowls and vessels.

AW 19:1, p16

Now we are into a red zone: large diameter (17"), heavy, out-of-round/balance blank. If the lathe can handle such a piece, I progress from a point just below vibration to a modest speed as it becomes more balanced. However, with a rim speed of 51mph at 1,000 rpm, I never find it necessary to crank up much speed.

The skill of the turner

With NASCAR racing and woodturning, a true professional can often work at higher speeds. As your skill and control improve, you can turn at greater speeds. However, unless you are a production turner working on a piece-rate schedule, high speeds are not really the answer—so be careful here. Even production turners have had serious accidents related to speed. In most cases, folks don't really care how quickly you made something—only how well it turned out.

The material

I often hear it said that you get a better cut at higher speeds. True to a point, but in reality there are still other factors related to the material that affect the quality of the cutting action. The moisture content is one (generally the wetter the wood, the cleaner the cutting action), orientation of the grain as well as consistency in grain direction (cutting against the grain or grain that is wild and erratic causes problems), and species (compare the cutting qualities of fir against pear—they don't even seem to be related). Sometimes I do get a cleaner cut by raising the speed (you are getting more cuts per inch of travel)—but other times I get better results by not raising the speed and only slowing my feed rate (I move slower, and thereby get more cuts per inch of travel). And add to this the question of tool sharpness, working at higher speed becomes a smaller component of the equation. Finally, too much speed contributes to the problem of ribbing or chatter when the material flexes or distorts.

Recommendations for choosing a speed

Yes, there are many variables. First, be aware of the speed your lathe is set to even before you mount a piece or turn it on. Some serious accidents have occurred by not heeding this warning.

Next, weigh all the factors for a particular piece on the lathe, especially diameter and mass. And the less stable your lathe and the less experience you have, get the blank as close to round and well centered before turning—this is primarily an issue in bowls, platters, vessels, and the like.

For between center work, I saw off the corners when the diameters go above 4"; below that, a large roughing gouge handles the "out of round" safely.

It is always better to start at the slower speeds with a piece and gradually bring up the speed.

This all raises the question: Can you turn too slowly? If the cutting action is choppy and labored, then speed up to the next level on your machine. If that next level leads to excessive vibration, you may have to live with turning at a slower speed. Always work at a speed that feels safe, controlled and comfortable for YOU. Finally, a sharp tool at the right cutting angle seems far, far more important than cranking up the speed to "do a better job."

*A past President of the AAW and an Honorary Lifetime Member, **Alan Lacer** has spent four decades as a turner, instructor, and contributing editor to* American Woodturner. *Visit Alan at www.woodturninglearn.net.*

SPEED OF LATHE-TURNED OBJECTS AT DIFFERENT RPM						
		250 rpm	450 rpm	600 rpm	1,200 rpm	1,800 rpm	3,000 rpm
RIM SIZE (outside dia.)	1/2" dia.	.4 mph	.7 mph	.9 mph	1.8 mph	2.7 mph	4.5 mph
	6" dia.	4.5 mph	8.0 mph	10.7 mph	21.4 mph	32.1 mph	54.0 mph
	12" dia.	8.9 mph	16.0 mph	21.4 mph	42.8 mph	64.2 mph	108.0 mph
	14" dia.	10.4 mph	18.7 mph	25.0 mph	49.9 mph	74.9 mph	125.0 mph

A Guide to Gouges

Understand the basics to master these essential tools

Looking through woodturning catalogs can be overwhelming—the choices in lathe tools alone are vast! One manufacturer lists over a dozen gouges in various sizes and styles. So, how do you choose? This brief guide will help you understand the basics of gouges and explain how to get the most from these indispensable tools.

Spindle-roughing gouge

Used for spindle turning only. The large cross-section at the cutting end is effective for roughing down square stock and for removing wood quickly. This tool is commonly sold in 1¼" and ¾" (32 mm and 20 mm). Size is determined by measuring across the flute. The inside profile of the flute is concentric with the outside of the tool. Wall thickness is consistently about ¼" (6 mm). The spindle-roughing gouge (SRG) is dangerous to use on bowl blanks because the shank has a thin cross-section where it enters the handle (see sidebar). (A notable exception is the SRG from P&N, an Australian manufacturer. The section that enters the handle is much heavier. Despite this, the tool should only be used on spindles.)

The SRG works best with a bevel angle of about 45°. A shorter bevel adds unnecessary resistance; a longer bevel creates an edge that is too fragile for roughing out work. The profile of the cutting edge is ground straight across, making sharpening a straightforward procedure.

In use, the flute faces up at 90° for the initial roughing cuts. In this position, the near vertical wings sever wood fibers as the large curved edge gouges away the bulk of the material. As the wood becomes a cylinder, the

Spindle-roughing gouge profile

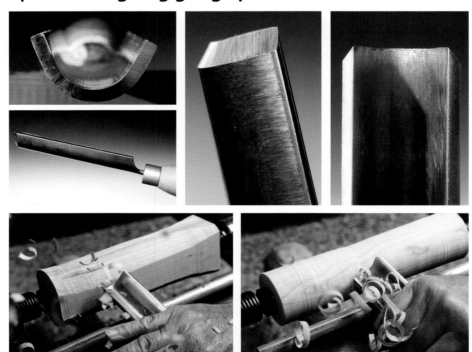

A spindle-roughing gouge (SRG) is used to turn a square spindle into a cylinder.

AW 26:5, p21

Spindle-roughing gouge

Until recently, spindle-roughing gouges were simply called roughing gouges. The name change/clarification came about because of the increasing number of woodturners who thought that a roughing gouge would be okay to use to rough out a bowl blank. Doing so caused numerous accidents when the small shanks of these large cross-sectioned tools snapped from the incredible force exerted by a rotating bowl blank.

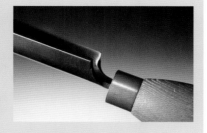

For safety's sake, a roughing gouge, more correctly called a spindle-roughing gouge (SRG), is used only for roughing out between-center spindle work where the grain of the wood runs parallel to the bed of the lathe.

tool can be rolled to use other portions of the cutting edge. With practice, the straight portion of either wing can be presented in a shearing-planing cut similar to the cutting action of a skew chisel.

Spindle gouges

Cutting coves in spindle-turned work defines what a spindle gouge does best; however, these versatile tools are also used to rough down stock, make V cuts, form beads, and hollow endgrain boxes. Richard Raffan uses a ½" spindle gouge for much of his work. He says, "Throughout my 30 years of teaching I've been saying that if you are limited to just one tool, that's the one. You can turn anything with a half-inch gouge."

A spindle gouge is measured by the diameter of the round rod the tool is manufactured from, which typically ranges from ¼" to ⅝"

(6 mm to 15 mm). The shape and depth of the flute, along with how the bevel is ground, help delineate the tool's cutting properties. Looking directly down the shaft of a spindle gouge, the profile of the cutting edge as it wraps around the flute resembles a crescent moon. The depth that the flute is cut into the rod reaches about midway through the rod in a traditional spindle gouge. The width of the flute is wider, relative to the rod, than for a bowl gouge. It is this rounded portion of the flute that creates the curved cutting edge that allows the wood to be gouged or scooped.

A subcategory of spindle gouges is the detail gouge. For detail gouges, the flute is shallower than for a regular spindle gouge, making the curve of the flute less pronounced. The result is a heavier cross-section of the bevel, which can mean more resistance when cutting wood. On

the other hand, the thicker tool provides more stability (the tool does not easily flex). A solution is to grind a double bevel: Resistance is diminished while at the same time the heavy cross-section supports an acute bevel angle. This thin cutting edge can then fit into tight intersections.

Most spindle gouges sold today have a fingernail or swept-back profile for the cutting edge. When looking at a spindle gouge with the flute facing up, the edge is usually shaped with the tip rounded and the edges curved toward the handle, the resulting profile resembling a fingernail.

The radius of the tip can vary; woodturners grind the shape of the tip to fit specific needs. For instance, if you were using the spindle gouge for cutting coves, a traditional spindle gouge with a gently rounded tip would be efficient. If you tried to cut deep V cuts with the same tool, however, the bottom cutting edge could make unwanted contact with the wood at the sharp intersection of

In general, spindle gouges are not meant for use with bowl turning, especially for a beginning turner. The shallow flute of a spindle gouge creates a different shape of the cutting edge than that of a bowl gouge and the bevels are generally ground at a steeper angle, making the cutting action more aggressive. Severe catches can result.

Spindle gouge profile

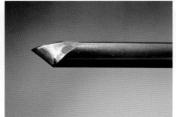
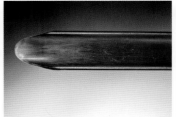

A spindle gouge cleanly cuts coves.

Detail gouge profile

A detail gouge is primarily used for spindle turning and is ideal for cleanly cutting tight transitions.

a cove and its adjoining element. In this case, a tip that is more pointed would work better. Some turners grind the profile of their detail gouges almost to a point and use them in much the same fashion as a skew chisel.

The overhang needed for the required depth of some cuts could cause the thinner cross-section of a traditional spindle gouge to vibrate and result in chatter. In this case, a detail gouge, ground with a double bevel and having a smaller-radius tip, would be the superior tool. Ground in this manner, the detail gouge is also ideal for turning beads.

Experienced turners will use spindle gouges on bowls and faceplate work, specifically for adding details such as beads and grooves. The flute should never face up, however. The cutting edge would be unsupported and a severe catch could result. If you keep the flute facing to the side or angled slightly, you will limit how much of the tool's edge will engage with the wood and a safe cut is possible for detailing a bowl.

For spindle turning, I recommend that beginning woodturners purchase a ⅜" or ½" (10 mm or 13 mm) traditional spindle gouge with a fingernail grind and a gently rounded profile for the tip. The bevel angle should be in the range of 35° to 40°. This is a useful general-purpose tool and this profile and bevel angle is a good compromise between cutting edge retention and the ability to reach into tight intersections.

Detail gouge Q&A with Michael Hosaluk

Q: *What are the features of a detail gouge that make it versatile?*

A: It is thick in cross-section resulting in less vibration, which means that the tool can hang off the toolrest more so than a traditional spindle gouge. This tool is useful for off-center turning and for cleaning up the sides inside deep vessels.

Q: *How does the shallower flute of a detail gouge compare to the deeper flute of a traditional spindle gouge?*

A: Thompson Tools makes detail gouges for me—the flute is slightly shallower than other designs, which allows me to reach into tight areas in a way that is similar to using a skew chisel. If the flute is too deep, that will limit this possibility. With the shallow flute I get more of a slicing action.

Q: *You are well known for using a double-bevel grind. What is the purpose of the double bevel?*

A: Since the detail gouge is thick in cross-section and has a shallow flute, if ground with one bevel, the bevel is very long from the heel to the cutting edge. Creating a secondary bevel allows easier reference from the second heel to cutting edge, which makes the tool less grabby. Some people remove the hollow grind altogether to create a radius that removes the reference of a heel.

Q: *What bevel angle do you usually use?*

A: The long bevel is 30° and the top bevel is 32° to 34°. The profile is like the fingernail on my pinky. I try to make the profile identical on both sides so that when I roll beads the result is the same. I have, however, seen them ground in every shape and get results. In the end, all that matters is what the turning looks like when you are finished.

Q: *Does the bevel vary depending on the type of wood? Does it vary for any other reason(s)?*

A: The longer the bevel angle, the sharper the edge and the further it can reach into tight spaces. Mine are factory ground to a specific angle that is good for general work, but never be afraid to change the angle of any gouge to suit the work at hand, after all they are just tools. When the technical aspects of turning are broken down to the basics, we turners (1) start with a revolving piece of wood, and (2) shape it with a tool. Where the two make contact you want the least amount of resistance.

Q: *Are there disadvantages to using a detail gouge?*

A: For turning bowls, a detail gouge is not as appropriate as a bowl gouge, but for spindles they are ideal. I do use a detail gouge on bowls, however, for finishing cuts. After you get to know woodturning tools, you will find you can use any of them for most aspects of turning, but we all develop preferences.

Bowl gouge profiles

Ellsworth

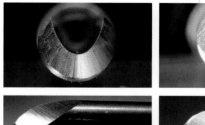

A roughing cut on the outside of a bowl.

Glaser

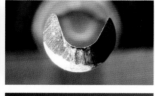

A pull cut is used to reach into a tight area and to clean up torn grain. For an even finer shear-scraping cut, rotate the tool slightly clockwise and drop the handle.

Traditional

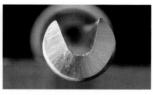

A light touch and a sharp edge will produce fine shavings and a cleanly cut surface on the outside of a bowl.

Bowl gouges

Bowl gouges are the workhorses of bowl turning. Their size, the profile of the cutting edge, and the angle of the bevel can be varied to meet individual needs. Large gouges are essential for roughing out a bowl blank, medium-size ones are ideal for refining the shape of the bowl, and smaller gouges assist in adding detail. Bowl gouges are commonly available from ¼" to ⅝" (6 mm to 15 mm), as measured by the distance between the flutes. They are made from round rod stock. A typical ½" (13 mm) bowl gouge is made from ⅝" (15 mm) diameter rod and a typical ⅜" (10 mm) bowl gouge is made from ½" (13 mm) diameter rod. (Some tool manufacturers, however, measure their gouges by the actual diameter of the tool steel.) The deep, relatively narrow flute produces a cross-section that is strong, much in the same manner that channel-shaped steel beams offer strength. The sturdiness of bowl gouges allows for overhanging the tool from the toolrest, which is important when hollowing deep bowls.

The shape of the flute can vary from a U to a V. Some U-shaped flutes have sides that curve inward. The bottom of the U or V has the smallest radius. The shape of the flute affects how effectively shavings are channeled and acts to break the wood fibers so that the shavings can be ejected. The U-shaped flute tends to eject shavings more efficiently than the V shape.

When looking at the tool with the flute facing upward, most bowl gouges have a fingernail-grind profile similar to that of spindle gouges. This fingernail grind (or swept-back or Ellsworth grind) makes the bowl gouge versatile. By rotating the tool and presenting the cutting edge at different points along the flute (from the tip to the side), the amount of wood that is gouged, scooped away, or finely shaved can vary from large to delicately fine. For instance, to achieve a fine shearing cut, use a deep-fluted bowl gouge with the flute pointed up and lightly cut the wood. Angle the tool slightly, add more force, and substantial shavings will fly, as when rough turning the interior or exterior of a bowl. In addition, a sizeable portion of the long swept-back edge can be used to efficiently gouge away the bulk of the material.

Alternatively, while working on the outside of a bowl when refining the profile or cleaning up torn grain, position the flute facing the wood and a shearing cut is possible using the trailing edge of the tool. With this cut, there is little chance of the tool catching; fine shavings and a clean cut are the result. The fingernail profile also allows access to the outside of the bowl near the base. By using a pull cut with the flute facing the wood (leading edge just clearing but not touching the wood), this area of the bowl can be shaped and cleanly cut.

Traditional-grind bowl gouge

Although it is versatile, the swept-back (fingernail) grind is by no means the only grind on a bowl gouge that is effective. When hollowing the interior of a bowl, professional turner Mike Mahoney believes the traditional grind is the best for hollowing the bottom third inside a side-grain bowl. "I use a traditional grind, which is ground straight across. You can grind the wings back minimally, but that can affect the cleanness of the cut. If the wings make contact, you are not holding the tool in the correct position. My argument to grind it straight across is to make it easier to sharpen," he comments. Although he understands that it takes more skill to use the traditional grind, he believes it's worth learning. "For me it cuts cleaner in almost all circumstances than the fingernail grind, but since it doesn't have a leading edge (like the nose of the fingernail grind) it is harder to control. The traditional grind, however, is less effective for bulk removal."

Cutting the interior of a bowl

For bowl turning, one area that is challenging to cut cleanly is the interior, where the side of a bowl transitions into the bottom. With a bevel ground at 60°, it is often difficult to keep the bevel in contact with the wood while rounding the corner—it is just not possible to swing the handle far enough to keep the bevel on the wood. Some turners advocate using a bowl gouge with a shorter bevel of 75° to 80° for tackling this juncture—the handle would not need to swing as far

to the left. Conversely, a ¼" (6 mm) bowl gouge with a long bevel (45° to 50°) will make a clean cut when turning the inside walls of a tall vessel.

I recommend a ½" (13 mm) bowl gouge with a fingernail profile and bevel angle of about 60° degrees as an all-purpose tool for beginning bowl turners. It is ideal for turning open bowl forms 8" to 10" (200 mm to 250 mm) in diameter. That bevel angle is nonaggressive and will allow the turner to maintain bevel-rubbing cuts on the exterior and interior of most bowls.

When selecting a new gouge, buy the highest quality tool you can afford—the quality of the steel varies from one manufacturer to the other. Look for the tool's cross-section to be uniformly shaped and the flute polished (mill marks removed). Seek help from experienced turners to

properly grind and sharpen your gouges, then practice sharpening.

As you practice basic cuts and gain experience, you will discover the versatility of bowl and spindle gouges. Different presentations or slight modifications in how the bevel is ground can make it possible to take just the right cut—don't be afraid to shape the tool to fit your needs.

I once received some excellent advice after purchasing a ¼" bowl gouge from JoHannes Michelsen. As I watched him grind the edge on a 6" (150 mm) grinder, freehand, with the easy grace that comes with mastery, he just smiled and said, "One way or another, you need to learn how to make the tools work for you."

Joe Larese is a member of the Nutmeg Woodturners League in CT. Visit Joe at www.joelarese.com.

Tool placement for cutting inside a bowl

To help explain proper tool placement for turning the inside of a bowl, I cut a bowl in half and photographed four bowl gouges, each with a different bevel angle and cutting-edge profile. The bowl's shape is relatively deep and has an undercut rim area. I selected this profile to better illustrate the broad range of tool placement needed to maintain bevel contact.

Three of the bowl gouges have a fingernail profile: a 1/4" (6 mm) Glaser bowl gouge with a 35° bevel, a 1/2" (13 mm) generic bowl gouge with a 45° bevel, and a 1/2" (13 mm) Ellsworth bowl gouge with a 60° bevel. The fourth is a 3/8" (10 mm) bowl gouge with a traditional-grind profile and a bevel of about 60°.

One photograph shows the four gouges together inside the bowl, which illustrates each of the four gouges placed where they work best. Additional photos show each gouge in five areas of the bowl.

Although bowl forms vary greatly, the area between #3 and #4 is typically the area that causes the greatest challenge to turners. Note the tool angle required for maintaining the bevel rubbing for this area for each tool. In the case of the Glaser gouge with a 35° bevel, this

long bevel, combined with the curved form of the bowl, means the inability to have the bevel support the cut beyond the wall area; the handle of the tool is outside the profile of the bowl.

Note: The toolrest is positioned in the same orientation for purposes of comparison. To obtain the least amount of tool overhang, the toolrest should be readjusted as hollowing proceeds.

The five areas are:
1. At the rim
2. Approximately 1/3 of the way down the bowl wall
3. Approximately 2/3 of the way down the bowl wall, just beginning the transition from wall to bottom
4. Lower portion of the bowl in the transition area between wall and bottom
5. Center of the bowl at the bottom

Medium bevel, positions one through five

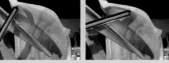

Ellsworth-grind bowl gouge

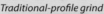

Traditional-profile grind

Glaser gouge, ground with a long bevel

Your First Bowl Gouge

Options abound but it's best to start with the basics

Illustrations: Angelo Iafrate and Roxanne LeMoine

AW 23:4, p56

For a beginner, buying turning tools can be a daunting task. Do you choose high-carbon steel, high-speed steel (HSS), or powdered metallurgy? What about cryogenically treated tools? Out of the confusion of tools available, which one do you really need? Sometimes it depends on what you turn, but even then, every turner seems to have a different opinion.

Before making a recommendation, I asked turners from beginner to professional what they own and what they would recommend for a beginner. Almost all recommended a 3/8" or 1/2" bowl gouge.

It's important to note that English gouges are designated by flute width while American gouges measure the diameter of the shaft. A 1/2" American gouge is about the same as a 3/8" English tool, so it's possible some turners were actually recommending the same tool.

What steel?
Because high-carbon steel doesn't hold an edge and carbide is too hard to sharpen, most professionals favor high-speed steel and powdered-metallurgy tools.

You won't find new gouges manufactured from high-carbon steel or carbide. You'll choose between standard HSS (most are M2) and high-wear steels (often in powdered metal) like 2030, 2060, A11, and V15. Although cryogenically treated tools offer an advantage in edge holding, they are expensive for a beginner.

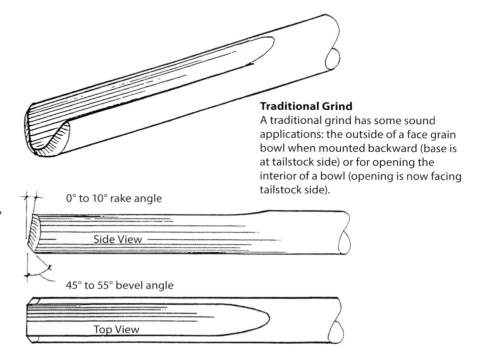

Traditional Grind
A traditional grind has some sound applications: the outside of a face grain bowl when mounted backward (base is at tailstock side) or for opening the interior of a bowl (opening is now facing tailstock side).

0° to 10° rake angle

Side View

45° to 55° bevel angle

Top View

This 3/8" bowl gouge has a fingernail grind.

The bowl gouge will become the most versatile tool in your toolbox. With a properly ground bowl gouge you can rough-turn a bowl, form the outside and hollow the interior, and shear-scrape it to a smooth finish. The gouge is also fine for roughing end-grain boxes and hollowing vases. (It tends to scrape rather than cut end grain.)

Some turners prefer a V-shaped flute, some a U-shaped flute, while others prefer the superflute, a shape somewhere between a V and a U. I have all three types at my lathe and find only minor advantages of one over the others. For a beginner, proper sharpening is more important than flute shape.

What profile?
Bowl gouges are available with tips ground to the manufacturer's standard profile or to a special profile developed by any of several well-known professional turners. The tip profile most often recommended for a beginner is the transition or fingernail grind. After experience (50-plus bowls), you may want to try

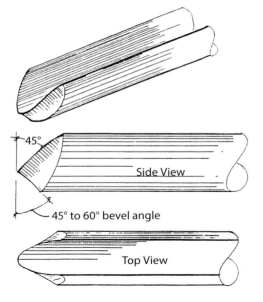

45°

Side View

45° to 60° bevel angle

Top View

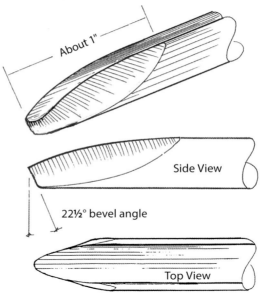

About 1"

Side View

22½° bevel angle

Top View

Irish Grind
Experienced turners may prefer the more complicated Irish grind. It's a good tool for roughing bowls, detailing (with the elliptical front), shear-scraping, and smoothing the transition from sides to bottom.

Transition or Fingernail Grind
Many turning instructors recommend the transition (fingernail) grind to new turners. You work the outside of a face-grain bowl regardless of the orientation. The ground sides allow limited shear-scraping.

the Irish (also known as the Celtic or Ellsworth) grind.

Using the Oneway Wolverine Sharpening System with the Vari-Grind Jig is an easy way to form a similar shape. Fundamentals of Sharpening, an AAW video, has excellent instructions on three techniques for sharpening a bowl gouge, making it easy to choose a method that works best for you. (For details, see woodturner.org/products.) The angles shown are typical ranges.

I'm confident that a ⅜" or ½" HSS or powdered-metal bowl gouge with a transition grind will get any beginning turner started on the road to enjoying bowl turning.

John Lucas is Shop Tips *editor for* American Woodturner *and a frequent demonstrator at regional and national AAW symposiums around the country.*

Allan Batty on angles of bowl gouges

What determines the grinding angle for bowl gouges is the type of bowl you are going to be making," writes Allan Batty in *Woodturning Notes*, an information- packed booklet available from Crafts Supplies (woodturnerscatalog.com)

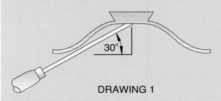

DRAWING 1

Drawing 1: "This is a shallow type of bowl. We have no restrictions placed on the gouge by the wall of the bowl. Therefore, none is placed on the angle of the tool."

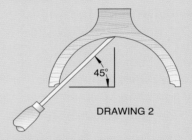

DRAWING 2

Drawing 2: "With this bowl, the wall restricts the gouge movement. As the depth does not exceed the radius, an angle of 45 degrees would be ideal to maintain bevel contact throughout the cut."

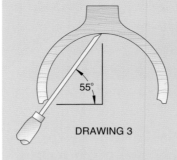

DRAWING 3

Drawing 3: "Here the restriction becomes greater as the depth has now exceeded the radius, which in turn, would require a shorter bevel angle of approximately 55 degrees. This would allow the bevel to contact right to the bottom of the bowl."

Drawing 4: "Now the depth has increased even further, which requires an even shorter angle (in this case approximately 60–65 degrees) to allow successful bevel contact."

"You can see that the determining factor is what type of bowl you want to make. An angle of between 45 and 55 degrees would be a good working compromise."

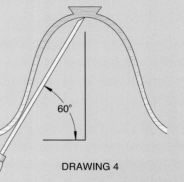

DRAWING 4

Humanizing the Skew Chisel

This essential tool is easier to use than you might think

I have yet to meet a woodturner whose skills weren't improved from learning to use a skew chisel. The skew teaches how wood is cut, and it teaches the importance of the bevel better than any other turning tool. Learning those two lessons will make anyone a more skillful woodturner, regardless of the kind of turning. In addition, the skew leaves the smoothest surface of any turning tool, and a sharp skew makes clean cuts easily in the most challenging of wood-grain patterns—more so than any other turning tool.

In the past, I described spindle turning as a skill to be learned before becoming a *compleat* and accomplished woodturner. There is one additional step, however: mastering the skew chisel.

The *skew* does not make these lessons easy. The very name

skew strikes fear in the hearts of woodturners, beginners and experts alike. We have all heard stories about the dreaded skew. Some will have mustered the courage to use the skew chisel, only to have a humongous catch that convinced them never to try again.

The reality is that the skew is no more difficult than whittling on a stick of wood or peeling a carrot with a knife. The only difference is the wood is spinning when the skew is cutting.

The tool

When you are learning how to use a skew chisel, practice with one that is at least 1" (25 mm) wide. Wider is even better—the wider the tool, the easier it is to see the cutting action and to control the cut. Additionally, a heavier tool causes less vibration. Save narrow skews for when you have mastered the use of this tool.

The cutting edge of the skew chisel *must be sharp*. Everything

else is a personal preference. The skew can have a round, oval, or rectangular shank; the cutting edge can be straight or curved; and the bevel can be concave, flat, or slightly convex *(Photo 1)*.

If the shank of your skew chisel has square edges, take it to the grinder and make the edges round and smooth. The skew has to slide smoothly along the toolrest, and a round edge will slide easily; sharp, square corners won't slide. It is worth the extra dollars to purchase a skew that already has rounded edges. There is an argument for rounding only one edge so the flat on top can be used as a reference for vertical cutting, but I prefer rounding both edges so they slide along the toolrest. An oval skew is fine just the way it is.

Sharpen a skew chisel

The skew should be the sharpest tool you own. A variety of machines can shape the bevels and form the cutting edges of skew chisels: a high-spseed

1 My favorite skew chisels: a 1¼"- (3 cm-) wide rectangular skew with a curved cutting edge and a concave bevel (top) and a 1½"- (4 cm-) wide oval skew with a straight edge and flat bevel.

AW 25:5, p32

2 The oval skew with the flat bevel is sharpened on a sheet of 600-grit sandpaper with some thinned mineral oil as a lubricant. The backing is a piece of particleboard that is ¾" (2 cm) thick.

3 The edge at the toe of the curved skew is at 90° to the top of the tool, and has a short (no more than ¼" [6 mm]) straight section before starting the curve.

4 The curved skew is ground on an 80-grit wheel, and then honed with a 600-grit India stone.

grinding wheel, a Tormek grinder, belt sander, or disc sander. Use a buffing wheel, slip-stone, bench stone, or sandpaper to hone—the wood doesn't know or care which was used. Honing will create a cutting edge that is razor sharp.

For skew chisels with a straight-profile cutting edge, I frequently hone or sharpen using a fine-grit bench stone or 600-grit wet/dry sandpaper placed on a piece of particleboard that is ¾" (19 mm) thick. I apply a few drops of oil to the sandpaper as a lubricant. I use a 50/50 mixture of mineral oil and kerosene (or mineral spirits) as a lubricant *(Photo 2)*. Over time, and after repeated sharpenings, this method gradually changes the bevel from flat (or concave) to slightly convex, which I believe is good; the tool seems to cut better.

For curved-edge skew chisels, it is important that the toe (long edge) meets at a right angle (90°) to the top edge of the shank *(Photo 3)*. This holds true for all skew chisels with a curved cutting edge.

To shape the profile of a curved-edge skew chisel, grind the bevel to create the desired curve, using a grinder, and then hone the tool to a sharp edge with a flat stone *(Photo 4)*. In addition to creating a sharper cutting edge, honing with a flat stone bridges across a concave

bevel, creating a narrow secondary flat bevel along the cutting edge. That tiny secondary bevel is what slides along the wood as the tool is cutting, making the tool easier to control.

Before applying the skew chisel to wood, make sure the top surface of the toolrest is smooth and free of dents and dings. A smooth toolrest is important when using the skew, more so than for larger-radii spindle and bowl gouges.

Carrots, rutabagas, and a permanent marker

A carrot is an excellent object to use when learning how to master the skew chisel. Carrots are easy to peel and there is no wood grain to catch. I give Ted Bartholomew of Tacoma,

WA, credit for introducing me to the benefits of turning vegetables; rutabagas are his favorite.

Buy a bag of large carrots, the larger the better, and a rutabaga—several rutabagas. Cut a carrot into pieces that are 4" (10 cm) long, and mount one piece onto the lathe, between centers *(Photo 5)*.

Select a sharp skew chisel, and then blacken both sides of the bottom half of the bevel that is closest to the heel (short edge) with a permanent marker *(Photo 6)*. This black mark is the *safety zone* for cuts that are made with the blade while not using the tip of the skew. The best and safest cutting will be somewhere near the center of this safety zone. For a 1"- (25 mm-) wide skew, this safety zone is ample.

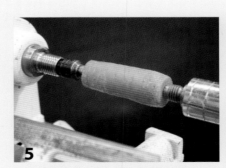

5 Cut a large carrot to about 4" (10 cm) long and mount it between centers.

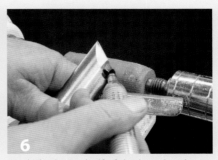

6 Mark the lower half of the bevel with a permanent marker. This will identify the safety zone.

With the lathe off, make a flat cut, checking that the bevel is supporting the cut in the middle of the safety zone. Adjust the height of the toolrest so that you can hold the tool handle in a comfortable and controllable position.

Make the same flat cut in both directions with the lathe off.

Now make the same flat cuts with the lathe running at a slow speed.

Make the same sequence of flat cuts with the toe of the skew chisel down. Note that the safety zone is now located on the opposite half of the bevel.

Practice flat cuts on a piece of wood. Run your lathe at about 1600 rpm.

The flat cut

With the lathe off, hold the skew with the shank at 30° to 45° from perpendicular to the lathe's centerline and with the heel closest to you. Roll the tool until the bevel in the middle of the safety zone rests flat on the surface of the carrot. Raise or lower the height of the toolrest so that you can hold the tool handle in a comfortable position. You have just gone through the ABCs of anchor, bevel, and cut. Now push the tool forward by sliding it along the toolrest, bevel touching the carrot, cutting edge engaged. A smooth curling carrot shaving should appear *(Photo 7)*.

Do this several times in both directions, and left and right handed *(Photo 8)*.

Now turn the lathe *on*. Have it running at about 100 rpm (or at the slowest speed possible if 100 rpm is not an option). A slow speed allows you to see what is happening with the tool. Position the skew to make the same cut as when the lathe was off. Move the bevel along the surface of the carrot with the cutting edge engaged. Practice this cut in both directions, and right and left handed, until the carrot is used up *(Photo 9)*.

You have just learned how to make a flat cut with a skew chisel. Repeat this cut until the movements become natural and you can make them without having to think about what you are doing.

Practice some more, but this time try the cut with the toe of the skew pointing down *(Photo 10)*. Some turners will find this is an easier way to hold the skew for turning square pieces of wood into cylinders. Note that when you are using the skew with the toe pointing down, the safety area is at the other end of the bevel.

Clean up all of the carrot peelings and mount a piece of wood onto the lathe. A section of a green tree limb is ideal, but any soft hardwood or construction lumber that is about 1½" (4 cm) square will work. At this point, avoid hard, dense wood. To begin, turn the spindle into a cylinder using a spindle-roughing gouge.

Then, do the ABCs, and make the same flat cuts as you made on the carrot *(Photo 11)*.

The round cut (beads)

The next vegetable to tackle is a rutabaga. Trim the ends first, using a knife, then mount the rutabaga onto the lathe between centers. A spur drive may be the best drive center to use in order to get a proper grip. With the lathe *off*, peel the rutabaga by following its curvature with the skew. Always cut downhill by starting at the larger diameter. The toolrest may have to be raised so you can hold the tool's handle in a comfortable position.

Swing, twist, and raise the tool handle to keep the cutting action located in the center of the safety zone. All the while, keep the bevel (at the point where the edge is doing the cutting) in contact with the rutabaga. Make this cut as many times as necessary until every peeling of rutabaga is continuous and is the same thickness, from the center around to both ends *(Photo 12)*.

Turn the lathe *on* at a slow speed (100 rpm or less), and make the same cut *(Photo 13)*. Make as many cuts, and use as many rutabagas as needed, until the swing, twist, and lift movement of the tool handle becomes a natural motion. It is much easier to learn how to move the tool using a rutabaga than with a hard piece of wood where catches can be inspirational events.

12 Practice peeling a rutabaga with the lathe off. This is a safe way to learn how to follow a curve with the skew, using the bevel to support the cut.

13 Make rounding cuts with the lathe running at a slow speed.

14 When rounding the end of a piece of wood, make sure the cutting action is taking place in the safety zone, with the bevel supporting the cut.

15 This is what the wood looks like when a catch happens… and they do! Use light pressure and make sure the safety zone area of the bevel is supporting the cut.

Remove what's left of the rutabaga and mount a length of wood onto the lathe, about the same diameter as the rutabaga. Turn it to a cylinder, and use the skew to turn a radius on each end *(Photo 14)*. Keep practicing until there are no catches *(Photo 15)*.

The V-groove

Mount a new piece of soft wood or another tree trimming onto the lathe. Turn it to a cylinder, using the skew as in *Photo 10*, or use a spindle-roughing gouge.

Move to the center of the cylinder to make V-groove cuts. Use the tip of the toe of the skew chisel. Hold the tool almost vertical to the toolrest (angle it slightly to one side or the other). Start the cut by holding the tip lightly to the surface until the tip starts to penetrate the wood. Angle the tool slightly in the

opposite direction and do the same thing to form the other side of the V. Keep making thin slicing cuts to widen and deepen the V *(Photo 16)*. V-grooves are made in a series of light cuts, first one side of the V, then the other.

Move a short distance away from the previous V, and do the same thing again to make another V that is separated by a short flat area *(Photo 17)*.

Round over the sharp edges at the tops of the Vs, using the rounding cut practiced with the rutabaga *(Photo 18)*.

You have just turned a bead using a skew chisel.

Now, grab another piece of wood and practice some more. If the wood is problematic, use another section of carrot or a rutabaga to practice V-grooves and beads.

Other cuts

There are four other basic cuts using a skew chisel: *peeling, facing, pommel,* and *cove*. These will be easier after mastering the flat, V-groove, and beading cuts, and gaining confidence with using the tool.

The *peeling* cut is an efficient way to make a tenon on the end of a turned furniture part, or to quickly remove a lot of wood. Hold the skew flat on the wood, with the bevel rubbing. Raise the tool handle to start and maintain the cut, similarly to how a parting tool is used. I find this cut is easiest to make using a skew chisel that has a curved cutting edge and a flat shank *(Photo 19)*.

The *facing* cut is made with the tip of the toe in the same manner as for the V-groove cut. The only difference is that the resulting shoulder is perpendicular to the

16 To make V-groove cuts, use the toe of the skew, holding the tool almost vertical. Make light cuts on either side of the V. I am using an oval skew with a straight cutting edge, but any skew will work.

17 Move down the piece of wood and make another V. Leave a flat area between the two Vs. This space will establish the width of a bead.

18 Round the edges of the Vs using the same cut you practiced with the rutabaga to create a round end. Note that the cutting action is taking place in the safety zone.

19 The peeling cut is made with the skew held flat on the toolrest. The 90° angle between the cutting edge and the toe of the skew is important to make this cut successful.

20 The facing cut is made like the V-groove cut except that the result is a 90° shoulder on the wood. Make sure there is a slight clearance between the wood and the side bevel of the skew.

21 The pommel cut is also like a V-groove cut and is used for making a transition from square to round.

22 To learn how to make a cove cut, practice first on the end of a piece of wood. Next try turning a complete cove in the center of the cylinder by cutting from both ends and meeting at the middle. Most likely, you will find that coves, especially smaller ones, are a lot easier to make using a spindle gouge.

axis of the lathe (*Photo 20*). If you are still getting catches with this cut, make sure you have enough (but not too much) clearance between the shoulder of the wood and the side bevel of the skew chisel. The bevel that supports this cut is underneath the toe, not the side bevel.

The *pommel* (sometimes spelled *pummel*) cut is a transition from square to round, as at the top of a table leg. It is a one-sided V-cut that may be either straight (90°) or slightly curved—the only difference is that the cut is started where the wood is square. It is made with the tip of the toe of the skew, the same as for a V-groove cut. Take a light cut and enter the wood very gently on the spinning square to avoid tearing the corners (*Photo 21*). A wood that splinters easily, such as oak, ash, or fir, can use some help from wrapping it

with a layer of glass-reinforced tape (strapping tape), and then cutting through the tape into the wood.

The *cove* cut with its concave curvature has been saved for the last; it is not an easy cut to make with a skew chisel. Everything just stated about following the bevel is ignored. As soon as the skew enters an inside curve the tool is touching the cutting edge and the backside of the bevel, and we already know that is a sure way to lose control of the tool and get a catch.

Additionally, it is challenging to start a cove cut because the skew will want to run away when making a shallow entry. Follow the rule of always cutting downhill from the larger to the smaller diameter (*Photo 22*). Cut downhill from both ends of the cove and have them meet at the bottom. Approach the cove cut with caution, and practice making the cut until you discover the limit

of the curvature that can be cut with the skew. Shallow, wide curves are easier. Trying to turn a cove using a skew will illustrate why many of us prefer to use a spindle gouge or small scraper for cutting anything but the long sweeping curves of a large cove.

A functional turned object

After following the instructions and practicing the exercises, you will know how to use a skew chisel and will have learned the importance of the bevel on a turning tool. Now it's time to incorporate the use of the skew chisel into your repertoire of turning accomplishments on your way to becoming a compleat woodturner. I suggest additional practice.

A good project for practicing the use of the skew chisel is the candleholder described in my previously referenced article. Simply substitute a skew chisel for the large spindle-roughing gouge, follow the instructions, and turn a candleholder (*Photo 23*).

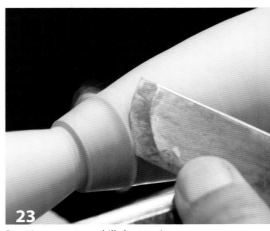

23 Practice your new skills by turning a candleholder with the skew chisel.

Russ Fairfield, who passed in 2011, was a respected turner, instructor, and member of the Inland Northwest Woodturners and the INW Pen Turners Association.

Using the Spindle Roughing Gouge

This handy tool could become your workshop favorite

Next to the small round skew that I use, the spindle roughing gouge (SRG) just might be my favorite woodturning tool.

Most people just use this tool to knock the corners off of stock for spindle turning and then grab other tools. But if sharpened and used properly, the spindle roughing gouge is capable of so much more than that.

In my woodturning shop, I use it for everything from roughing square stock and turning the icicles on my Christmas ornaments to turning Rude Osolnik-style candlesticks. My SRG is perfect for long sweeping curves and for 1/16"-diameter tenons.

Because I primarily work on small-scale projects, I make extensive use of a 1/2" SRG manufactured by Ashley Isles tools. But, the principles are the same for all roughing out gouges whether they be 1-1/2", 3/4", 1/2", or 3/8". Most turners have a 3/4" SRG in their tool kit, and I used one for many years, but my overall favorite is still the 1/2" SRG.

Sharpening

Sharpening the roughing out gouge is really quite easy. But like any other tool, you have to know what you want the finished product to look like before you begin grinding. In the case of the SRG, you want the tool sharpened at about a 45-degree angle. See the tip box "Technique counts for more than tool angle"

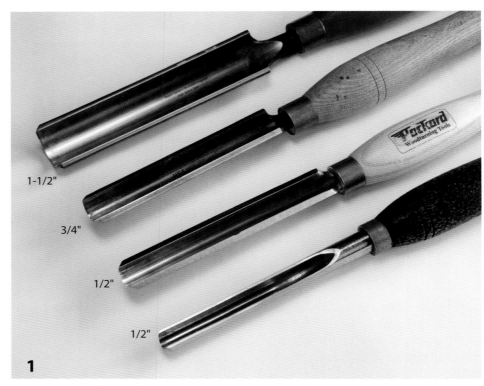

1

If you've limited the use of the spindle roughing gouge to knocking the corners off stock, you're missed some sweet turning experiences. For Christmas ornaments and other small work, I prefer the 1/2" gouge, which is not always easy to find.

about the importance of your grinding angle.

I've met a fair number of people who grind their SRG as though it were a spindle gouge. Experience tells me you lose the effectiveness of the gouge unless it's ground straight across—the straighter the better. If you look at the SRG from the front, you will see that it is horseshoe shaped with a rounded area and two

2

For freehand grinding, use one hand as a fulcrum, then rotate the tool with your other hand. Apply light pressure.

flats. The flats are what I find to be the most useful in my turning.

There are three ways to sharpen the SRG: freehand, on a large platform, and with a sharpening jig.

AW 21:1, p46

Getting Started in Woodturning

3

When sharpening with a large platform, press the tool down with one hand while rotating the tool with the other hand.

4

When using a V-arm with a sharpening jig, use one hand to keep the tool in place and the other hand to roll the tool.

5

Touch the tool to the grinder, then check to see if the angle you selected removed all of the bevel blackened with a felt-tip marker.

Freehand. Most grinders include a standard platform (about 1×3") that locks in front of the wheel. If this describes your platform, you can still sharpen the SRG on it with practice. When I sharpen using this method, I create a fulcrum with my fingers.

As shown in *Figure 2*, place one hand on the tool rest and the tool on top of your hand. With your other hand, hold the tool and rotate it while grinding.

Now, lower the tool handle, touch the tool to the wheel, then raise the handle until you are sharpening the bevel—not the edge.

When I started turning, I never quite grasped the idea of sharpening the bevel and not the edge, but it's really quite simple when you think about it. If you sharpen the bevel, the bevel will always remain the same. But if you sharpen the cutting edge, you slowly change the bevel, making the tool angle blunt and unusable until you regrind a new bevel. Save yourself time at the grinder and learn to sharpen the bevel.

Large platform. You may be fortunate enough to own a grinder with a platform about 3×5". If so, sharpening the SRG is easier. Adjust the platform so that its angle approximates the 45-degree bevel. Now, place the SRG on the platform. With your thumb or fingers, hold it flat on the platform and rotate the tool with the other hand (*Figure 3*).

Here's a reliable way to test that the platform angle is correct. Mark the SRG with a felt-tip marker, then touch the tool to the grinder. If you have a parallel shiny grind line, the angle is perfect. If the mark resembles a little triangle, adjust the platform up or down. I usually do this by tapping my tool handle on the platform.

Sharpening jig. Some turners prefer to sharpen with a jig such as the Wolverine jig. Actually, I'm kind of spoiled and do most of my sharpening using a jig. This jig system includes a V-arm that adjusts in or out (*Figure 4*).

Place your SRG in the V-arm pocket and make a rough setting. Use the felt-tip marker method described earlier, then touch the tool to the grinder. As with the platform method, a parallel grind line tells you that the setting is perfect. Got a triangle marking on the grind? Move the V-arm in or out until you nail a perfect angle. Now, sharpen the bevel (*Figure 5*).

With all of these methods, a light touch of the tool to the grinding wheel is all that is required. Once you have established the desired bevel, you only want to touch it up at the wheel.

If you generate a lot of heat when sharpening, you are pressing down too hard. Unless I am changing the bevel angle of a tool, I use little or no downward pressure when sharpening.

5 ways to put the spindle roughing gouge to use

The simplest use of a spindle roughing gouge is to true up a cylinder. That is to take a square block of wood and make it round. If I think back to my days as a fledgling turner, this was a major accomplishment. Here are some tips to help you master this tool.

When you turn with an SRG, the wood grain should run parallel to the

Technique counts for more than tool angle

That bevel on your spindle roughing gouge should be at about 45 degrees; anywhere from 48 degrees to 42 degrees is acceptable. More important is how you use the tool: Lower the tool handle, rub the bevel, then slowly raise (pivot) the handle until it starts to cut. Think about this routine every time you take a cut until it's second nature to you.

If the angle is a degree or two from 45 degrees, it will make no difference in your cut. Technique does matter.

bed of the lathe, not perpendicular as though it were a bowl.

The SRG was not designed for and will not work well for roughing out or turning bowls. Don't even think about it! See the tip box "Let's get it right" for more details.

Roughing cylinders. When you rough down a cylinder, place the tool on the tool rest, point the flute of the tool in the direction you intend to cut, rub the bevel (not cutting yet), then slowly raise the handle until the tool begins to cut. That will give you the proper cutting angle. If you do this each and every time you approach the wood, it will soon become second nature to you, and eventually you will not think about it.

Trueing stock. You can then begin to true up the stock you are working on. When you move the tool toward the headstock, point the flute in that direction. When you are cutting toward the tailstock, point the flute in that direction. You will eventually develop a rhythm to cutting (*Figure 6*).

Smooth tool rest. Take a few minutes and closely examine your tool rest. If it has lots of nasty nicks and dings in it (from other turners, obviously not from your work), you need to remove them with a file and 220-grit sandpaper.

These nicks will translate directly into your work. Another little trick that will keep the tool moving along the tool rest is to occasionally rub the rest with a chunk of paraffin wax (available where canning supplies are sold). If the wax builds up, simply clean it off with your fingernail and reapply fresh wax.

Shaping. If you intend the cylinder you turned earlier to become a weed pot, the SRG can be helpful. I use a spindle gouge to shape the body of the weed pot, but I rely on the SRG to shape the neck of the weed pot. In *Figure 7*, I am doing just that. You

When trueing a cylinder, point the tip of your spindle roughing gouge toward the tailstock, as shown in the photo. Rotate the tip toward the headstock when you true in the opposite direction.

For turning the neck of a weed pot, roll your spindle roughing gouge on its side. This tool isn't designed for turning tight curves, but is excellent for long, sweeping curves.

1/2" spindle roughing gouge: Hard to find

Most woodturning catalogs sell standard spindle roughing gouges. However, the 1/2" SRG is a bit harder to find. Packard Woodworks (packardwoodworks.com) sells a 1/2"-wide version of the 3/4" SRG. My favorite is the Ashley Isles round-bar style. One U.S. source is Tools for Working Wood (toolsforworkingwood.com).

If you buy the tool with a handle, I highly recommend knocking off the factory handle and making a new one at least 2" longer. This will increase the leverage of the tool, and it will work much better for you.

—*Bob Rosand*

8

For delicate work like the icicle segments of a Christmas ornament, turn the spindle roughing gouge on its side. With a soft touch, you can complete this piece supported only by the chuck (no tailstock).

9

How small? With a 1/2" spindle roughing gouge turned on its side, you can turn these 1/16×3/8" ebony perches for ornamental birdhouses.

10

The details of this acorn birdhouse were turned with a spindle rouging gouge.

can use the spindle gouge to do this shaping, but the spindle roughing gouge does it better. Note that the tool is very much on its side, and I am taking advantage of the flat areas of the SRG to make a nice smooth neck on the weed pot.

Delicate work. I also turn delicate work—like the icicles on my Christmas ornaments—with an SRG. As shown in *Figure 8*, the turning stock is clamped in a spigot-jaw chuck and is not supported by the tailstock.

Turn the SRG on its side, taking advantage of the flat area. I turn about 90 percent of the entire icicle with an SRG before cleaning up the shape with a 1/4" round skew or 1/2" skew. If I had ground the SRG back as though it were a spindle gouge, I could not have accomplished this.

Despite its name, this tool is capable of refined work. *Figures 9 and 10* show a 1/16 × 3/8" ebony scrap being turned for an acorn birdhouse. I turned this detail with my 1/2" SRG rolled on its side. With a light touch and a sharp tool, you, too, can accomplish this.

You can produce the same work with a parting tool or skew laid on its side, but the SRG—especially when properly sharpened—does it much better.

Let's get it right: It's a *spindle* roughing gouge

Roughing gouge? Gives us the shivers. Roughing-out gouge? Also wrong.

Nick Cook, Alan Lacer, and Bob Rosand are among the many woodturning teachers who agree that the terms roughing gouge and roughing-out gouge are big problems. Some new woodturners—left to their own devices—believe they can attack bowl stock with this tool. Not true! Worse: It's dangerous!

This is a tool for spindle work only. Please join our campaign to attach the correct name onto this tool: spindle roughing gouge.

The 1-1/2" and 3/4" tools are probably better suited for rough work, but you can accomplish a lot of detail work with a 3/4" and 1/2" SRG. As with any other tool, all it takes is practice and an effort to learn the tool's capabilities.

A previous member of the AAW Board of Directors, **Robert Rosand** *is an instructor and frequent contributor to* American Woodturner. *Visit Robert at www.rrosand.com.*

Getting the Most from Scrapers

Real woodturners do use scrapers...a lot

On the first day I turned wood, as I entered his workshop, Douglas Hart said, "You might have heard that real woodturners never use scrapers, but we find them pretty useful." That was 1970, and I hadn't a clue what he was talking about. I forgot his comment until seven years later when I was told by a turner destined to be a renowned pedant, that I had interesting techniques but scrapers should never be required. By then I'd come to regard scrapers as essential for many jobs and had developed a range of scraping techniques using gouges.

I continue to meet novice turners who feel guilty that they even own scrapers, so the myth is perpetuated. It makes me wonder if the perpetuators are limited in their turning activities and abilities, superstitious, or merely ignorant. Whatever the reason, their assertions are of little benefit to the craft.

As a turner of bowls, endgrain boxes, and scoops, I've always found that scrapers enable me to arrive at the shapes I want with maximum speed, efficiency, and above all, with control and minimal sanding. Scraping techniques frequently produce glasslike surfaces right off the tool, especially on the endgrain of tropical hardwoods such as cocobolo or African blackwood. On bowls, scrapers will often improve a gouge-cut surface: The inside of the claret ash bowl in *Figure 1* couldn't be cut much cleaner.

It's certainly true that when turning spindles, scrapers should not be required, but they make life a lot easier when hollowing endgrain— try using a gouge to square the inside of an endgrain box, or turn a flat-bottomed dovetailed rebate for an expanding chuck.

Selecting scrapers

The scrapers I use all the time are shown in *Figure 2*. The scraper I use in a given situation will have a radius only slightly tighter than the curve I'm intending to cut. The scrapers with broad-radius edges (top of *Figure 2*) are primarily for bowls, while the tighter radiuses (bottom of photo) are for hollowing into endgrain.

The square-end and spear-point scrapers (to the right) are for convex curves and getting into corners when hollowing boxes or detailing around beads.

The standard square-section scrapers I use are high-speed steel (HSS) or Kryo steel and mostly ⅜" (9 mm) thick for cuts more than 2" (50 mm) over the toolrest. The narrower tools, 1/2" (13 mm) or less wide, although used very close to the toolrest, are never less than 3/16" (5 mm) thick, with 1/4" (6 mm) thick being preferable.

Heavy scrapers, 1/2" to 3/4" (13 mm to 19 mm) thick, are worth avoiding, however inexpensive. They are tedious to grind and offer

AW 27:2, p20

strength and weight not required on such short tools. A better option for working a long way over the toolrest is a boring bar with a replaceable square cutter, but make sure the cutters are the same width as the bar and are on top of it.

Controlling leverage can be a problem so it pays to have long handles. An old rule-of-thumb says a handle needs to be four times the length of the distance between the toolrest and the cutting point of the edge.

Shaping and grinding

All my scrapers start off with bevels of about 45°, which on rounded edges steepen until vertical on the side. If you're grinding on a 6" (150 mm) wheel, however, an edge can become very fragile, so a double bevel is preferable. Those in *Figure 3* are typical. I don't want a long bevel on the side of a scraper because that makes it too grabby.

Before grinding any scraper, I hone the top. This can be accomplished using a diamond hone, but generally I use the well-worn 180-grit sanding disk stuck between my grinder rests (*Figure 4*).

For decades I've used an edge straight off a 60-grit wheel, only honing the edge for very hard and dense timbers at one end of the spectrum, and very soft woods at the other. For the easy-to-work timbers suited to production work (ash, cherry, teak, yew, and fruitwoods), I've used an edge straight off the wheel and get shavings like the ones in *Figure 1*. But all that might be about to change: A couple of times I've used the new-to-turners cubic boron nitride (CBN) grinder wheels that seem to produce a much finer edge with less chance of burning an edge. They're expensive, but getting my serious consideration.

For scrapers that are near square-ended, you can adjust the platform to the desired angle, then keep the

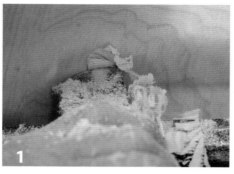

The inside of this ash bowl barely needs sanding after a gentle sweep with a bowl scraper.

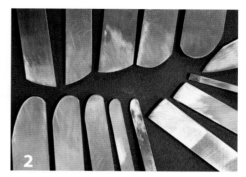

Bowl/facework scrapers (top); tools for hollowing endgrain (bottom); square-end and spear-point scrapers for convex curves and getting into corners (to the right).

tool flat on it as you ease the edge into the wheel (*Figure 5*). The idea then is not to force the edge into the wheel, burning the thin cutting edge. Think in terms of letting the wheel come to the tool with minimal tool pressure against the grinder wheel. With the platform set in position, touching up an edge should take only two or three seconds. On my high-speed grinder I have my platform set for skew chisels, so for all other tools I'm using only the top of the platform to support the tool. I bring the bevel heel onto the wheel, then raise the handle until I see sparks come over the top of the edge. With HSS and Kryo tools, there are few sparks, so when the edge changes color slightly, stop grinding, (*Figure 6*).

To grind a round profile to the cutting edge, I tend to push the tool up the wheel (*Figures 7, 8*) rather than swing the handle sideways, as the edge is less likely to catch or flatten out.

General approach

As a general rule and to avoid catches, scrapers should be used flat on the toolrest—that is, not tilted on edge. After that, make sure the blade tilts down slightly so the angle between the wood and the top of the tool is less than 90°. The currently popular negative-rake scrapers aim to make scrapers more forgiving and you don't need to be quite so

careful about the blade angle, but I'd still aim to keep the edge down, especially on a flat face or in the bottom of a bowl. I see no advantage in a negative-rake grind when all you need to do is raise the handle of any standard scraper to achieve the desired angle between the wood and upper bevel.

Use a straight rather than curved toolrest. On a curved toolrest inside a bowl, a scraper must be kept horizontal or tilted up, which can be dangerous: If you drop the handle, the scraper is supported where the sides contact the toolrest, but the edge points up and is likely to catch. If you raise the handle to drop the edge, then the flat blade rocks on the curve of the toolrest and that also leads to catches. Curved toolrests and scrapers don't go well together.

I have lots of scrapers of various ages, widths, and lengths, and I never use one longer than is necessary. To cut flowing and smooth curves, I choose a tool with an edge that has a radius only slightly tighter than the curve I'm cutting. I find creating a long curve using a narrow round-nose scraper really difficult, no matter how smoothly I move the tool. I also try never to have the tool blade at 90° to the surface I'm cutting. It's usually much easier to have the blade at an angle to the surface you're cutting so you can drag or push the edge

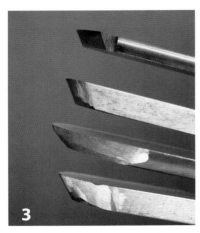

The bevels on my scrapers start at about 45° on the nose, becoming near vertical on the side.

The bevels on my scrapers start at about 45° on the nose, becoming near vertical on the side.

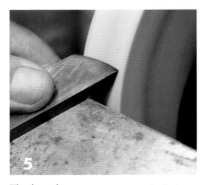

The bevels on my scrapers start at about 45° on the nose, becoming near vertical on the side.

around a curve or across a face of a bowl base.

Used aggressively for rough hollowing bowls or enclosed forms, square-end scrapers can shift a lot of waste in seconds. Using a 1" square-end scraper, it took me about 45 seconds and five cuts to hollow most of the 4" × 8" (10 cm × 20 cm) bowl in *Figure 9*. Provided cuts are directed nearly parallel to the lathe axis, toward the headstock and

within the diameter of the chuck or faceplate securing the job, you can be quite aggressive and force the edge into the wood. Negative-rake scrapers are not so efficient here because the corners are not on top of the tool.

At all other times, and especially when making finishing cuts, you should think in terms of letting the wood come to the tool (rather than pushing the tool into the wood). You need to hold an edge firmly in position so the wood is shaved as it comes onto the edge. And, as the wood is shaved, ease the edge forward. Don't use more than half the edge at a time, and even less as you cut beyond the diameter of the chuck jaws and farther from center.

For finishing cuts, use the same scrapers for delicate stroking cuts. Tool pressure against the wood is about the same as when you rub your hands under a hot-air dryer.

Scrapers on bowls

Figure 10 illustrates a number of ways scrapers can be used for refining surfaces on a bowl. Both the round-nose and V-shaped spear point are more often used tilted on edge to shear scrape. Each of the others has a radius slightly tighter than the curve it's cutting.

Working into corners or around beads, skewed scrapers enable you to get better detail (*Figure 11*). To shear scrape up to a bead or into a corner you need a spear point.

I try never to use scrapers on the upper half of a thin bowl, especially if it's a thin open form, as the wood is inevitably flexible. Catches are almost guaranteed if the scraper is flat on the toolrest. I prefer to cut in from the rim cleanly using a gouge. If, however, scraping techniques are the only way to eliminate chatter marks and torn grain (other than sanding), never attempt to use a scraper flat on the toolrest near a rim. Instead,

shear scrape by tilting your scraper on edge (*Figure 12*). I support the rim as I clean up the inside using an asymmetric round-nose scraper. Dropping the speed a few hundred RPMs makes the task less exciting when things go wrong.

Long before I began shear scraping with scrapers (which for years I wrongly thought too dangerous), I used gouges for similar cuts to great effect, mostly for eliminating small bumps on bowl profiles. The gouge must be rolled right on its side so it doesn't catch (*Figure 13*), and I still prefer this technique for truing up a bowl rim that's running slightly out of whack, or to cut the rim of a face or base in preparation for a shear cut using a scraper.

Hollowing endgrain

The scrapers I use on and into endgrain form the bottom row in *Figure 2*. All my round-nose scrapers are asymmetric with the left wing longer than the right because I always work inboard (to the right of the headstock) so I never need a symmetrically domed scraper. These are ground with a 45° bevel on the nose that becomes ever steeper to the side like the bottom two scrapers shown in *Figure 3*.

These scrapers are not profile cutters: If you get the entire edge in contact with the wood at once, you'll have a big catch. The idea is to use only a small portion of an edge at a time, and by swinging the handle around you can use all of the edge at some time.

I use an edge with a radius only slightly tighter than the curve I'm trying to cut, which makes it easy to develop smooth and flowing curves. When finishing an interior of a hollow like the one in *Figures 14, 15,* and *16,* I opt for the larger scraper (to the left in the photos) and avoid using the narrower scraper (to the right). In this situation the tool

To grind a rounded edge, use the top edge of the toolrest to support the tool and push the tool up the wheel.

Using a 1" square-end scraper, it took me about 45 seconds and five cuts to hollow most of the 4" × 8" (10 cm × 20 cm) bowl.

Working into corners or around beads, skewed scrapers enable you to get better detail. Spear-points enable you to shear-scrape right into corners.

Never use a scraper flat on the toolrest near a rim. Instead, shear scrape by tilting your scraper on edge.

To shear-scrape using a gouge, the tool must be on its side.

moves out from the center, and in from the rim, barely brushing the wood to remove little more than dust and tiny curly shavings. If you move the tool smoothly with minimal pressure against the wood, flowing curves should follow. And if you get it right in a couple of passes, be grateful and get sanding. Don't feel you have to stick the tool in the hole again. At the rim of the hollow form, you can have the edge tilted up slightly, but at center it must be tilted down. On a tighter curve, a slightly smaller round-nose is used, but again, I use the largest-profile scraper I can fit in without having the whole edge in contact with the wood at once.

My square-end scrapers are actually slightly skewed to the right for getting into corners of a flat-bottomed box (*Figure 17*). This enables me to get into the corner without the right corner of the tool messing up the flat endgrain. The slightly curved edge of a "square end" means you can turn a flat surface without having both corners of the edge in the wood at once.

Enclosed forms

When hollowing enclosed forms I use standard scrapers if the opening is large enough to accommodate them (*Figures 18, 19*). The main irritation in using these tools in this situation is that the large shavings are not easily extracted with the lathe running. Initial roughing is with square-end scrapers (see *Figure 9*), then I complete the inside curves with a round-nose that is as large as can reach the area I'm completing. The more the rim is undercut, the narrower the tool you need.

When there are smaller openings or undercut rims that I can't reach with a straight blade, I resort to the undercutting tools,

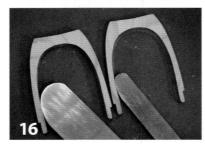

Use as large a tool as possible (left) with a radius slightly tighter than the curve you want to cut.

My square-end scrapers are actually slightly skewed to the right for getting into corners of flat-bottomed boxes. The profile of the round-nose scraper is such that the entire cutting edge does not make contact with the wood all at the same time.

which still produce a decent shaving and remove waste in a hurry (*Figure 20*).

If you've been taught that scraping is not something real turners do, I'd urge you to give it a go.

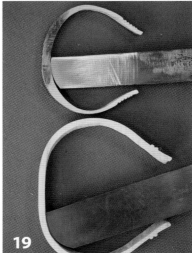

Standard straight blades can be used through quite small openings.

Kelton Undercutters and similar tools let you reach where straight blades cannot.

Richard Raffan, *now semi-retired and living in Australia, is the well-known author of classic woodturning books and videos from the Taunton Press. Visit Richard at www.richardraffan.com.*

Using the Point Tool

This finesse tool shines in delicate situations

The point tool is used for both spindle and faceplate work. It is also useful for details such as texturing and making designs in the bottom of bowls and hollow forms. I find myself picking this tool up in dozens of situations where I need access and don't want to risk a catch with a detail gouge or the point of a skew.

This is a finesse tool, not a hogging tool. The point tool really shines on delicate, high-definition spindles such as finials, boxes, clock parts, and chair parts. It was originally used on small objects made of ivory, bone, or on extremely dense, fine-grained hardwoods such as ebony or boxwood. There are four basic cuts that can be performed with this tool: The V-groove, the bead, the facing cut, and the planing cut.

V-cut

Use the V-cut for detailing and as the beginning step in forming a bead. Examples of detailing are the signature lines in the bottom of a bowl or vase and the delicate line marking the transition between flats and beads in spindle work. V-cuts are also a fast, efficient, and controllable way to produce texture.

To make a V-cut, place the point tool on the tool rest perpendicular to the surface of the wood. Rotate the handle until a triangular face is up. Drop the handle until this cutting face is almost horizontal. Push the tool straight in as shown in the photo *V-cut.*

Bead

There are two classic bead shapes: Greek (elliptical) and Roman (semi-circular). Begin either by making a V-cut. For a semi-circular bead, the V-cut depth should be about one-half the width of the bead. For the elliptical shape, the V-cut must go a little deeper.

To scrape a bead, simply make a V-cut and swing the handle toward the center of the bead keeping the triangular face horizontal. Pulling the handle back slightly allows the edge to follow the curve without the point touching the adjacent side of the V-groove. Repeat for the other side.

To cut a bead, make a V-cut and begin swinging the handle very slightly toward the center of the bead. This pulls the point out of the groove so that it will not catch the opposite side. Drop the handle as you roll the tool slightly away from the bead. This brings up the cutting edge and rotates the bottom face toward the bead. This lower triangular face should float over the newly cut surface acting as the rubbing bevel. This face starts out almost vertical and ends up horizontal. You are rolling the bead uphill from the V-cut rotating the tool toward the center of the bead as you progress (like a windshield wiper with a twist). Control the cut by varying the amount you drop and roll the handle. Reverse these motions to cut back downhill.

Allan Batty recommends pointing your index finger along the tool for increased fine motor control. If you are right handed and are rolling the right hand side of a bead, you need to place this "pointing finger" along the right side

V-cut: With a triangular face up, push the tool straight into the stock between centers.

Bead step 1: After making a V-cut, swing the handle slightly toward the center of the bead.

Bead step 2: Drop the handle slightly as you roll the bead "uphill."

Facing cut: On an end-grain surface, align one triangular face with the surface. Drop the handle, then arch the cut toward the center.

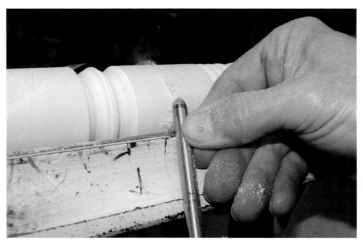

Planing cut: Place the triangular face of the tool flat on the surface. Advance the handle slightly in the direction of the cut.

of the tool so your hand can rotate from vertical to horizontal as you roll the bead upward. For the left side of a bead you would start with the "pointing finger" on top of the handle so you can rotate smoothly to the right as you go from the V-groove to the top of the bead. Everything is just the opposite for us lefties.

One advantage of this tool is that you can move back and forth (both uphill and downhill) over a surface until you get the shape you want. This is the only tool I am aware of that will cut uphill on a bead. As you would expect, the downhill cut is smoother. The usual practice is to rough one side of the bead going uphill from the beginning V-groove, then to refine and finish with a downhill cut. Repeat this procedure for the other side of the bead.

As with any complex cut, practice may be necessary to get all of this coordinated. I recommend practicing on a nice green branch until you get the hang of it. Begin with beads about the diameter of the tool. The challenge is to make smaller and smaller beads.

Facing cut

Align one triangular face of the tool with the surface you wish to face off (usually an end grain surface). Drop the handle until the upper cutting edge is almost horizontal. Push the cut straight in, arcing the point of the tool toward the center of the spindle. This should produce a cut almost as clean as the skew with less chance of a catch.

Planing cut

This is useful in tight places where you can't access with a skew or gouge (for example, the flat separating a cove and a bead). Make this cut by placing one triangular face of the tool flat on the surface to be planed. Advance the handle slightly in the direction of the cut and push the tool along the surface. The cutting edge should be about 45 degrees from vertical or horizontal. Try to maintain a slight feather or fuzz in front of the cut. As with a skew, keep the cut at the heel of the cutting edge (away from the point).

---

*A member of the Central Texas Woodturners Association of Austin, **Stacy Hager** is a respected instructor, maker of his own woodturning tools, and frequent contributor to* American Woodturner.

Carbide Cutters

Learning to use long-lasting carbide is worth the effort

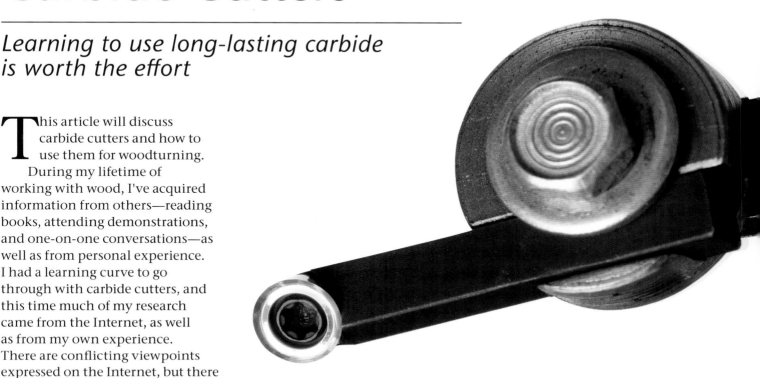

Photos by David Speckman Photography

This article will discuss carbide cutters and how to use them for woodturning. During my lifetime of working with wood, I've acquired information from others—reading books, attending demonstrations, and one-on-one conversations—as well as from personal experience. I had a learning curve to go through with carbide cutters, and this time much of my research came from the Internet, as well as from my own experience. There are conflicting viewpoints expressed on the Internet, but there is consensus enough to support my conclusions.

History

A few years ago, Mike Hunter asked me to consider using carbide cutters on my boring-bar system. In spite of my initial comment, "No thanks, carbide does not get sharp enough for turning," Mike began my education. He described the new technology of nanograin carbide. "Okay," I said, "prove it." And he did—my assumption was wrong.

Carbide cutters have been in use for decades: metal machining, military, sports, plastics, wood-production duplicators, and in flat woodworking for tablesaw-blade tips. The earliest mention I found for carbide was in the 1860s, but the woodturning tool market did not accept carbide until recently.

The first commercially produced use of carbide for turning that I know of was when Dennis Stewart put a carbide tip on his slicer tool, sometime in the early 1990s. It was the precursor of the coring systems used today. While it had wear resistance better than HSS or carbon steel, it would not get as sharp. For the use Dennis intended, however, it was perfect. Then why didn't other uses of carbide take off with Dennis's example? The answer is: *That carbide did not get as sharp as high-speed steel, and a diamond hone was required to sharpen it.*

Metallurgy

There are many different carbides and grades of carbide. Carbide is not just carbide. The quality of the manufacturing varies greatly, and the particles that make up the carbides are different sizes. A microscope is needed to see the difference. Let's break down carbide cutters into two categories. First is *tungsten carbide*. It is formulated from a gray powder and the result is three times stiffer than steel.

The second category is the new *nanograin tungsten carbide*, sometimes referred to as *micro-grain carbide*. The nanograin, as you might guess, is made of much smaller particulate than for tungsten carbide—the difference in grain size is that of BBs to beach balls. Nanograin carbide grains are cemented with another metal, usually cobalt *(Figure 1)*. Generally, there is 6% to 12% binder in the carbide. With optimum grade selection, submicron-grain-size particles of tungsten carbide are manufactured to have a razor edge. What does this have to do with us in the turning world?

Start with a sharp edge

In woodturning, we begin with a sharp edge on our tools, and the instant we start turning, the

---

sharpness of the edge degrades. Let's do some math. Take a 10"-diameter bowl and calculate the circumference: 10 × 3.14 = 30+". Thirty inches of wood are passing the cutter every rotation. Let's say we are turning at 1,000 rpm. In one minute we have just cut 30,000" of wood—almost one-half mile or 500" per second. Will any tool retain its sharp edge very long?

After the initial sharpened edge is gone, the structure of the base material the cutter is made from is left. This remaining cutting edge is called the *land*. With carbide, the base material is very wear resistant and the tool will cut reasonably well for a long time on the land before the edge deteriorates enough to become unusable.

With nanograin carbide, the finer particulate will allow the edge to be even sharper to begin with than with the old carbides—manufacturers are able to produce a razor-sharp edge. The land edge left after the initial nanograin razor-sharp factory edge has been used to cut wood will still be sharp because the fine grain structure is resistant to wear.

How can you tell if your tools are made from the old-style carbide or the new nanograin carbide? The nanograin carbide is manufactured under high heat and high pressure. The surface ends up with a mirror or glossy finish. The old carbide will have a dull, flat-gray appearance. To confuse the distinction, some carbide manufacturers apply coatings to enhance sharpness. These coatings are usually yellow or gold in color and they are intended to mask the dull gray. The coating wears off quickly and the tool is now cutting with the land made of the same base metal structure.

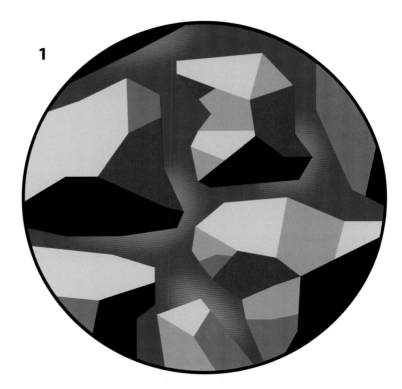

1

Magnification of carbide: Illustration of (gray) carbide cemented with (red) cobalt under high magnification.

Grain sizes and sharpness

I spoke with Tom Walz, President of Carbide Processors Inc. in Tacoma, WA, to compare nanograin carbide to HSS. He said, "Consider that the sharpness level of HSS is in the range of 1 to 20, with 1 being the sharpest possible for HSS starting out. Nanograin carbide, on the other hand, starts out at 2 or 3 sharpness. Turning with both for the same amount of time, HSS is dull and has reached a 20 while nanograin carbide is still sharp at a 4 or 5 in the 1 to 20 range." My conclusion is that the finer structure of nanograin carbide will begin with and hold a sharper edge than the old carbide and stay sharper longer than HSS. This is demonstrated to me in daily use of the Hunter nanograin carbide tools on my boring-bar system.

With HSS tools, the sharpened edge will degrade rapidly, but we can go quickly to the grinder and constantly renew the sharp edge

to optimal performance. The sharpened edge of HSS tools will be sharper than the old-style carbide ever gets. You also can use a burr on HSS tools that is not present on carbide. Other steels like stainless and composites have the same trade-off. The knife industry has been struggling with this issue for centuries. The old carbon-steel knives would get sharper and last reasonably well for culinary needs, but they rust and their appearance was a problem. Flat woodworkers have been arguing forever about the best tool steel for router bits and carving tools.

Why use carbide?

Nanograin carbide tools cannot be resharpened to their original razor-sharp factory edge; they are designed to be disposable. They are, however, economical because they last so long. I believe they will wear up to 100 times longer than HSS.

Nanograin carbide cutters leave a much better surface on the wood than the old carbide. Why? Because it begins and remains sharper, and we can use a slicing cut that leaves a cleaner surface on the wood.

How woodturners use carbide tools

There are two types of cuts we can make while turning wood: a scraping cut or a slicing cut. It does not matter whether the tool is HSS or a carbide. The rule for scraping is the cutting edge must touch the wood at a 90° angle or less. Cutting at the centerline with the scraper held flat on the toolrest, the 90° angle is achieved by having the handle slightly up from horizontal (nose of the tool pointing slightly down). As the wood passes by the cutting edge, it scrapes some wood off. If we touch the wood with any sharp edge at more than a 90° angle, handle down with a scraper, the tool will dig in, starting a catch.

The rule for a slicing cut is the bevel behind the cutting edge must be supported against the wood. If you are slicing on an angle without bevel support, the cutting edge will grab, dig in, and skate across the wood's surface until you get a catch. This is a critical concept to understand and when you understand it, tool catches will become a thing of the past (see *Figure 2*).

The two different carbides are used for different cuts for different reasons. The old carbide is used in the scraping mode. Carbide cutters are especially useful for beginners. Learning to use a scraper is easy, and they can scrape for hours and their tool will still be sharp enough.

Old-style carbide cutters are also great for what they were originally made for—roughing out. The turner just presents the tool to the wood in a scraping mode and just pushes it into the spinning wood and scrapes away, keeping the handle slightly up, never violating the 90°-angle rule. The old carbide cutters are wear resistant, so going through dirty bark and miles and miles of waste wood, they will hold their edge for a long time, longer than HSS scrapers. The trade-off is that the old carbide cutters are not as sharp as HSS scrapers or bowl gouges, which is okay—we are using them as roughing tools.

The new nanograin carbide can be used for either a scraping cut or a slicing cut. Professional turner Mike Jackofsky has set up the nanograin cutters to work only in the scraping mode with

2

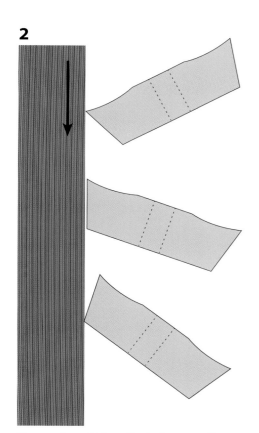

Nanograin carbide cutter in three positions tilted to cut wood (or not).

A

Figure A. Carbide cutter clock positions for a nanograin cutter on ³⁄₁₆" (5 mm) square shaft to be used with swiveling-head boring bar.

Figure B. The carbide cutter is shown cutting under the shoulder of a vessel. The cutting motion can be in both directions, as indicated by the arrow. Notice the swivel has positioned the cutter to allow scraping at the 9:00 position. This means the carbide cutter is cutting at the 9:00 position and is directed toward the tailstock when cutting under the rim of the vessel. Note the obstacle created by leaving the waste wood behind the cutter, which could easily become a problem later.

B

3

The direction of cut is to the left when the carbide-cutter insert is angled to the left. The ring visible in the photo shows the transition shoulder between the surface of the wood just cut and the wood ahead of the cutter. Notice the large thickness of the shaving. The cutting motion is slightly pulling away from the tip, on a taper, across the bottom of this vessel. This hogging-off cut is aggressive and removes large quantities of wood quickly.

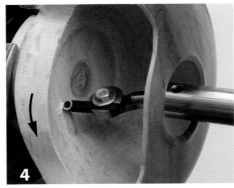

4

This bevel-supported cut in the bottom of the vessel is made with the cutter at the 12:00 position, angled to the left, and the direction of the cut is to the left. Note the fine shavings as a light cut is taken.

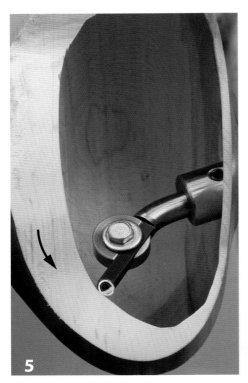

5

A light cut, riding the bevel, and slicing part way up the side of the hollow form produces a smooth surface. The cutter is cutting at the 12:00 position and the cut is to the left.

6

This is the correct way to undercut a shoulder by removing the waste wood from behind the cutter before working on the underside of the shoulder. The cutter is at the 12:00 position, riding the bevel, and slicing up the side wall to the left.

a tip angle dedicated to scraping across the bottom, inside a hollow form. Mike Hunter developed his new Hercules tool to scrape in this manner, which works better than the old carbide because it is sharper.

Mike Hunter, Trent Bosch, Eliminator, or Jamieson tools have set up the nanograin carbide inserts so the bevel can be used in a slicing action to get a smoother, cleaner surface on the wood. It acts as a hook tool or ring tool to slice through the endgrain fibers of a hollow form or lidded box. Mike Hunter has great tutorials on using nanograin carbide for slicing and scraping in bowls and hollow forms on his website, hunterwoodturningtool.com.

Nanograin carbide: Three cuts possible

The new carbide tool is one complex little workhorse. The 3/16" (5 mm) nanograin carbide cutter is efficient and in this case, smaller is better. Larger cutters stress the wood and the chucking method. Using this small cutter, it is easier to hollow deeper vessels without vibration. The turner takes many smaller cuts quickly rather than slowly grinding away with a larger cutter bit.

If you set it up as I do in my captured boring-bar system, there are three different cuts possible.

Let's envision the cutter assembly locked in a boring-bar swivel assembly and positioned straight forward. Looking toward the headstock and down on the cutter, imagine a clock face *(Figure A)*. When presenting the 8:30 to 9:30 section of the cutter to the wood, the cutting action mimics that of a negative-rake scraper *(Figure B)*. The arrow indicates we can cut in both directions while scraping.

The second type of cut is to use the cutter from the 10:00 to 12:00

section. The result is an angled slicing action that is efficient and easy to cut with (Figure 3). In fact, this is the workhorse section of the cutter that gets most of the use and abuse; wood can be hogged off. There is no bevel support for this cut or for the scraping cut. Note the arrow in Figure 3: Only cut to the left.

At the 12:00 position of the cutter, a bevel-supported cut is the result. It is a slicing action and leaves a smooth and clean surface behind. This cut is intended for removing only a small-shaving slice to clean up tool marks and prepare to sand, if needed (Figure 4). To make a bevel-supported cut, you must swing the handle to keep the bevel on the surface of the wood to make a curved shape inside a hollow vessel. As indicated by the arrow, the cutting action is to the left.

Even if the entry hole is small, the swivel will allow the 12:00 position to be used in any quadrant of the vessel, bottom, side, or top. This will require working in stages as you move the swivel often to position the cutter to use the bevel at the 12:00 position. The inside contour achieved from this method is really sweet because it is easy to pick up the line from a previous stage and carry it through the next stage (Figure 5). With a little practice, the line that the bevel and cutter follow will be superior to scraping cuts. (A laser-measuring device will help monitor the transition from stage to stage and keep a uniform wall thickness.)

The cutter will not cut in the 12:00 to 3:00 position. If you present this quadrant to the wood, it will just rub the shaft and the bottom edge of the cutter, and may even result in some chatter and/or vibration.

One caution to keep in mind: Do not combine the ride-the-bevel and the hogging-off cuts—that combination removes too much

wood, too fast, and starts some vibration going. Doing both cuts simultaneously stresses the chucking method, stresses the wood, and stresses the boring bar. The trick to hogging off fast and easy is to cut with a slight sweeping or scooping motion to pull away from the bevel slightly as you cut. This will create a slight curve to the inside surface of the vessel (see Figure 3).

Learning curve

HSS cutters attached to the end of boring bars can be directed left, right, in, or out to produce a cut. With a nanograin carbide cutter, however, there is a bit of a learning curve. For example, the cutting action of the carbide cutter will always be to the left if it is angled or facing to the left. The direction the cutter is facing dictates the direction of the cut. It will try to "climb" if you try to cut in the opposite direction. Going the wrong way will not usually produce a catch, but it will cause the cutter to skate.

When hollowing under a high shoulder, make sure to get the waste wood out of the middle behind the shoulder of the vessel (Figure 6). Figure 2 shows the incorrect way to hollow by leaving the waste wood in the way behind the cut. Removing the waste wood will prevent an inadvertent skate should you bump the wood behind the cut with the back side of the tool.

Figure 4 shows the correct direction for cutting the endgrain on the bottom of a hollow form. Figure 6 shows the correct direction of a cut coming up the side of a hollow-form vessel. The cutter needs to cut pulling toward the shoulder of the vessel when the cutter is swiveled to the left. And in Figure 6, "left" is actually pulling the cut toward the tailstock. Figure 2 shows the negative-rake scraping cut used to undercut the shoulder area.

The shearing/slicing cut of the nanograin carbide cutter produces a shaving. A scraping cut would produce sawdust. Try one of these little cutters on the nastiest wood you can find and you will be a believer. These nanograin carbide cutters excel in wet wood, dry wood, hard wood, and soft wood. There is no sharpening and they are economical. I find them to be easy and fast for hollowing, and I like it that there is less sanding required. It takes making a few vessels to master the cuts, but it is worth the effort.

Lyle Jamieson is a sculptor, instructor, and frequent contributor to American Woodturner. *Among his contributions to the craft is the boring bar and laser measuring system bearing his name. Visit Lyle at www. lylejamieson.com.*

The Parting Tool

Helpful insight for using this turning workhorse

Sometimes we forget that we did not start out as professionals. I was reminded of this while teaching a class a few years ago. As I talked about the tools we would be using, a student was furiously putting masking tape on the handles of her tools and then writing on the tape. When I asked what she was doing, she said she was writing the names of the tools so she wouldn't forget them. This stuck with me and I try never to forget that there was a day that I could barely turn a block of wood into a cylinder.

With that in mind, I would like to discuss the use of a basic, important tool: the parting tool. My intent is not to write the definitive word on tools and tool use, but to pass on a few tidbits I have learned over the years in order to help novice turners enjoy their turning experience and avoid some of the mistakes I've made.

The primary function of the parting tool is to do just what the name implies, divide or separate one piece of wood from the other while the lathe is running. (Furniture makers mostly use the parting tool for parting into the wood in order to establish dimensions for various elements on a spindle.) When I first started turning, we just had parting tools. Now we have thin-walled parting tools, parting tools with flutes, diamond parting tools, mini-parting tools, and parting tools made from bandsaw blades and old knives.

The kind of parting tools you own and use depends on the type of

Shown here is an assortment of the author's parting tools. (Left to right) Nick Cook tool with a flute (Sorby), standard diamond parting tool (Sorby), standard thin-walled tool (no flute), shopmade mini tool, Bonnie Klein mini parting tool, and shopmade parting tool.

turning you do. I have all of them because I make a variety of objects, but I consider the diamond parting tool to be my workhorse. It costs more than a standard parting tool because the diamond profile requires more machining. What's nice about the profile is that it minimizes binding and heat buildup. A standard parting tool does not have a diamond profile so it tends to bind and generate heat, particularly in deep cuts.

A thin-walled parting tool is about 1/16" thick, but the blade is wide, which helps give the tool strength. I like to use these tools when I am turning lidded boxes. The

The diamond parting tool on the right is too blunt. The bevels need to be reground (lengthened) for the tool to be used properly.

AW 24:2, p36

thin blade minimizes waste when I separate a box lid, which helps keep the grain pattern intact between the lid and body of the container. I'm especially fond of my thin-walled, fluted parting tool which has come to be known as the Nick Cook parting tool. The little spurs on the flute cut cleanly. It's a relatively expensive tool, so I primarily use it when I want a very clean cut, even when parting through wood.

Sharpening parting tools

When any tool first comes from the factory, plan on sharpening it. Toolmakers make great tools, but for the most part they are not woodturners, so your tools need to be modified. I do my initial grinding with a 36-grit wheel which allows me to remove metal quickly to get the shape I want. I find that the factory bevels on most parting tools are too blunt, so I lengthen them. Once I have the bevel about where I want it, I switch to an 80- or 60-grit wheel to do a final touchup. I do all

With the handle held too high, the wood is being scraped, not cut, with the tool.

of my sharpening at 1,725 rpm. I like this slower speed because it allows me more time to refine the edge of the tool. You could easily use a jig for sharpening, but all that's really necessary is a good eye, a steady hand, and a substantial platform in front of the grinding wheel.

The parting tool has a cutting edge, a bevel, and a shoulder or heel. To sharpen it, place your fingers on the toolrest and use them as a fulcrum. Touch the heel of the tool to the grinding wheel, and then lift

the handle of the tool until the curve of the bevel fits the curve of the grinding wheel. You want to sharpen the bevel, not the cutting edge. If you sharpen just the cutting edge, the tool will be sharp, but the bevel will eventually become so short that the tool will be virtually unusable (it will be blunt) and you will have to regrind it to make it useful again. Sharpening the bevel—not the edge—is an important concept that took me a long time to comprehend. If you learn it sooner than I did, it will serve you well.

While sharpening the parting tool, I also look at what I am doing from the side so that I can see the gap closing between the bevel and the wheel of the grinder as I lower the bevel onto the wheel. You do not need or want to exert a lot of pressure when sharpening. Let the grinder do the work. You might also want to try using a set of magnifying lenses so that you can see what you are doing up close and personal. The older I get, the more I find myself taking advantage of visual magnification. Good lighting is helpful, too.

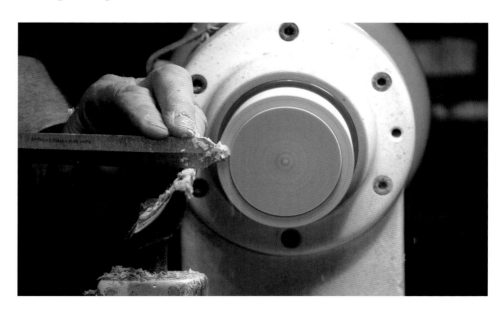

To properly cut with a parting tool, hold the handle of the tool down and arch the cutting edge into the wood to start the cut.

Using a parting tool

Using a parting tool is fairly simple, but a surprising number of people use it as though it were a scraper rather than a cutting tool. They are keeping the tool handle high when starting their cut, rather than dropping the handle down and feeding the cutting edge into the wood. The scraping method *will* part the cylinder of wood, but it creates sawdust rather than fine shavings. It also generates more heat, dulls the tool quicker, and takes more brute force to remove wood. You *can* part wood this way, but it is not as satisfactory as cutting.

To part or separate a cylinder of wood, let's say for the lid for a container, place the parting tool on the toolrest, drop the tool handle down (in a lowered position), and rub the heel of the bevel on the cylinder. At this point, nothing will happen. Slowly lift the tool handle up until the cutting edge engages with the wood. This is the proper cutting

As the cut progresses, raise the handle of the tool and feed the cutting edge into the wood.

angle. To finish the cut, continue lifting the tool handle and at the same time advance the tool forward, in an arching motion, moving toward the center point of the cylinder of wood. There is a rhythm involved and it takes practice to master. My recommendation is to take a short piece of green wood and practice, practice, practice. Yes, even with a parting tool.

Other uses for parting tools

Once you have mastered the basics of the parting tool, you will discover that it is capable of performing other cuts. When I am turning perches for Christmas ornaments, I use the parting tool in the same manner as a skew chisel to clean up the perches. It's a time-saving measure because the edge of the parting tool is similar to that of a skew chisel.

Often I will turn the parting tool on its side and make a cut similar to using the long point of a skew chisel. This allows me to cleanly part a finial or perch from the turning stock without changing tools. When I make spindles for ornaments, I grind the cutting edge of one parting tool at an angle to look like a skew chisel. This allows me to undercut finials for a better fit. With practice, you can even turn partial beads with the parting tool. The point here is to become familiar with your tools and how they work. When you do, the possibilities abound.

A previous member of the AAW Board of Directors, **Robert Rosand** *is an instructor and frequent contributor to* American Woodturner. *Visit Robert at www.rrosand.com.*

Choosing the Right Drive Center

Understand your options to make the right choice

Four-prong center

Two-prong center

Stubby screw-on center

Oneway Mfg. safe-drive center

As is the case with most woodturning tools, devices for holding wood onto the lathe have evolved considerably, especially in the past fifteen years. Faceplates, chucks, and drive centers have all come a long way. Drive centers, as simple as they may seem, are varied and their use is often not fully understood. While I was going through my toolbox, pulling out different drive centers accumulated over the course of twenty-five years of turning, I had good and not so good memories of some of those tools. The innovators who have developed new and, in many cases, improved tools have made our lives easier and safer while working with the lathe. All drives work well in some situations. Variables such as timber hardness, size, and shape all come into play.

The *four-prong center* is the most common center and is supplied with most lathes. The adjustable center point makes it ideal for all timber densities. The four sharp prongs are designed to bite into the wood. Whether turning spindles or forming the outside of bowls, this type of drive center is effective with softer timbers. The four-prong center is a good all-around method of holding between-center work. The downside is that it will not penetrate into hard woods as deeply as you might like. As a result, light cuts will be necessary.

A *two-prong center* works well with natural-edge bowls. It will seat deeper into the wood than a four-prong center. Additionally, it allows for easier repositioning of the bowl blank. Two prongs offer half the holding power of four, however, so when aggressive cuts are made, it can quickly become a drill bit.

The heavy-duty 2" (50 mm) Stubby brand *screw-on center* screws onto the lathe spindle. It is ideal for starting medium or large bowls or mounting hollow forms between centers. The spurs can be removed for regrinding or replacement. The drive center can be used with two or four spurs. To suit either hard or soft timber, the center point is easily adjustable by loosening the setscrew and it can also be reground or replaced. The sheer size of this drive offers superior holding pressure. Because the spurs can be reground, this drive has a big advantage over conventional four-prong drives, in particular when working with hard woods.

Oneway Mfg.'s *safe-drive centers* are ideal for beginning turners when safety is the prime concern. The safe-drive center provides sufficient grip, depending on the amount of tailstock pressure applied. Designed for nonaggressive turning, the beauty is that the workpiece will slip

AW 26:3, p24

or stop if a catch occurs. The spring-loaded center point and circular design of the end prevents splitting the work piece. These drives work very well for their intended purpose, nonaggressive cuts; however, they do not provide enough holding pressure for most of my needs.

An *arbor-screw center* is ideal for holding small items such as bowls or boxes because the screw is ground to provide maximum holding power. The workpiece will require a predrilled hole. They work well when production turning a number of pieces—just drill all the center holes at once, and mounting and dismounting is quick and convenient. The bottoms of boxes can easily be finished without rechucking. These small screw arbors, however, have limited holding power in larger work.

Oneway brand's *screw drive centers* are designed for holding small items such as doorknobs. The #8 or #10 center screw can be changed to any length to suit the workpiece. Small parts can be drilled and held with the same screw size that will be used for installing the piece when it is finished. As with the arbor-screw center, these drives are ideal for completely finishing the piece while it is initially attached.

Mini drive centers are ideal for between-center turning of dried flowerpots, vases, or almost any small between-center project. Small is the key here, as the prongs are delicate and will break or bend if they are overworked.

Stebcenters are available in a number of different sizes and feature a serrated drive ring with a spring-loaded center point. By varying the tailstock pressure, the workpiece can be stopped for inspection while the lathe is still on. The circular head design prevents splitting by distributing the pressure evenly around the drive ring. Light pressure from the tailstock will still drive the work and in the event of a catch, the workpiece will stop rotating. The Stebcenter drive works great with all timbers that I have tried, including hardwoods such as cocobolo. The spring-loaded point makes finding the center a breeze because the point significantly protrudes, making it easy to position the tip directly into a center-punched hole. For small to medium spindle work they are ideal.

Similar to the Stebcenter but designed to be mounted in most four-jaw chucks, the *Stebdrive* eliminates the need to remove the chuck for between-center work.

The *Elio safe drive/faceplate* has three adjustable pins making this drive center versatile. It is ideal for large logs, natural-edge and regular bowls, or spindle work 2½" (65 mm) in diameter or larger. The three countersunk holes make it perfect for small faceplate work. Three adjustable pins allow for a firm grip with both hard and soft timbers, as well as with thick bark. This is the drive I use most frequently. It is, however, not designed for small-diameter between-center work.

Most of these drive centers are available through all woodturning tool supply retailers with the exception of Oneway Screw Drive (oneway.ca), the Stubby Screw-On Drive Center (stubbylatheusa.com), and Elio Safe Drive/Faceplate (onegoodturn.ca or langercraftworks.com).

Brian McEvoy is a professional woodturner from Canada, well known for the diversity of his artistic woodturnings. He teaches woodturning and generously shares his knowledge and techniques in presentations throughout the U.S., Canada, and Australia. He has also produced instructional DVDs. To learn more about Brian and view his work visit onegoodturn.ca.

Arbor screw center/chuck

Oneway Mfg. screw drive center

Mini drive centers

Stebcenter

Stebdrive

Elio safe drive/faceplate

Faceplates

A primer for putting them to work safely and effectively

Faceplates are a practical and effective way of mounting work on the lathe. They have many advantages over other methods.

- They are inexpensive.
- They allow for multiple remounting of the work without loss of alignment.
- They can be sized to the project.
- They are often used in place of a scroll chuck for mounting bowl blanks.

Safety considerations

Faceplates are simple mounting devices; however, there are things you need to consider in order to make them work safely and properly.

- Match the size of the faceplate to the size of your project. The faceplate and glueblock must be of sufficient size to properly support the work, especially while being roughed out and off balance.
- Use steel faceplates for larger, heavier projects. Steel does not deform or flex like aluminum might.
- Match the screw size to the faceplate holes. Using the largest diameter screw possible prevents the faceplate from shifting slightly during use, especially when catches happen.
- Use machine screws when your faceplate has chamfered holes. This also reduces shifting.
- Predrill glueblock holes. This eliminates "mushrooming" of the wood next to the back of the faceplate, allowing the glueblock to lay flat. It also reduces the possibility of splitting the

glueblock when threading the screw into the wood.

- Avoid using MDF, plywood, or soft woods for glueblocks. Those materials will fail on large or heavy projects.
- Don't use an endgrain glueblock. Screws do not hold well in endgrain and may pull out. Additionally, the glue joint will be far weaker when your bowl stock is glued to endgrain.
- For your glueblock, use wood that is thick enough to accept a long screw and will still allow enough thickness to turn away part of the glueblock if need be.

When purchasing a faceplate for your lathe, be sure its threaded shaft is of sufficient length to seat properly on the shoulder of the lathe's headstock shaft in order to provide proper registration. If the shoulders don't meet flush, there will be alignment problems, and a remounted project may not register properly. If the faceplate happens to have a shaft that is too short, add a flat spacer between the headstock and the faceplate to ensure better alignment. Some lathe manufacturers sell washers for this purpose. They are machined

Glueblock with holes not pre-drilled. Mushrooming of the wood will prevent getting a good glue joint.

The threaded shaft of this faceplate is too short for the faceplate's shoulder to rest on the shoulder of the lathe's headstock.

AW 24:1, p50

to be flat enough for provide proper registration and alignment of faceplate shaft to lathe shaft.

When attaching a faceplate to your lathe, be sure it is securely seated on the spindle. I back off the last quarter turn and retighten with a quick jerk to be sure of tightness. A hexagonal treaded shaft or a hole for a tommy bar is important for easy removal of the work.

Faceplate, glueblock, and platter, assembled and ready to turn.

Considerations for the use of screws

Many accidents have occurred from the use of inappropriate screws when attaching a glueblock to the faceplate. In addition to selecting screws of large enough diameter to fill the screw holes in the faceplate, the following are some other points to consider.

- Drywall screws may snap off during installation or during use.
- Use chamfered head screws for faceplates with chamfered holes and flat machine head screws for faceplates with holes that are not chamfered.
- Square drive screws provide the most control on installation and removal. The driver will not slip or tear the head of the screw.
- Be cautious of iron/steel screws when attaching wet wood. The screws will eventually rust, discolor the wood, and freeze to the steel faceplates. They may weaken due to rusting.

Jim Rodgers, author of A Lesson Plan for Woodturning *and past President of the Bay Area Woodturners Club, is the Director of turning programs for Mt. Diablo Unified School District. Visit Jim at www. jlrodgers.com.*

Types and uses of common faceplates

Custom made locally

Many turners have found local individuals who make inexpensive faceplates. While these faceplates might not be perfectly true, the use of a screw-mounted glueblock, trued up on your lathe, solves this problem. However, be sure not to mount this faceplate on other lathes unless re-trued to that specific lathe. Projects may not be easily moved from one lathe to another with these faceplates.

Locally made faceplate with threads relieved.

Back side of the locally made faceplate.

Commercial aluminum faceplates

These faceplates also are inexpensive and, when used for smaller projects, will perform very well. Some even have holes for tommy bars to aid removal and set screws for securing to the spindle of your lathe. Be aware, though, that with heavy projects mounted, these aluminum faceplates may deform and cause problems.

Commercial aluminum faceplate.

Commercial steel faceplates

These are the more expensive faceplates, but they are also more reliable, especially for larger-sized projects. Many of the larger ones have abundant screw holes to securely mount your project. The better brands of steel faceplates will have set screws to secure them to the lathes for reverse turning.

Commercial steel faceplate.

Understanding Your Bandsaw

Safe setup and operating tips for using this versatile tool

There is potential danger lurking in the corner of woodturning shops, waiting for the most inopportune time to injure or maim. For some, the thought of operating a bandsaw strikes fear; we have all heard horror stories of bandsaw accidents. The bandsaw's negative reputation, however, is largely undeserved. If we follow a few guidelines, the bandsaw can be one of the safest, and most versatile, of all stationary woodworking equipment. Let's see if we can demystify this machine and acquire a comprehensive understanding of how to operate it safely.

Know your machine

Before operating any power equipment, it is imperative to have a basic understanding of its functions, adjustments, and maintenance and safety procedures. Read and periodically review the owner's manual; it contains necessary information required to properly set up and maintain your bandsaw. If you have misplaced your owner's manual, many manufacturers make copies available online. Excellent books and articles on setting up and operating bandsaws are also available (two books are listed at the end of this article). If you are unsure of any bandsaw function, most turning clubs have experienced operators who will be willing to give proper instructions. Under no circumstance should you operate a piece of power equipment without proper training, when tired or under the influence of alcohol or medications, or when the equipment is not in good working condition.

Safety

While there have been many publications written about the bandsaw, very little information on bandsaw safety, as it applies to woodturners, is available. This article will focus on safe bandsaw operation and will cover the basic cuts employed by woodturners.

Before using any power woodworking equipment, ensure a clean work area free of obstructions. Remove rings, watches, and other jewelry. Avoid wearing loose-fitting clothing or shirts with long baggy sleeves, and if you have long hair, securely tie it back. Always wear eye protection (a faceshield is best). Even when every precaution is taken, you may find yourself in a dangerous situation. Be sure the on/off switch

is located in a convenient, easy-to-reach location.

Establish and adhere to the concept of a danger zone (*Figure 1*). This zone is an area where an operator's hands are not safely placed when cutting wood. The red area indicates the danger zone, as seen from above the saw's table. Keeping your hands out of the danger zone will significantly reduce chances of injury while operating the bandsaw. As obvious as this may seem, nearly all bandsaw accidents occurred because the operator placed his hand directly in the path of the blade (in direct line of the cut).

Good posture and body position are important; you may inadvertently place your hands in danger if you lose your balance. Stand with a relaxed posture, feet balancing your body so that you are squared up in front of the table. Avoid reaching too far forward or to the sides. I recommend an open stance while cutting large pieces. This gives you the ability to react in any direction. Avoid standing flat-footed. Imagine you are resisting someone pushing: feet together, no resistance and easy to push over. Open stance, good resistance and balance.

Condition of the bandsaw

Cutting bowl blanks safely begins *before* the bandsaw is turned on. The condition of the saw blade is of utmost importance; many accidents are the result of the operator

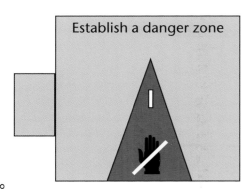

Establish a danger zone

Figure 1. The red triangle illustrates the danger zone area: the area where it is not safe to place hands and fingers when making cuts on the bandsaw.

AW26:4, p28

attempting to cut with a dull blade. Never operate a bandsaw with a dull blade. Resist the temptation to take just one more cut when you *know* the blade needs replacing. For every action, there is an equal and opposite reaction: If you are pushing hard, trying to make a cut with a dull blade, as the blade exits the wood, the bowl blank will jump forward, possibly pulling your hand directly into the path of the blade. The blade may be dull, but it will still cut off a finger.

When installing a new blade, disconnect the saw from the power source, then adjust the tension, blade guides, and rollers to the bandsaw's and blade's specifications. At the same time, inspect your saw and make necessary adjustments or replace worn parts. The following are things to check before and during installation:

- Check the condition of the rubber tires on each wheel. Obvious cracks, chunks of missing material, or a loose rubber tire indicate replacement is required. If the tires are in good condition, clean each tire using a thin piece of scrap wood or stiff nylon brush.
- Thrust bearings play a role in proper bandsaw setup and use. The thrust bearings are located behind the blade (one above and one below the table), and they should move freely so that a slight pressure from the back of the blade against it during use will keep the blade from moving too far back. The bearings should not rotate while the saw runs idle, but should begin to rotate the instant the cut begins.
- Most bandsaws are equipped with upper (above the table) and lower guide blocks (below the throatplate) or with ball bearing rollers. Guide blocks/ball bearing rollers play a critical role in the performance of your bandsaw and

Bandsaw blade terminology

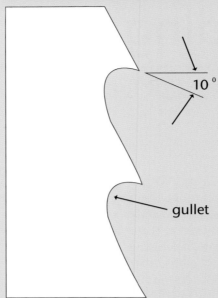

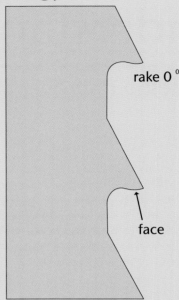

Hook-tooth blade
A hook-tooth blade has a deep gullet and widely spaced teeth that have a 10° undercut face, which helps the blade cut well. The gullets tend to curl the chips. Hook-tooth blades, alternate set, are good for harder woods.

Skip-tooth blade
A skip-tooth blade has a zero degree rake (a straight 90° tooth) and a sharp angle at the junction of the tooth and gullet. The large distance between the teeth aids in breaking up and clearing chips. Skip-tooth blades, raker set, are good for general-purpose woodcutting.

Terminology

Alternate set: How the teeth are set—in an alternating right, left pattern.

Gauge: The thickness of the material used to fabricate the bandsaw blade.

Gullet: The space within the curved area between two saw blade teeth. This space serves to remove chips.

Kerf: The slot created when a cutting tool parts through material.

Rake angle: The angle that the tooth face makes with respect to a perpendicular line from the back edge of the blade. The angle is positive when the tooth angles forward in the direction of

the cutting action and negative when it angles backward from the direction of the cutting angle. A hook-tooth blade has a positive rake of 10 degrees.

Raker: A pattern of offsetting the teeth, one tooth right, one tooth left, one tooth unset. (Also referred to as *raker set* or *raker tooth*.)

Set: The bending of bandsaw teeth to right and left of center. The set allows for clearance of the back of the blade as it cuts, which enables the blade to cut straighter and to clear chips from the kerf.

Tension: The direct pull in pounds on the bandsaw blade.

TPI: Teeth per inch, also referred to as *pitch*.

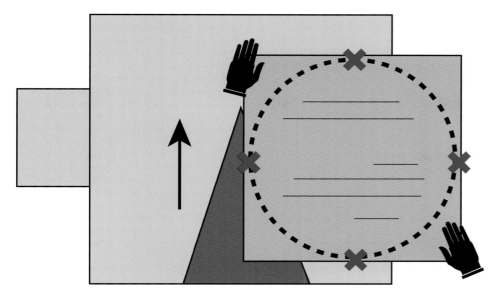

Figure 2. Position your left hand behind the sawblade and your right hand outside the danger zone as you cut a bowl blank. The Xs represent the four places where the blade will exit the wood, potentially making the bowl blank jump forward.

must be in top condition. Inspect them for wear or deep grooves and replace if necessary. Keep them adjusted so that the sides of the blade are supported but not pinched.

- Bandsaw blades, by their nature, are flexible, so the greater the distance between the upper and lower blade guides, the greater the chance the blade has to flex or develop a bow while cutting. Any maladjustment of the blade guides will only exacerbate the problem. If the guides are adjusted too far forward, the set of the teeth will be removed. If they are adjusted too far to the rear, or set too loosely, the blade won't steer properly.
- Make sure the throatplate does not have an overly large opening. An opening that has become too wide can cause a small piece of wood to fall into the opening, get caught, and possibly break a blade.
- An additional safety consideration is the distance between the top of the wood and the blade guard. When cutting bowl blanks of uneven thickness, that gap might be significant for part of the cut.

Adjust the guard to be as close as possible to the top of the wood.

Bandsaw blades

Blade type and width are important. Make sure the blade you use is capable of cutting the radius required for each size bowl blank. It is good practice to install a bandsaw blade that will allow at least three teeth to be in contact at all times with the material being cut.

The teeth on bandsaw blades are manufactured with a *set*, each tooth offset alternately right-left-right-left. This set is important because it produces a kerf that is wider than the thickness of the saw blade, which allows for clearance between the wood and the blade so that the blade does not bind. This clearance also gives the blade the ability to cut along curved or circular lines. A blade that has lost its set (a dull blade) will not cut properly and will overheat, weakening the blade and burning the wood.

For cutting large chunks of green wood, a 3 tpi, ½"- (13 mm-) wide blade is a good size that will hold up well to heavy use. For

cutting smaller stock, a ⅜"- (10 mm-) wide, 4 or 6 tpi works well. Bandsaw blades for cutting wood are available in hook-tooth or skip-tooth configurations. (A standard-tooth blade is a good choice for cutting thin stock or nonferrous metals.)

Hook-tooth blades, available in alternate or raker set, have a deeper gullet than skip-tooth blades. Their positive-tooth rake cuts more aggressively than a comparable skip-tooth blade. The deep gullet works well for eliminating shavings when cutting thick, green wood. A ⅜"- or ½"-wide skip-tooth blade, alternate set, is a good selection for general resawing, cutting round sections to length, or cutting bowl blanks.

For inexperienced bandsaw users and for cutting soft wood, I suggest using a blade with a skip-tooth design, raker set.

Deconstructing an accident

Woodturners primarily use the bandsaw to cut bowl blanks, so it's not surprising that many bandsaw accidents occur while performing this operation. Cutting bowl blanks involves both ripping cuts along the grain, as well as cutting across the grain; it is important to understand the effect this change in grain direction has when cutting round bowl blanks. Ripping cuts require more force than crosscuts because the blade is pushing into endgrain fibers. In crosscut operations, the blade feeds freely with little operator effort (assuming the blade is sharp and the bandsaw is set up properly). The change of grain direction is a leading contributor to bandsaw injuries while cutting bowl blanks— the operator does not take into consideration the difference in the amount of push required. If a dull blade is added to the equation, injury is even more likely.

Let's examine a common bandsaw accident in order to

understand what went wrong. In almost every accident, the saw blade exited the wood at one of the points near the edge *(Figure 2, blue Xs)* while the operator's hand was positioned in the danger zone. Just slightly before the blade exits a piece of wood, resistance abruptly ends, the wood jumps forward (still pushed by the operator), and the operator is unable to react quickly enough to stop his or her hand from being cut, if it is in the danger zone. Keep your hands away from the danger zone and be aware at all times when the blade is about to exit the wood so that you can ease up on the pushing pressure and cut the last bit of wood with a slow, controlled push.

Forcing a bandsaw blade through the cut with a dull blade stretches the back of the blade and compresses the front edge, allowing a bow to develop in the blade while attempting curved cuts. Once the blade begins to develop a bow, it becomes even harder to follow a curved line; there is so much pressure on the inside of the cut that the blade will have a tendency to cut in a straight line instead of following the curve of the bowl blank. The more force the operator applies to turn and cut the blank, the more the blade begins to bow and an accident is in the making.

Most turning blanks made from log sections are rectangular or square in shape, so when cutting a circular shape from the half-log, there are two or four points during the cut where the blade is close to the edge of the wood. Not coincidentally, these points are where the grain direction change occurs and where nearly all accidents happen. Be aware at all times when the blade is about to exit the wood and ease up on the pushing pressure.

Safe cutting method

Figure 2 illustrates the method I advocate for cutting bowl blanks. Notice that the operator's left hand is behind the saw blade as the blank is rotated toward the danger zone, where the blade is most likely to exit the blank. In the event that the blade exits the cut at that point, the operator's left hand has already been placed beyond the cutting edge of the saw blade, completely out of harm's way. Having a slight bend at the left elbow keeps the operator's arm well away from the blade. By following this method of cutting blanks and planning your hand position in advance, chances of being injured while cutting bowl blanks will be significantly reduced.

Other considerations

Always ensure that bowl blanks (or any wood being cut) sit flat on the table of the bandsaw. Any gap between the blank and the table where the blade enters the wood will cause the wood to be pulled toward the table with enough force to damage or break the blade.

It is common practice to mount a fixture to the bandsaw table that utilizes a stationary pin to cut circles. A divot is created in the center of the blank, which is then placed over the pin. The stock is pushed through the blade while rotating on the pin, and the result is a near-perfect circular shape. This setup works fine for thin stock, but never, under any

Cutting large-diameter logs

When cutting round stock on a bandsaw, unsupported material can be caught and rotated, pulling it into the blade with a good deal of force. This can result in serious injury and/or jamming the blade, stalling the bandsaw motor, or kinking the blade, rendering the blade useless.

For small-diameter round stock, a simple V block works well. For larger stock, V blocks do not sufficiently support and stabilize the log, so for safety, I use a modified sled.

For the bottom two boards, use 2" × 4" lumber, screwed to the miter gauge at 90°. To that, attach with screws 2" × 2" cross pieces, spaced as wide apart as possible, yet still making contact on both sides of the log. This spacing may need to be adjusted for larger or smaller diameter wood.

Some logs are crooked or have knots and do not rest in the carrier as safely as I would like. For those, I use a bar clamp to hold the log securely to the fixture. Placing screws into the log and the carrier is another option, as are wedges hot-melt glued onto the log and carrier.

A refinement to the fixture would be to use ½" plywood for the bottom instead of the 2" lumber, which would allow cutting of even larger-diameter pieces.

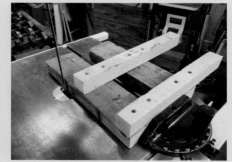

Ripping wide stock

a

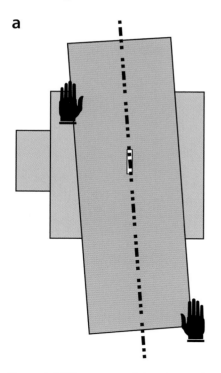

b

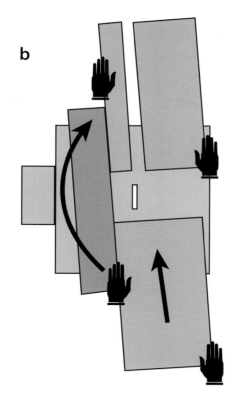

Figure 3. (a) The operator's hands are placed correctly to avoid the danger zone. (b) If cutting a long board, the cut can begin with hands placed as shown in the lower portion of this illustration. As the cut proceeds, move your left hand to the back side of the blade, as shown on the top of this illustration.

Ripping narrow stock

a

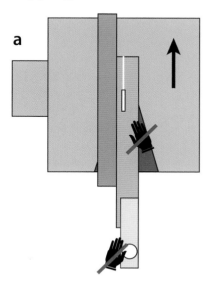

b

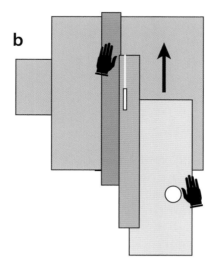

Figure 4. (a) The operator's hands are not positioned correctly even though a push stick is employed. (b) The operator is using a push stick (depicted in light brown) and has placed both hands correctly to avoid an accident.

circumstance, should you attempt to cut bowl blanks while using a pin guide such as the one described. The bowl blank must be allowed to "float" on the table, which helps compensate for blade drift and flex. Turning blanks do not have to be perfectly round—that's the lathe's job.

If you find yourself in a situation where the blade is having trouble following the desired line and the blade is in danger of exiting the blank, don't continue to force the cut. Ease up pressure on the cut, be sure your hands are out of the danger zone, and carefully steer the blade out of the side of the blank.

Ripping wide stock

Woodturners often find it necessary to cut large blocks of wood into smaller pieces for pen blanks, furniture legs, or bottle stoppers. Properly tuned, the bandsaw is ideal for this. It provides a better yield and is safer than using a table saw.

Very few bandsaw blades cut in a perfectly straight line, though, even when new. That tendency to cut on either side of a straight line is known as *drift*. To compensate for drift, a bandsaw should be equipped with a fence that is capable of being adjusted to compensate. An easy way to determine the amount and direction of drift in a bandsaw blade is to draw a straight line, parallel to one edge, on a piece of flat scrap wood *(Figure 3, a)*. As you guide the blade through the cut, notice the angle of the stock in relation to the square table. Set your fence to that approximate angle and make another test cut, keeping the stock against the fence and the guides close to the wood. With minor adjustments of the fence, the blade will cut cleanly through a long piece without binding or drawing the stock away from the fence. You are now ready to rip your stock to width *(Figure 3, b).*

Pay attention to the hand positions in the diagrams. Similarly to cutting bowl blanks, the left hand is moved to a position behind the blade, while the right hand is never in the path of the blade. In the event of a slip, there is little danger of operator injury.

Ripping narrow stock

When cutting a board into narrow stock, your hands can come dangerously close to the bandsaw blade. It is good practice to use a push stick to guide your work through the blade. Even then, it is important to position your hands away from the danger zone. *Figure 4 (a)* shows the operator using a push stick; however, both hands are potentially in the blade's path.

A safer method is placing your left hand behind the blade to secure the stock, while your right hand is safely off to the side of the blade holding the push stick *(Figure 4, b).* By the time the cut is completed, your right hand will be beyond the cutting edge of the bandsaw blade as well, out of harm's way.

There are many circumstances where a small piece of wood requires cutting on the bandsaw, and there are many ways to safely cut each piece. For example, a wooden clamp is useful for holding small objects safely while they are being trimmed to length. You could use a piece of scrap wood and use hot-melt glue to temporarily affix the small item to the larger piece of wood, sacrificing the scrap wood instead of your fingers.

Cutting round stock (cylinders)

Another cut frequently employed by woodturners is cutting cylinders, such as tree limbs, into manageable lengths. Cutting cylinders on the bandsaw, however, is a potentially dangerous operation. Aggressive saw blades may work just fine for cutting bowl blanks, but that same blade will cause an unsecured round piece to roll rapidly into the blade, possibly carrying the operator's hands with it. There is also the possibility that the workpiece will roll with enough force to break the saw blade. Even something as small as a ½" (13 mm) dowel rod can break a bandsaw blade.

There are several ways to prevent injuries when cutting cylinders. (A chainsaw may be a safer alternative when cutting large-diameter logs.) A shopmade V block will help stabilize smaller pieces and allow them to be cut safely *(Figure 5).* A miter gauge, in combination with the V block, is a good choice as well. Never attempt an unsupported cut on round stock. The material to be cut must be sitting flat on the bandsaw table.

A common, and incredibly unsafe, mistake made by some woodturners is attempting to shorten a too-long tenon on the bottom of a bowl blank using the bandsaw. The saw *will* pull the stock down to the table, rolling the round bowl at the same time. Even the most experienced bandsaw operator should never attempt this cut.

Do not attempt to cut a sphere using the bandsaw unless you know how to correctly and securely attach it to a jig.

A last word of caution

There are two categories of woodworkers who receive the most injuries, beginners and, oddly enough, the most experienced operators. It's possible that experienced operators begin to take the bandsaw for granted since they've made thousands of cuts without incident. It is easy to become complacent and gradually let your guard down. Always use common

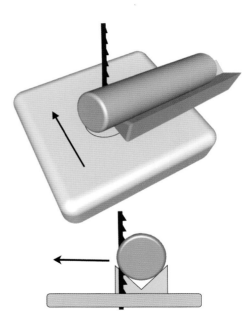

Figure 5. Never cut a cylinder without supporting it in a jig of some sort. This cylinder is correctly supported in a V-block jig. (Do not attempt to cut spheres using a bandsaw without the use of a proper jig—a V block is not sufficient support for cutting spheres.)

sense and think safety first. If it is used properly, you will discover the bandsaw is a versatile, safe machine.

Suggested References

The Band Saw Handbook by Mark Duginske, Sterling Press, 1989.

The Bandsaw Book by Lonnie Bird, Taunton Press, 1999.

*An award-winning turner, **Keith Tompkins** operates a woodturning studio, teaches, and contributes to* American Woodturner *and* Woodturning Design. *Visit Keith at www.keithptompkins.com.*

Cutting Green Wood Safely on Your Bandsaw

The surprising bandsaw can do a lot in the shop

Give me a lathe, a grinder, and a bandsaw and I'm a happy woodturner. But despite the importance of lathes and grinders, we sometimes overlook the bandsaw's role in turning. Here are some bandsaw tips for a wide range of turning applications—from preparing stock for small tops to larger green wood bowls.

Sensible bandsaws for woodturners

I've had poor luck with bandsaws with smaller than 14" wheels, and no luck at all with the three-wheel models and resaw bandsaws with wide blades. My recommendation is a 14" or larger saw—preferably with a minimum of 8" under the blade guide.

One excellent choice for a woodturner turning modest-sized pieces is to purchase a 14" saw with the optional riser block kit (allowing approximately 12" under the guides). There also are a number of 16", 18", and 20" saws capable of doing great work for the turner, but costs escalate.

I steer most turners away from the large classic bandsaws of 30" and 36" because the forces are so great and the saw is too unforgiving when something goes wrong. For 14" saws, I prefer at least a one horsepower motor for the gusto required to cut through wet wood. And I like a tilting table for tasks

including sawing off corners of large turning squares and cutting tapered bowl blanks.

Options and accessories
- Good light to shine directly onto the cutting area.
- Brush for the lower wheel to minimize build-up on the tires.
- A brake, which is a wonderful safety feature usually found on 20" or larger saws.

Bandsaw safety

I probably know more turners injured at their bandsaw than at their lathe. The message: Learn the saw's habits, develop sound

AW 19:3, p60

Bandsaw blades for turners

- For green-wood cutting, I prefer a skip or hook-tooth blade with as few teeth to the inch as I can find—usually 3 or 4 teeth per inch (tpi). Both tooth styles have advantages and disadvan-tages. The hook tooth does not clog as quickly, but the aggres-sive cut pulls stock into the blade. The skip tooth is gentler to operate, but clogs more frequently. Try both types to determine which suits you best; you'll like either one better than a regular blade.

- I don't recommend narrow blades of 1/4" or less, nor blades greater than 1/2". For preparing bowl blanks, turners don't need a narrow blade to cut exactly on the circumference. However, we want a blade that is not prone to jamming when cutting a radius. In balance, a 3/8" or 1/2" blade satisfies turning work.

- Blade thickness also is a concern for resistance to twisting and metal fatigue. Generally I avoid any blades less than 0.025" thick. For my 20" bandsaw, I prefer something closer to 0.030".

I purchase blades from a local saw shop that welds them to length from good quality basic stock. If you go through a lot of blades and have a frugal bent, consider learning how to silver-solder blades from rolls of coil stock.

But what about the low-tension, bi-metal, or carbide-tipped blades? Because I often cut wood with bark attached—which dulls blades—I can't justify the more expensive blades in these categories for rough-cutting stock.

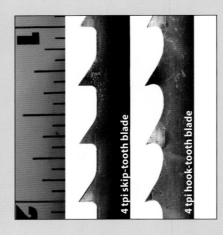

4 tpi skip-tooth blade

4 tpi hook-tooth blade

While teaching bandsaw techniques, I recommend drawing or painting a 1"-wide strip on the bandsaw table that extends from the blade to the edge of the front table. Hands and arms must stay out of this zone. Unless using a pushstick, never push with the hands or fingers in this zone.

To reduce exposure to injury, I work from the side when cutting bowl blanks, turning the piece \into the blade rather than pushing.

One more suggestion: Develop a routine to pull the stock through the bandsaw rather than pushing. Doing so reduces the chance of injury.

practices, and acquire a healthy respect for this machine.

Who is probably most at risk for a bandsaw accident? Two prominent groups generate the most accidents: the novice who does not understand the bandsaw's behaviors and the seasoned veteran who thinks he or she has mastered all and therefore can't get hurt.

I operate from two essential rules. First, hands and arms must stay out of the Red Zone—the area in line with the blade. See the box *at right* for more details.

Second, work with supported stock—not stock that wobbles, rolls

or flips while cutting. Just as in turning wood where an unsupported edge causes a dig-in, serious bandsaw accidents happen with lightning speed when the work is not supported below the cut.

I know a lot of turners like to crosscut short, round objects on the bandsaw. But there are serious risks here unless you take precautions. If larger than 3" in diameter, I prefer to crosscut stock with a chainsaw.

It is possible on some sizes to rig up V-blocks to cradle the round stock. If the round stock is small (under 2") and shorter than the table is wide, I suggest securing the piece in a parallel (handscrew) clamp that stays flat on the table as shown *at right.*

For making multiple blanks 2" or smaller, crosscut stock with your bandsaw miter gauge. Clamp smaller pieces of wood against the miter-gauge fence and cut away—a good technique to remember for making multiples.

The problem with crosscutting round stock is that on entry, the piece tries to roll like a wheel—pulling the work quickly into the blade and sometimes twisting the blade. Either of these situations can result in a broken blade or worse—an accident caused by shooting the wood from the saw or pulling your body parts into the blade.

One additional note: It makes my hair stand on end when I see or hear about a turner going to the bandsaw to cut the waste off the bottom of a turned bowl. This sounds like an emergency room visit in the making. A better plan: Remove the nib off the lathe with a Japanese pull saw.

Bandsaw bowl stock

Because bowl turning is still the most popular interest, let's review the process of bandsawing a small log to produce a face-grain bowl.

I recommend crosscutting the log to length (slightly longer than the diameter) with a chainsaw or even a hand bow saw. Next, halve the log using wedges and a sledge hammer, a chainsaw, or bandsaw.

At the bandsaw, there are several options for halving a log. One is to cut into the side of the log (end grain on table) as shown *at right.* I suggest this technique on logs 6" or larger in diameter and no longer than the height under the upper blade guide.

Another strategy is to cut head on to the end-grain as shown on the following page—truly a ripping cut.

To crosscut short round stock, securing material in an adjustable parallel (handscrew) clamp is a solid solution.

With 6"-diameter or larger stock, you can bandsaw logs upright to halve the material. Note safe hand position.

This cut on supported wood avoids the danger of the piece rolling like a wheel as noted in crosscutting. If using this method, I recommend looking for a face of the log that has support on the bandsaw table along the entirety of the cut. Also, the face of the log that first contacts the blade should be as flat as possible to maximize support under the blade.

Next, cut the half log into a disc. The safest way I have found is a cutting template attached to the curved section of the half log.

I recommend making a set of patterns for the smallest bowl you think you will ever turn to the largest capacity of your lathe. Patterns from 1/4" plywood or hardboard are ideal. Make a set in half-inch increments, drill a hole through the center to accept a nail, and identify the size of each template as shown *below*.

Bandsaw with a template

Select the appropriate template, nail it to the half log (flat face down on the bandsaw table) and cut around the outside of the template as shown *below right*. Don't try to cut the circumference in one pass—it's too easy to jam the blade or even twist it. I nibble away with 6 or 8 cuts that appear to be straight.

If you're new to bowl turning or you're turning at a lightweight lathe, take your time to make the blank round; doing so reduces effort at the lathe. For mounting stock to the the faceplate, use the same template to mark the center on the flattened face.

I can think of no other saw that is so versatile as the bandsaw. It easily rips, crosscuts, cuts circles and arcs, works logs or other thick stock, and cuts angles—all quietly and effortlessly compared to other power saws.

But just like other power tools, the bandsaw demands full attention and control. Focus on the task at hand—not your lathe work— while bandsawing.

*A past President of the AAW and an Honorary Lifetime Member, **Alan Lacer** has spent four decades as a turner, instructor, and contributing editor to* American Woodturner. *Visit Alan at www.woodturninglearn.net.*

A recommended ripping procedure: The downward pressure of the bandsaw blade reduces the tendency of the log to roll side to side.

Spend a few minutes to make a set of cutting patterns, shown above, for your lathe's swing capacity. The 8" pattern is shown at right on a birch log.

Sweet and Simple Chucking Strategies

Learn to attach and cleanly remove blemish free bowls

One of the first challenges for the turner who wants to make bowls is attaching the block of wood to the lathe. Once the bowl has been shaped, another major challenge is how to finish off the bottom. When people pick up a finished bowl, they invariably turn it over and examine the bottom. Instinctively they realize that's where the bowl must be held on the lathe and they want to figure it out. Good technique means the foot or bottom will be as well finished as the rest of the bowl, and there should be no detracting indication of how the bowl was attached, or chucked, to the lathe.

Of course, in between the first and second challenge, there are plenty of other challenges, but I would like to concentrate on chucking methods here, based on my own experience. I'll address basic chucks first, and then reverse chucks.

Basic chucks

There are several chucks on the market in the $150-$300 range available to fit most lathes. These are usually multipurpose affairs with expanding and contracting jaws. I bought one, and after paying another $50 to have it properly tapped for my headstock spindle, I used it once or twice only. It now sits on the shelf waiting for the special case, which never seems to come, where its complexity is needed. While I am sure these chucks are good and serviceable, I prefer the KISS approach—Keep It Sweet and Simple. I have found that two chucks are all that are needed: a screw chuck and a faceplate.

The screw chuck—A good screw chuck will securely hold large blocks of wood. The basic design is straightforward: Usually it's a 3/4-inch-long screw extending from a small faceplate. A matching hole is drilled in the wood and the wood screwed onto the chuck. I have seen designs for home-made units where hardware-store lag screws are used, centered through wooden faceplates. However, the critical success factor for this chuck is the design of the screw, and here one product is preeminent. Glaser Engineering's screw is designed with a shallow pitch and large flanges that grip the wood almost without fail. Glaser makes two sizes of screw—one with a 3/8-inch outside diameter, the other with a 1/2-inch outside diameter. Both fit his chuck body; the complete unit is the Glaser Screw Chuck. I use the 1/2-inch o.d. screw, and so I drill a 3/8-inch hole in the face of the woodblock (approximately 1 inch deep) and spin the block onto the screw chuck. Some persuasion may be necessary, depending on the hardness of the wood. Once the block is tight, this screw will hold wet woods of large diameter, which are really heavy. (For safety considerations, see the sidebar.)

When the outside of the bowl has been shaped, a 3/4-inch-deep hole can be drilled into the foot, and the block reversed on the chuck. The design of the bowl should allow for 1 inch of waste at the foot, which will be parted off. I fitted a 3/8-inch long-bore drill with an old tool handle, but I've also held a regular drill with a vise-grip. You have to be careful not to drill too deep, or the drill hole will go through the eventual bottom of the bowl, which is not recommended.

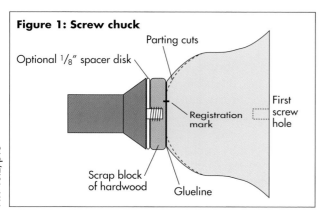

Figure 1: Screw chuck

Optional 1/8" spacer disk · Parting cuts · Registration mark · First screw hole · Scrap block of hardwood · Glueline

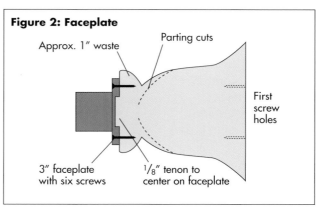

Figure 2: Faceplate

Approx. 1" waste · Parting cuts · First screw holes · 3" faceplate with six screws · 1/8" tenon to center on faceplate

AW 10:2, p16

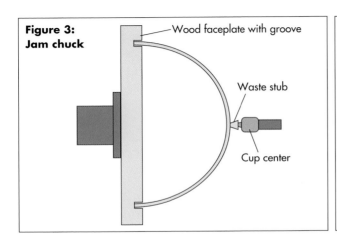

Figure 3: Jam chuck

Wood faceplate with groove

Waste stub

Cup center

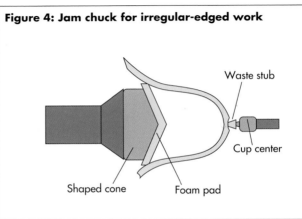

Figure 4: Jam chuck for irregular-edged work

Waste stub

Cup center

Shaped cone

Foam pad

Immediately one benefit of the single screw hole can be seen—the reversed block should be almost perfectly centered. Work can now begin on the inside.

We can extend the approach even more by using scrap blocks of hardwood glued to the (flattened) bottom of the bowl via cyanoacrylate glue, and drilling the hole in this after starting a hole with a narrow gouge (Figure 1). This is useful if the design requires using the full block of wood. Hardwood scraps are necessary; plywood separates and fiberboard crumbles. The scrap is turned to a circle and eventually parted off.

Another tip here is to use a 1/8-inch plywood disk on the chuck to shorten the screw penetration into the wood. This is particularly useful for small pieces. If the wood is soft, a few drops of thin cyanoacrylate will harden up the drill hole.

Mark the position of the scrap relative to the bowl with a pencil or black marker, in case the bowl breaks off after a catch, or when it dries and warps.

Which brings us to another major advantage of the single-screw chuck: Once the bowl has dried for three or more months and stopped warping, and you now need to remount, true up, and finish it, the single hole is there for you, centered and ready.

The faceplate—For large blocks, which even a Glaser-style screw will not hold, a faceplate and screws will be required. Large faceplates are not necessary except for starting on really big blanks (greater than 20 inches in diameter). It's hard to get a large enough flat surface on raw blanks, and a large faceplate limits access when used on the bottom of a bowl. A 3-inch faceplate is best, but it should be drilled for six screws. And the type of screws is important—sheet-metal screws with a uniform shank and square-drive pan head are my preference. Drywall screws are tempting because they are sharp and easy; however they are also brittle

Safety considerations

- Blocks of wet wood are heavy and uneven. Use the tailstock with revolving center to keep the wood up against the chuck, especially with the single screw, but also with the faceplate, until the block is true.

- Start with very slow revolutions; a variable-speed DC motor makes a great difference here.

- Always wear a face shield (not just goggles).

- Stand aside from the plane of rotation.

- Be able to stop your lathe as soon as there is a problem—use a foot switch or a switch placed near the tailstock.

and will shear under stress, so they should not be used. Six 1-1/4 inch screws, which penetrate through the faceplate and 1 inch into the wood, will hold most blocks other than decayed, punky wood, which can be hardened with cyanoacrylate. When the faceplate is used for the initial shaping, it is attached to the face of the block; and then it is attached to the bottom of the bowl, either to the wood itself (Figure 2), or to the scrap block if required by the design. It is sometimes necessary to drill pilot holes in the scrap block.

It is helpful to raise a 1/8-inch-long tenon on the bottom of the blank, its width equal to the inside diameter of the faceplate. This will assist in centering the faceplate.

Reverse chucks

There are several approaches to completing the foot of the bowl. I will discuss three: the jam chuck, the vacuum chuck, and the ring chuck. Each requires investment in time and money before it can be used, but this investment has to be made if the job is to be done right.

The jam chuck—This is the simplest device for reverse chucking: it is a wooden disk with a groove turned into it to match the diameter of the bowl. The bowl is reversed onto the disk and held in the groove by a snug fit, the groove serving also to center the bowl. The tailstock is brought up to help keep the piece in place. At low revolutions and with

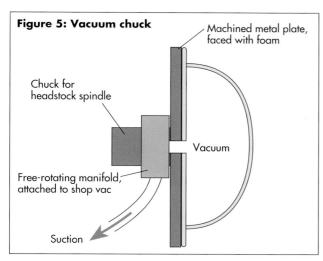

Figure 5: Vacuum chuck

Machined metal plate, faced with foam

Chuck for headstock spindle

Vacuum

Free-rotating manifold, attached to shop vac

Suction

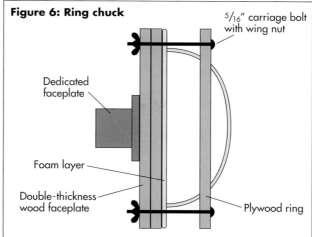

Figure 6: Ring chuck

5/16" carriage bolt with wing nut

Dedicated faceplate

Foam layer

Double-thickness wood faceplate

Plywood ring

light cuts, the foot is shaped, leaving a small stub at the tailstock point (Figure 3). This stub will finally be chiseled off and the spot sanded to blend in.

The wooden disk can be held via faceplate or screw chuck. It can be any material—plywood is fine. One jam chuck disk is used per bowl, so you end up with a pile of disks of various diameters, but they can be reused with smaller-diameter bowls.

The tailstock support also works for irregular- or natural-edged bowls, when a foam-padded cone is used inside the bowl to jam against (Figure 4). The cone is readily made from scrap wood to match the unique size and shape of the bowl; at its simplest it is the waste block left behind when the bowl is parted off.

This approach is pretty straightforward and works well, except that you have to find large disks of scrap wood and cut the groove to match, and fuss with the little stub at the end. By comparison, the vacuum chuck is more attractive.

The vacuum chuck—This is an advance over the basic jam chuck: atmospheric pressure holds the bowl against the faceplate, thus obviating the need for a groove (since the workpiece can be easily centered) and the tailstock (since air pressure is strong enough to hold it in place in most cases).

There are two types of vacuum chuck: One uses a suction tube centered in a wooden faceplate and fed through the headstock spindle. It uses a small vacuum pump. The other uses a shop-vac attached to a rotating collar behind a metal, engineered faceplate faced with a foam pad (Figure 5). I chose the shop-vac unit since shop-vacs are easily found (KISS again), and although I have not been using it for long, I like it despite the noise. For the right shape of bowl, the suction is tight and allows fast, effective finishing of the complete bowl foot. For larger bowls and odd shapes, or designs with uneven edges, this chuck is not so suitable, and I sometimes resort to using the tailstock for reinforcement. I intend to build, as needed, special-purpose wooden enhancements to the suction plate to deal with more complex shapes such as vases, although in these cases I find I can just as well use the tailstock and avoid the din of the shop-vac.

The ring chuck—Tried and true, the homemade ring chuck consists of a faceplate disk and a wooden ring which holds the bowl to the plate via bolts and wing nuts (Figure 6). Various lengths of bolts, and various diameter rings, are made to accommodate any bowl of diameter less than that of the faceplate.

Readily constructed in an afternoon out of plywood, the faceplate is double-thick and covered with thin foam rubber. The rings are of the same diameter as the faceplate, and have three matching holes for the 5/8-inch carriage bolts; register marks on each ring ensure the bolt holes line up. The inner diameter of the rings varies from narrow to wide; three or four can be made and the inner edges rounded over with a router to prevent marring the bowl.

The reversed bowl is held in place via the appropriate ring and length of bolt. The closer the ring can be to the faceplate, the more secure the bowl is against being bumped out of true. The bowl is then centered carefully (bring up the tailstock to register it) before tightening the bolts. I have seen designs where a stepped cone is added to the center of the faceplate to provide for rapid centering. When the lathe is turned on (at low revs, I hasten to add), the foot is wholly available for finishing. Again, light cuts with small gouges are recommended.

Summary

For the primary attachment of wood to a lathe, you can get by in most cases with a Glaser-style screw chuck, some scrap hardwood disks, and the ubiquitous, invaluable cyanoacrylate glue. To finish the bottom of a bowl, hold it against a large home-made faceplate by the tailstock, suction, or a ring, the latter two leaving the foot completely clear for proper attention.

Peter Smith is a 14-year AAW member who lives in Princeton, NJ.

Mastering the Four-Jaw Scroll Chuck

A convenient and smart choice for securing wood

Of the many ways that woodturners can mount stock onto a lathe, nothing seems to generate more interest—or debate—than the popular four-jaw, self-centering scroll chuck. It's fair to say that scroll chucks are the first choice to secure wood for turning as well as the number one lathe accessory, in large part because turners appreciate their convenience, versatility, and time-saving qualities.

This handy and practical device came into widespread use on wood lathes in the mid 1970s, derived from the gear-driven chucks that had been used in metalworking for many years. After its introduction, woodturners quickly shelved their faceplates and jam chucks to enthusiastically adopt the scroll chuck—and the turning craft hasn't been the same since.

Properly used, scroll chucks offer significant advantages over traditional methods:
- Screw holes are eliminated from the bottom of turned items, making more creative designs possible.
- Chuck jaws can grasp both a round tenon (also called *spigot* or *foot*) as well as square spindle stock.
- Indexing and off-center turning can be enhanced through the use of some scroll chucks.

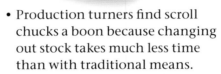
Open-back Talon chuck with key.

- Production turners find scroll chucks a boon because changing out stock takes much less time than with traditional means.

This article explores the uses of the four-jaw scroll chuck for the beginner (and perhaps intermediate) woodturner. It is not an endorsement or ranking of any particular make, model, or manufacturer, but rather an overview of what is available, and the pros and cons of various designs.

Limitations of chucks
Scroll chucks have their limitations. Perhaps chief among them is the potential for mishaps that can result in injury to the turner or damage to the turning. For larger work, and when the absolute best holding power is required, using a faceplate is still the safest way to go. As David Ellsworth tells his students, and notes in his recent book *Ellsworth on Woodturning*, "If the piece of wood is tall or heavy or out of round, or if it looks like it would smash your foot instead of just crunching a toe, don't even think twice—just stick it on a faceplate.

The bottom line is that nothing holds a piece of wood to the lathe stronger and with less vibration than a faceplate."

Varieties of chucks
A plethora of chucks and chuck accessories is available in today's market. This is evident by opening any woodturning catalog or by perusing online woodworking forums where no one is shy about expressing blunt and candid opinions about chucks. Turners are enticed by various brands of scroll chucks—with a wide range of prices—as well as vacuum chucks, donut and jam chucks, collet and Jacobs chucks, eccentric chucks, and more. In addition, four-jaw chucks have an array of extensions and attachments of every configuration, including screw chucks, Stebcenter and spur drives, and jumbo jaws of various sizes. The world of chucks can be a confusing place to navigate, even for experienced woodturners.

That world has expanded considerably in recent years. The leading industry manufacturers include Oneway, the Canadian company that produces the Stronghold and Talon models; Vicmarc, a manufacturer in Australia

Screw chuck attached in a Talon chuck.

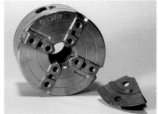
Talon chuck showing safety slots and pin in jaws.

Photos and drawings by Ed Kelle

AW 25:1, p47

Getting Started in Woodturning

Template guides for turning safe tenons and recesses

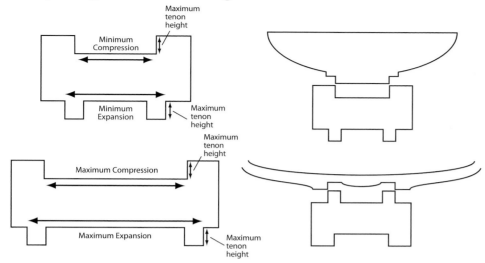

of the VM 100, 120, and 150 series; Robert Sorby, the English lathe tool producer that makes the Patriot brand; New Zealand-based Teknatool, maker of the Nova and Titan chucks; and Axminster, the British toolmaker that offers the Clubman and Super Precision chucks.

Increasingly, manufacturers in China and other Asian nations are bringing to the market less expensive scroll chucks that are gaining admirers for their rugged qualities, high performance standards, and their interchangeability with more established brands. These include several models made by Grizzly Industrial, the Barracuda line from Penn State Industries, and Pinnacle and WoodRiver chucks sold by Woodcraft, among many others. For lighter duty applications and for beginning turners, these chucks

Axminster engineering workshop and Axminster chuck.

afford commendable quality and are certainly less demanding on the wallet.

What is a chuck and how does it work?

A *chuck* is a mechanical device that holds material during various stages of processing. Applied to woodturning, this primarily means a four-jaw scroll chuck. This design allows the four centering jaws to work in unison—unlike metalworking chucks in which the jaws may operate independently to accommodate off-center work.

Four sliding base jaws, or *travelers*, are engaged by matching channels that are grooved into the chuck body. The chuck's top jaws that grip the wood attach to these slides. At the opposite end of the chuck is a threaded insert, cut to match the thread of the lathe's headstock spindle nose. The centering results from a machined spiral, or *scroll*, that rotates inside the body of the chuck and shifts the jaws in and out as the lathe operator tightens the grasp on the work.

A turner activates the rotational movement using a geared chuck key, hex T-wrench,

or dual tommy bars, rodlike levers that are pulled counter to each other to encircle and secure the work. While lever-operated chucks are generally faster than key-operated chucks, and lower in price, they are less convenient and not as intuitive to use. Opening and closing mix-ups can easily occur if the user is not paying close enough attention because achieving a reliable hold takes more effort. Thus, the majority of chucks sold today use a single key, which allows a major advantage: one-handed operation.

Quality control

While manufacturers take care to produce accurate products, any affordable chuck that has moving parts will exhibit some wobble or *slop,* which is built-in tolerance that results in a slight amount of run-out that is especially noticeable in larger-diameter pieces. The only way to completely remove this tolerance would be to engineer chucks to such a high degree of precision that few people could afford to purchase one. Metalworking chucks, for example, can cost thousands of dollars and weigh hundreds of pounds to eliminate tolerances in performance.

Many turners insist that some run-out is inevitable in wood lathe work anyway, because of spindle misalignment and the nature of wood itself. If a chuck shows signs of run-out that is noticeable to the naked eye, the first thing to check is whether the spindle adapter is improperly aligned or loose. Even the slightest run-out at the spindle will be magnified considerably in the turning itself. And, taking a blank out of the chuck and remounting it will almost always produce noticeable run-out. Some turners place a mark on the chuck's edge and a corresponding mark on the tenon so that they can remount the work exactly where it was originally. *Repeatability* is important in chuck performance, so that when pieces

The diameter of this tenon is too large, causing the jaws of the chuck to stick out so far that they become a safety hazard. Additionally, if the tenon were slightly longer, the jaw would have more surface on which to grip.

The diameter and height of this tenon will hold the bowl blank securely and safely. The jaws are not protruding too far; the tenon is not touching the bottom of the chuck; and there is a flat shoulder on the bottom of the bowl that rests evenly on the top of the jaws.

are reversed in the lathe they will require a minimum of reshaping to eliminate wobble.

Manufacturers compensate for these quality control issues by working to perfect a chuck's fit and finish so that the device will provide a lifetime of consistent service. External surface coating is applied to improve smoothness of operation and reduce chances of rust and corrosion. Materials are chosen for compatibility, balance, and resistance to wear. The scroll, base jaws, and top jaws use different metals that have surfaces tempered by heat and tough electroplating. Chucks come in both open- and closed-back designs, which may affect their operation somewhat. An open-back chuck leaves the gears exposed, which may allow grit and grime to impede the tightening of the jaws, but also facilitates cleaning. Oneway claims that after producing the Talon and Stronghold chucks for many years, no chuck was ever returned because of its open-back design. Vicmarc chucks, which have closed backs, have convenient indexing holes drilled around the outer edge of its chucks. The back can be removed for inspection and cleaning of the gears.

Safety considerations and gripping power

Various safety measures have been built in to prevent the jaws from loosening or flying off the chuck. For instance, Oneway has added grooves that are cut in the face of the chuck in which a pin rides as the jaws move.

A shorter groove keeps the jaws from extending beyond the body of the chuck—a benefit in schools or beginner classes to protect knuckles from the spinning steel. A longer groove allows maximum travel while not interfering with easy disassembly if required. Nova and Vicmarc employ a pin in the jaw travel slot. These designs usually reduce jaw travel and, as a result, more top jaw sets are required to cover a range of diameters.

Chucks should have set screws of hardened steel to securely attach them to the lathe's spindle. Moreover, because many turners increasingly use reverse, or clockwise, turning, it is *critical* that the chuck attach tightly to the headstock spindle to prevent the work from unwinding right off the spindle.

In addition, to mitigate the prospects of a failure, experienced turners seldom rotate chuck-mounted stock at high speeds, especially in the roughing-out stage. So long as one is getting a good clean cut, slower is safer. And, prudent users know to crank in the live center from the tailstock to provide additional support when turning a bowl blank.

When a bowl is properly mounted in a chuck by its tenon and the turner experiences a catch or dig-in, the tenon must stay attached in the chuck (even if the bowl itself breaks off). To reduce the chances of a failure, chuck designers have created

several innovations that have been adopted by most manufacturers. The most crucial aspects of these are the gripping powers of the top jaws—the ones that clamp the wood. No matter how good, smooth, expensive, cheap, large, or small—if the top jaws are not capable of holding the blank securely, then the chuck is essentially useless.

Types of jaws and mounting the stock

Perhaps the most contentious issue among veteran turners is which of the two main types of jaws on the market has superior holding power. The most common style is the dovetail shape used by Vicmarc and other makers. The other is the patented Oneway grooved cam-milled design and the various adaptations of Oneway's design.

Jaws are made to clamp externally on a round tenon (or glue block) in what is known as a *compression* hold, or to extend internally into a hollowed recess, known as *expansion* or *tension*. How well a jaw grips depends on the fit between the jaws and the tenon (or the dovetail shape in the event you are using the chuck in expansion

Vicmarc chucks and accessories.

Using a parting tool to turn a tenon works well to create a 90° shoulder and a flat base surface. If dovetail-style jaws are used, the sides of the tenon should match the jaw shape.

Place marks on the bowl blank that relate to the jaws of the chuck so the bowl blank can be remounted in the same position. Doing so will help keep the bowl blank in alignment for "repeatability" and will minimize wobble.

A platter or bowl blank also can be expansion-mounted; the jaws of the chuck are placed inside a turned recess.

mode), the jaw diameter, and the diameter of the wood. Every jaw, with the exception of Oneway's patented top jaws, is designed to fit only one size and one dovetail shape. Any other size or shape will compromise holding power to some degree.

Wood is held more strongly in compression than in tension. For turning bowls and vessels, most turners use a tenon to hold the piece in compression mode. For plates and platters, a recess is often used, and—as long as the jaws are not overtightened in the recess and as long as no major catches occur—the use of the recess with the wood in tension is suitable.

Don't apply too much force when tightening the jaws in either expansion or compression mode. Many turners tighten the chuck so

Nova chuck

much that they split the recess or they crush the fibers of the tenon, thus decreasing the holding power of the chuck and jaws. Crushing the fibers of the tenon is also a prime culprit for introducing unwanted vibration and chatter into the turning process. With that said, however, when holding green wood, it is necessary to periodically tighten the jaws as turning progresses. The tenon will loosen as jaws sink deeper into the wet fibers as the wood dries during the turning process.

Wood should be held in a concentric grip, which arguably should occur when using a scroll chuck. Many turners, however, insist that the best way to ensure a concentric grip is to hold the tenon in the jaws and tighten the chuck just enough to hold the piece snugly. Then, rotate the chuck to the opposite side opening and then tighten a bit further, repeating the process on each side. Progressively tightening in this manner makes it more likely that all the jaws will compress equally and will be concentric on the tenon.

Tenon size and recess

The size of the tenon or recess should be proportional to the intended finished size of the object and the size

of the jaws being used. Most chuck jaws are manufactured in such a way that maximum gripping power is achieved at only one diameter: when the jaws are nearly closed. At this point the maximum amount of jaw surface is holding the tenon. At larger openings, less and less of the jaws' surface is gripping the stock.

A useful rule of thumb is to make the tenon about 30%–40% as wide as the largest diameter of the stock. Large bowls 12"–20" (30cm–50cm) in diameter, for example, require a tenon 3½"–6½" (9cm–16cm) in diameter. Bowls that are 4"–12" (10cm–30cm) in diameter can be held on a tenon that is 1¾"–4" (45mm–100mm) in diameter. Tenon height should be a maximum of 3/16"–7/16" (5mm–11mm). In general, the better the fit of the wood blank to the design of the chuck, the better it will hold. Experienced turners make a template out of cardboard or plywood with a semicircular cutout of the minimum and maximum distances that their chuck will accommodate to facilitate a proper fit.

Tenon or recess profile

The walls of the tenon or recess must match the profile of the jaws. On chucks with a dovetail design, the tenon or recess must correspond to that shape. Other manufacturers machine the profile of the jaws such that a straight-sided tenon or recess must be used.

The bottom of the tenon should not rest on the inside bottom of the chuck. Rather, the shoulder around the bowl's tenon should sit in solid contact with the top of the chuck's jaws. Since the exposed surfaces of the jaws are machined flat, a corresponding flat area must exist on the wood immediately surrounding the tenon. This ensures maximum holding power and safety by providing sideways support for the bowl blank during turning.

Design diameter is the size that the jaw was machined to before separation into the four quadrants. The simplest way to check design diameter is to open the chuck to ⅛" (3mm) between the sides of the top jaws. Measure across the circumference and you have design diameter. When the owner's manual claims that a certain jaw has a range of 2"–3" (50mm–75mm) you can be sure only of one thing: design diameter is somewhere in between, probably 2¼" (60mm).

The Oneway jaws are a radically different design in two areas. For external gripping, the milled, serrated profile will grip any diameter within its capacity (not just design diameter) with eight nearly form-fitting contacts. For internal chucking, the jaw shape is a 10° dovetail. Additionally, Oneway mills a small circular ridge on the outside of the jaws that bites deep in the dovetail recess for extreme holding power in the least visible area of a recess.

Process for mounting and turning a bowl

It is commonly accepted in today's turning world that the bottoms of bowls be finished in such a way that the method of holding the blank is no longer a visible feature. Usually, this means that a tenon is removed after hollowing or is incorporated into the design.

At the start of the turning process, a bowl blank also can be held with a large screw, upon which the blank is threaded using a predrilled hole. Screw chucks are usually provided as accessories and, when used, are held in the chuck's jaws. Alternatively, the blank can be mounted on a faceplate, using screws. Held either way, and with the tailstock brought up for extra security, a tenon can be turned on the bottom of the bowl. The outside of the bowl can be completely

finish-turned before the blank is reversed and attached by its tenon to the scroll chuck for hollowing.

When the bowl is complete, the tenon is removed, either by turning or by sawing it off. If a lathe is equipped with a vacuum chuck, that is often the fastest and easiest approach. Other options are the jumbo or mega jaws marketed by several chuck manufacturers. These jaws hold the rim of the bowl with rubber buttons. Last but not least, the bowl can be remounted onto a jam-fit chuck, then secured with the revolving tailstock center for removal of the tenon. The small nub left in the center can be carved off.

Chuck maintenance

Modern-day chucks can take years of daily use, and even abuse, and still perform admirably. But over time, plus exposure to the normal abrasion of metal on metal, compounded by the introduction of dust or rust, moving parts will show wear; safety will be compromised. To minimize this, one can periodically disassemble the chuck, remove all dust, dirt, and grime and administer a dry lubricant to moving parts. Manufacturers usually offer detailed instructions on taking a chuck apart and reassembling it, and it is a very instructive process. Any novice taking on this job would be wise to have on hand someone who has done it before.

Some turners clean their particularly dirty chucks by

Use the tailstock for support as long as possible while roughing out a bowl blank to provide maximum safety.

The bottom of a bowl can be turned by mounting the bowl in jumbo jaws in expansion or compression modes. Whenever possible, use the tailstock for added support and safety.

submerging them in mineral spirits or acetone for a half hour to loosen accumulated residue, then using an air hose to blow them out. At a minimum, experienced users recommend periodic spraying with a dry, Teflon-based lubricant rather than using oils or greases.

When maintaining the chuck, remember to inspect the screws that hold the jaws to the slides. These should be checked with every use to ensure that they are tight and fully seated. Also, examine the grooves and dovetails as well as the heads of the screws that join the jaws to the slides. If they are packed with sawdust, clean them with a short blast of compressed air or a scratch awl. If care is taken, chucks should provide many years of use.

A previous board member and an Honorary Lifetime Member of the AAW, **Dick Gerard** *is a member of the Central Indiana Chapter. Visit Dick at www.dickgerard.com.*
Stan Wellborn, *a longtime journalist, is a member of the Capital Area Woodturners in Washington, DC.*

Oneway Stronghold chuck and key.

Grinder Wheels

A simple way to make sharpening easy

Most people don't realize they might need specialized grinder wheels when they begin their adventure with woodturning. The first thing they think of is usually a lathe. Next, turning tools and wood. Maybe sharpening enters into the process at some point, but grinder wheels? Nobody thinks of them.

Having proper wheels on your grinder makes woodturning simpler and more pleasant than struggling to sharpen tools with improper equipment. Quality wheels that are balanced and suitable for your needs will make sharpening easy. Sharp tools make turning fun.

The old pros can sharpen successfully with just about any grinder and grinder wheel. They probably don't even use a jig to hold the tool at the proper angle. Decades of practice make it easy for them to roll the tool over the grinder wheel by hand and get a perfect edge, whether it is an old gray grinder wheel or the latest ceramic ones.

The rest of us, however, appreciate all the help we can get. When we are starting, it is particularly important to simplify the process and have the most appropriate equipment.

I spent more than a decade as a production turner and used a wide variety of grinder wheels. I have tested all the popular types—and some not so popular. Some wheels work quite well, but I have a cabinet full of wheels that do not. Now I want to share those experiences with you.

Grinder size and speed

I have used 6" and 8" (15 cm and 20 cm) grinders both high and low speed. Which is best? Probably the one you have. The main difference between the 6" and 8" grinder wheels is the amount of use you get out of them. When a 6" wheel gets down to 5" (13 cm), I generally change the wheel. But I use an 8" wheel until it is about 6", which is a substantial amount of extra grinding. Yes, it costs more to begin with, but you quickly recoup the extra cost. Is it

worth buying a new grinder, though? Probably not, unless you are in continual production mode.

More important than the wheel size is the speed of the grinder. There are high-speed (3450 rpm) and low-speed (1725 rpm) grinders. Low-speed grinders are increasingly popular with woodturners because of the lack of heat buildup during use. At a lower speed, there is less chance of *bluing*—heating the metal to a blue color. In the old days, this was considered a terrible thing to do, with good reason. The carbon-steel tools—all we had until the last twenty years—lose their temper if the metal turns blue from heat buildup when grinding. The tools would not hold an edge and had to be ground back significantly to get rid of the soft metal, wasting metal and grinding grit.

The newer high-speed and powdered-metal tools are much less susceptible to overheating, but it can still happen, especially if you put some pressure on the tool and take it beyond the blue stage. Many people recommend dunking a tool in cool water to keep the heat level down. I have done this and seemed to get away with it; however, it can lead to microscopic cracks in the sharp edge. It is better to use a light touch when sharpening a tool to avoid heat in the first place.

If you have a high-speed grinder, there are wheels made specifically for them. Oneway Mfg., for example, sells wheels recommended for use with high-speed grinders. These wheels tend to be harder than the low-speed ones, so don't mix them up. Personally, I prefer the lower-speed wheels because I tend to grind off less of my tool at each sharpening.

AW 26:2, p23

Three aluminum oxide wheels are currently available. The gray one on the left came on a new grinder and is meant for grinding soft steel. The white wheel in the center was also on the grinder and is a little too coarse for woodturners' sharpening needs, but would be suitable for major reshaping of a tool. The blue stone is distributed by Oneway Mfg. and is a type that is designed for woodturners' needs. Note: it is rated for 4,140 rpm, so is meant for a high-speed grinder. Stones are also made specifically for slow-speed grinders.

Dressing the wheel

Speed is not the only thing that causes heat. A dull wheel is a major culprit. Dress your wheel as soon as it is not cutting efficiently. When the abrasive particle contacting the steel is sharp, a metal shaving is milled from the steel and ejected. This removes a significant amount of generated heat in a spray of red sparks. A wheel with dull grit ploughs across the steel and transfers much of the heat to the steel. Hard wheels are particularly prone to getting dull.

Gray wheels

As I mentioned, those who have been turning for quite some time can do a good job of sharpening using the hard gray wheels that normally come with a grinder. For many of these turners, this was all they had, so they learned to live with the grinder wheel's limitations. Gray wheels are designed to stand up to the terrible punishment associated with metalworking shops where thick steel plate is ground, bolts shortened, and other heavy-duty jobs performed. Heavy pressure is usually put on the wheel and the metals are soft. Gray wheels are very hard, so they can do these jobs while lasting a reasonable length of time. They

also tend to heat up the metal, which is not a problem in most applications.

We woodturners, however, are performing a light-duty job on very hard tempered steel—simply renewing an edge on an already sharpened tool. The tool's hardness and the resulting heat are our enemy. Gray wheels tend to glaze over easily and stop cutting efficiently. When that happens, the normal reaction is to press harder, increasing the heat. If you have to use a gray wheel, clean it often and use a light touch when grinding.

White wheels

White wheels became popular about twenty years ago. They were considered a solution to all of our sharpening problems. And, to a certain extent, they were. They were soft and did not burn hard steel tools as readily. (Most were about an H grade.) The softer the wheel, the less heat buildup.

There was a downside, however. It was easy to wear a groove in a white wheel. As a result, more time was spent dressing the wheels to get rid of grooves, causing most of the wheel to be ground away by the dresser, removing ripples and grooves on the face of the wheel, white powder piling up. The wheels did not last long but did a good job of sharpening. Another

Ceramic wheels. On the left is a Norton SG wheel and on the right, the 3X wheel. Both cut faster and cooler than aluminum oxide wheels. The SG wheel lasts a very long time. In fact, the wheel on the left has been in daily use for over two years.

problem was that with the quick wear, my grinding jig had to be constantly readjusted in order to maintain the same angles on my tools.

Blue wheels

After white wheels came blue wheels, which are still popular. They are harder, but not hard enough to cause major problems with overheating the steel. They sharpen tools quickly and easily. They are great workhorses and last longer. I continue to use them. They are a great compromise for light use on hard metals.

Wheel grit

All these wheels are made from aluminum oxide, the workhorse of the metal industry, and they are relatively inexpensive and do a good job. The blue wheels are the wheels beginners will probably like best. I keep an 80-grit wheel on one side of a grinder and 120 grit on the other side, the first for shaping tools, and the second for creating a fine edge. The edge produced by the 120 grit is sharper than that produced by the 80 grit. It looks almost like a honed edge, yet the edge will not break off the high-speed tools we use, as it used to with carbon-steel tools.

Ceramic wheels

There are new and interesting wheels on the market. The ones made from a ceramic alumina compound are better than the regular aluminum oxide wheels. The grit on these wheels is not made from your granny's ground-up teapot, even though it is called a ceramic. Each manufacturer closely guards exactly how it produces the material, but basically, the manufacturer converts a colloidal dispersion of hydrosol containing goethite into a semi-solid gel, dries this gel to a glassy state, crushes it to the required grain size, and fires it at between 1200° C and 1600° C. The final product is an abrasive grit of alumina microcrystals.

A major reason why these wheels work so well is that the grits are microcrystalline. This means that each piece of grit is composed of a clump of hundreds of tiny sharp crystals. They continually break away as they are used, exposing millions of fresh sharp cutting edges. These wheels cut cool and leave a fine finish on the tool bevel. By comparison, each piece of aluminum oxide grit is one crystal, which may or may not fracture under pressure and break down to expose smaller edges as they wear. Blunt abrasives rub, which overheats tools.

Ceramic wheels are expensive, but they produce a wonderful edge. I find that when sharpening with 80 grit, the edge looks almost like it was sharpened with a 120-grit wheel. (The finest wheel I can find in ceramic is 80.) They grind almost twice as fast as aluminum oxide (so use a light touch) and produce a keen edge. The wheel self-sharpens as it grinds, it wears slowly, and requires minimal dressing. They can last five times longer than a white wheel, so they are cost-effective.

Because the ceramic is expensive to produce, it is mixed with regular aluminum oxide before being pressed into a wheel. The wheels I am referring to are 50% ceramic, such as

Three diamond wheels. On the left is the wheel with 1/8" (3 mm) of diamond/nickel on the rim. The polished spots caused by sharpening high-speed steel are visible. In the center is an unused resin-bonded wheel and on the right (diamond plated) is the one I found most suited to my needs. It started out as an 80-grit wheel and after a year, I am using it as a fine-honing wheel. Note that there is no identification on the two wheels on the right.

the Norton SG wheels sold by many suppliers. Norton also manufactures a wheel that has only a 30% ceramic content, the 3X. While these cut cleanly and run cool, some people have found the wheel wears faster than they would like. Some who have had problems say their wheel has a bond hardness of I. Mine has a bond hardness of K, and has not been a problem. To me, they are good value for money, however, the SG, with its higher ceramic content is well worth the added expense.

Diamond wheels

Some woodturners use diamond wheels. The theory seems to be that diamond can cut anything. In theory, it does. It is great for cutting ceramics, stone, and aluminum. But diamond wheels do not cut steel efficiently. All the manufacturers agree it should not be used to sharpen the steel we woodturners use—in fact, anything with iron in it. On metals with a ferrous content, the diamond literally disappears.

Diamond particles have a fatal attraction to the iron in the steel. The iron attracts away the carbon in the diamond one atom at a time. The two actually bond at the molecular level, which means a minute amount of the diamond gets carried away with the chip. It sounds like a slow process, and at room temperature it is—thus hand-held diamond honing stones last a long time. Start adding heat, however, and the process speeds up dramatically and catastrophically and you will find a mist of black dust around the base of your grinder, all that is left of your precious diamonds. If you put much pressure on your tool—pushing it into the diamond—you can go through the diamond layer in minutes. If you are gentle, you can get a year or so out of a diamond wheel in use daily, but it will slowly

change from an 80-grit wheel to a 120-grit wheel, and eventually will only be good to use as a hone.

I have tried several brands of electroplated diamond wheels, as well as resin-impregnated ones, and an expensive wheel with 1/8" (3 mm) of diamond embedded in nickel around the rim. They all behaved the same way: The diamond quickly wore down to a finer grit and some wheels seemed to need a lot of dressing.

Cleaning them with an old aluminum oxide wheel can restore diamond wheels. That worked on all wheels I tried, but I was reluctant to use the aluminum oxide on the electroplated wheel—there is only one layer of diamond. In fact, that wheel needed less attention than the other types—just cleaning with WD40.

The wheel with the diamond/nickel mixture wore away the old aluminum oxide grinder wheel faster than my daughter's large cat inhales food. It looked great and cut well after this treatment. What happens is that the aluminum oxide wears away the bonding agent in the diamond wheels, exposing more of the diamond. If I sharpened a few 5/8" (16 mm) gouges on the wheel, however, the surface seemed to deteriorate into a finer grit and the nickel became highly polished. It always looked like it needed cleaning. I eventually took that wheel off the grinder and will give it to a stone carver. That is a $400 loss.

The resin-bonded wheel also lost its edge quickly, but would clean up well with the aluminum oxide dressing stone. The stink of hot resin in the shop was intolerable. That noxious odor was even present when I was sharpening tools. I finally gave the wheel away.

To summarize, the electroplated wheels caused the least amount of trouble. It took about a year to permanently wear them down from 80-grit to honing-wheel condition. The electroplated and resin-coated

CBN wheels, my favorites. They cut cleanly, quickly, and smoothly. They have been in continual use for over a year and show no wear.

wheels cost more than $200 apiece, so I do not consider them cost effective.

CBN wheels

Manufacturers recommend wheels made of CBN—not diamond—for sharpening tool steel. CBN is cubic boron nitride and it is almost as hard a diamond—it will actually scratch diamond. And, it does not have the fatal attraction that diamond has for iron. I have had a pair of these wheels on a grinder for over a year now and can detect no wear. Of course they will eventually wear out, all things do, but the 80-grit is still an 80-grit wheel and the 180 grit is still 180 grit. (I have found I can use the 180-grit wheel to keep my powdered metal tools, like the ones made by Doug Thompson and Dave Schweitzer, sharp as a razor.) The steel is hard enough, yet flexible enough, to maintain a scary-sharp edge, reducing dramatically the need for sanding.

CBN is used widely in industry where precise sharpening and shaping is required. Aircraft manufacturers use distinctively-profiled wheels to sharpen end mills and other precision machining tools to strict tolerances. The CBN sharpening wheels have to perform exactly the same job, with no significant measurable wear, shift after shift, day after day. That is why they last a long time in a woodturning shop.

The CBN wheels I have came prebalanced. I did not have to fuss with dressing and shaping the wheel when it was first mounted. Maintenance of CBN wheels is simple: Scrub them once in a while using a toothbrush and kerosene or WD40. This removes varnish and CA glue that gets transferred from turning tool onto the wheel. I have never had to use aggressive cleaning techniques on these wheels.

If I use a CBN wheel, I never have to adjust my sharpening jig. I can leave it set exactly the way I want, and since the wheel never gets smaller, I get the same grind every time. One light pass over the 180-grit wheel is enough to sharpen a tool to razor-blade quality most of the time. If my tool is really dull, then one pass over the 80 grit wheel, followed by a light pass over the 180 grit wheel will return the edge to perfection.

CBN grinder wheels come in almost any shape desired. The choice is endless . . . except for simple bench grinder wheels. (The shape of a standard bench grinder wheel is generally called 1A1 for diamond/CBN.) Bench grinder wheels are available, but you have to search for them. Check with your local metalworking shops.

I intend for this brief survey of grinder wheels to accomplish three objectives. First, to provide information to help you buy grinder wheels with more confidence. Second, to make your turning experience more pleasurable. And third, to help you save money—I know—I have spent far too much on grinder wheels over the years. It is my own fault, of course, but I am too curious for my own good!

After thirty years as a writer and editor, **Bill Neddow** *spends his retirement creating bowls and demonstrating. He lives in Ottawa, Canada, with his wife and 3,500 rough-turned bowls.*

CBN bench grinder wheels (6" by ¾" [150 mm by 20 mm] only) are available in Britain from Peter Child Woodturning Supplies.

In North America, they are harder to find. Dave Schweitzer of D-way tools just started carrying CBN wheels. Another source is the one I found after searching for six months—the supplier was in my own backyard! Cuttermasters (800-417-2171 or cuttermasters.com) has both 6" and 8" (15 cm and 20 cm) wheels in a variety of grits and they ship worldwide. One major woodturning supplier is actively searching for a good source, but there has been no announcement yet.

Another source is Northwest Super Abrasives in Eugene, OR (541-683-0801). Reed Gray (robo hippy) provided this source. Reed is an active and knowledgeable contributor to woodturning forums. Reed adds, "My 80-grit (CBN) wheel is four-plus years old and until last year, I was turning maybe 800 bowls per year, along with other things. It might be halfway used up. That amount of sharpening would have worn out at least one standard grinder wheel per year."

I have tried getting the wheels from the salesmen for all the big name companies, including Norton and 3M. They all say they can deliver, but not one has called back. These companies produce CBN wheels, but it appears that bench-size grinder wheels are not part of their regular production lines.

Identifying grinder wheels

Most manufacturers use a system for identifying grinder wheels. There are variations—a number of manufacturers modify the identification system to meet their needs, and not all use the complete sequence of identifying codes. Some wheels carry an absolute minimum of information. It is possible, however, to figure out the code on most wheels.

There are two systems, quite similar. One is for identifying bonded wheels (made of such substances as aluminum oxide and silicone carbide). The other is for diamond and CBN (superabrasive) wheels.

I have tried to simplify the systems to cover only the types of wheels woodturners generally use.

Identifying a Bonded Wheel
Number and Letter Sequence

Prefix	51
Abrasive Type	A
Abrasive Grain Size	80
Grade (Hardness)	K
Structure	5
Bond Type	V
Manufacturer's Record	05

Prefix: Manufacturers' symbols indicating the exact kind of abrasive. This is optional, and often manufacturers do not use it.

Abrasive Type: Identifies the primary grain used to make the wheel.

A	Regular Aluminum Oxide
WA	White Aluminum Oxide
Z	Aluminum Zirconium
C	Silicone Carbide
SG	Seeded Gel (Ceramic)

Abrasive Grain Size: Indicates the size of grit particles going through a screen. For example, 80 grit is what goes through one row of screen with 80 wires in one linear inch. 120 grit means there are 120 lines of screen, making the size of the grit going through a 1" (25 mm) linear line of screen smaller. The measurements range from coarse to very fine. I have found that woodturners use the medium-grit range (46, 54, 60) and fine (70, 80, 90, 100, 120, 150, 180). We most commonly use 46 grit for shaping a tool and 80 grit for sharpening. Some turners use a finer-grit wheel to keep the tool sharp, such as 120 grit.

Grade (Hardness): Hardness is rated from A to Z with A being the weakest bond and Z being the strongest. A weaker bond is preferred for grinding harder materials like tool steel. Most of the wheels we use are in the I to K range. An increase in the hardness grade by one or two letters can make a dramatic difference. A move from an H to an I, for example, could double the life of the wheel.

Structure: Basically the spacing between abrasive grains, represented by a series of numbers, with the structure becoming more open as the number increases. A 1 would be very dense. We are after a more open structure, which would probably be 5 or above.

Bond Type: The most common bond types are vitrified V and resin B. Vitrified is basically a vitreous glass much like pottery or glassware fired in a kiln, which is why there is such a fuss about not using a chipped or dropped stone

made with this material—it may be cracked and can blow up. Resin is more commonly found in cut-off wheels, but can also be found in diamond and CBN wheels. There are other bond types such as Rubber R and Silicate S.

Manufacturer's Record: A private manufacturer's marking to identify a wheel. The use is optional.

Identifying a Superabrasive Wheel
The marking system for superabrasive grinder wheels is somewhat different.
Number and Letter Sequence

Abrasive Type	D
Abrasive Grain Size	80
Grade (Hardness)	N
Concentration	100
Bond Type	M
Bond Modification	77
Abrasive Depth	⌧
Manufacturer's Record	4

Abrasive Type: The letter D indicates that the abrasive is diamond. The letter B or CB is used for CBN.

Abrasive Grain Size: The number 80 represents the average grain size fitting through a linear inch of wire mesh (e.g., 120 grit would mean 120 lines of mesh).

Grade (Hardness): Like conventional wheels the letter N identifies the hardness of the wheel. Resin- and metal-bonded wheels, however, are produced with almost no porosity and the grade of the wheel is controlled by modifying the bond formulation.

Concentration: The number 100 is known as a concentration number, indicating the amount of diamond abrasive contained in the mix in the wheel. The number 100 corresponds to an abrasive content of 25 percent by volume. For CBN wheels, the number represents a concentration of 24 percent by volume. Concentration numbers of 75 or higher are are preferred. For CBN wheels, Norton drops the concentration section. Norton refers to the concentration as the grade and uses the letter W for 100 concentration, T for 75 concentration and Q for 50 concentration.

Bond Type: The letter M or N indicates the bond is metallic. Another bond is resin, represented by the letter B or R. There are also vitrified wheels V.

Bond Modification: This is the manufacturer's notation of any special bond type or modification. It is optional information.

Abrasive Depth: The working depth of the abrasive section, generally measured in inches. For example: ⅛" (3 mm). This is very important in determining the life of the wheel and its initial cost. A bond layer of ⅛" provides about half the life of a bond layer ¼" (6 mm) thick.

Manufacturer's Record: As with the bonded wheels, this is optional information on the manufacturer's private identification code for the wheel.

Safety Note
Grinder wheels can explode as they rotate at high speed. It is absolutely necessary to wear an impact-resistant faceshield when using a grinder.

Section 3: Techniques

The things I make may be for others, but how *I make them is for me.*
—Tony Konovaloff

After the lathe is set-up, the tools are in-hand, and the face shield
is on, it's time to learn the *how* of woodturning. This section is full
of valuable lessons on fundamental techniques that will get you off
to a great start and last a lifetime. The detailed, practical advice
in these next pages range across the many challenges and problems
that all beginners encounter from how to avoid a catch to how
to properly finish your first project so it's safe to use with food.
There is nothing more enjoyable than learning the techniques to
make something with your own two hands. As a result, the sincere
pleasure that woodturners take from their craft is infectious.

Twenty Ways NOT to Turn a Bowl

Helpful advice for guaranteed success

When it was suggested that I write this article, I wondered if it was because someone thought I didn't know how to turn a bowl. I was assured that I drew this assignment not because I'm inexperienced at bowl turning but rather because I have had so many woodturning students.

I have been teaching woodturning for more than 20 years, and many of the classes have been basic, for beginners, or an introduction to woodturning. You can ask anyone who has been involved in one of these classes and they will tell you that my most frequently used direction is: "Stop, don't do that!"

Anyone who teaches basics at John C. Campbell, Appalachian Craft Center, Arrowmont, or Anderson Ranch Craft Center expects to have raw beginners in a class. We also expect novices with just a little experience and even expect a few who have been turning for a number of years.

The teacher's challenge is getting all of the students on the same page in the same book at the same time. Adult learners seem to have their own ideas about how to turn, and some are not the least interested in how I want them to turn. Some are self-taught; some

No matter how eager you are to turn your first "keeper," don't begin turning with large or expensive stock. The 8"-diameter stock on the headstock is more appropriate.

Photos: Marisa Pruss

have attended other classes. Others have read woodturning books and watched videos.

And others...must have been time-traveling to their eighth-grade shop classes when someone was attempting to instruct them.

The right stock

One of the biggest problems teachers face is that many students are itching to turn a really large bowl the first time they step up to the lathe. Or, they lug in something that cost them big bucks.

Getting Started in Woodturning

Stop! Don't do that!

1 Too big. You will learn a lot more about turning techniques by turning lots of small, shallow bowls than you ever will by turning one or two really large pieces.

2 Too valuable. Whatever you do, do not pay fo;r practice wood. There is plenty of free wood out there—the stuff really does grow on trees. Ask around at your AAW chapter; you'll find a resourceful group with plenty of practice pieces.

3 Too hard. Green wood is a great way to start. Wood lots and local tree cutters are great sources for practice materials.

4 Too deep. Start out with a small (8"-diameter) platter before attempting any type of bowl. When you are comfortable with that, transition to a shallow bowl—just slightly deeper, but still about 8" in diameter.

Keep the form open rather than making the openings smaller. The smaller the opening, the harder it is to cut the interior.

5 Not ready for prime time, (or finish). Don't worry about applying finish to anything—that will come later. Think practice pieces. I suggest that you use a screw chuck or faceplate and turn shapes that resemble bowl forms until you get to the point of becoming comfortable with the bowl gouge. When you get to where you do not have to think about what the tool is doing, you are ready to turn a bowl. Once you get a few decent-looking forms, turn the bowl around and begin hollowing the interior. Then, get out the finish.

The right speed

Too often, novice woodturners go from turning spindles to turning bowls without adjusting the lathe speed. Too big and too fast is a deadly combination.

Here's a good habit to develop: Before you turn on your lathe, always stand to the left or right of the chuck.

Stop! Don't do that!

6 Too much speed. Before mounting stock between centers or on a faceplate or chuck, switch on the lathe without anything mounted. This will give you the opportunity to see where the speed was set when the lathe was last used. Developing this habit will prevent an accident.

I encourage students to reduce the speed of their machines at the end of every turning session. This is easy on variable-speed lathes, but I meet resistance to this when students are learning on machines with step pulleys. Do it anyway; it's never too early to develop good safety habits.

7 Too much of a hurry. Another problem that can ruin your day occurs when you have a large piece on the lathe and stop the machine too quickly. This happened to my friend Andy Marinos, who suggested adding this tip to the Don't Do! list.

To turn the bottom of a bowl, Andy mounted his large flat jaws on his scroll chuck and mounted the rim of the bowl in the jaws. Without checking the speed, he turned on the lathe. It was going much too fast for the task at hand. Andy quickly hit the stop button on the machine, and the motor stopped. But, the chuck and the bowl had enough momentum to keep spinning—even with the lathe stopped. When it came off the spindle, the assembly caught his hand between it and the tool rest. Andy's wound required numerous stitches.

Here's a safer plan: Start the lathe at a low speed or use the setscrew in the chuck to lock it onto the spindle.

8 Standing in the wrong place. You should always stand to one side of the workpiece (out of the path of the spinning blank) when you turn on your lathe as shown in the photo.

The right tool

Before anyone stands in front of a lathe, I review all of the tools, their uses, and how to sharpen each. I identify each tool, explain how it is used, show how to sharpen it, and also show the various cuts that can be made. I also explain what each tool is not designed to do. But sometimes, that's not enough.

Stop! Don't do that!

9 **No roughing-out gouge for bowl work.** For bowl turning, never turn with a roughing gouge. This should be a no-brainer, but I have seen it done. In my mind, this tool should be referred to as a spindle roughing gouge.

Here's a classic example. One student mounted a large, square blank on a lightweight lathe and turned it on at too high of speed. Needless to say, I screamed from across the room, "Stop, don't do that!" When I got to where he was working, I also discovered that he was about to attack the piece with a 1¼" spindle roughing gouge. Oh, and it wasn't sharpened yet; it had just come out of the box.

You should not use the skew on a bowl either!

10 **Big gap at tool rest.** One of the most common problems is extending the tool too far out over the tool rest. Many times, students will continue cutting without moving the rest any closer to the blank. Once the tool extends more than 1" or so beyond the rest, stop the machine and move the tool rest closer. Lathe tools have been known to break over the tool rest—a very bad thing.

The height of the tool rest is determined by the tool you are using and your height and stance. Always place the tool on the rest first, touch the back of the tool to the blank, then gently lift the tool handle until

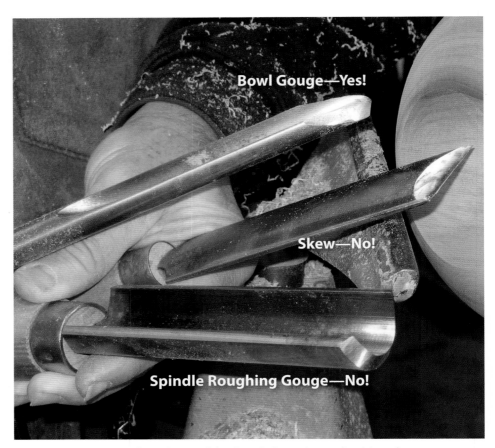

The bowl gouge, top, is the only one of the three lathe tools you should use for your bowl projects.

As your bowl takes shape, stop the lathe frequently and move the tool rest to about 1" from the stock.

the bevel makes contact with the wood. This will ensure the bevel supports the cutting edge. You will be less likely to get catches this way.

11 Moving tool rest with lathe running. Don't even think about it! Never move the tool rest with the lathe running.

12 Not following the curve. It is not uncommon for a beginner to make straight cuts along the length of the tool rest, correctly move the rest closer but continue to cut in a straight line. To produce better profiles, move the tool rest around the shape of the bowl. The result is a cone-shaped bowl. This is where a curved tool rest can be helpful, although not a necessity.

Work on a continuous curve—not thinness.

13 Wrong direction. For face-grain bowls, cut uphill or from bottom to top on the exterior of the bowl. On the interior of your bowl, cut downhill or from the rim to the center.

14 No body movement. You are not bolted to the floor. To produce better curves, use your body and move it through an arch. Learn that "woodturner's sway."

Place the tool handle against your hip and hold the handle with your right hand near the shaft and your left hand on the tool rest. Keep your left hand on the tool rest throughout the cut to provide additional support. Remember, if you move your feet, you move the pivot and lose the curve. Learn to swing your body, but don't move your feet.

15 Dull tools. Beginners also have a problem determining whether a tool is sharp or not. It takes experience to be able to tell. Different woods react differently to being cut. Most beginners merely increase pressure as the cutting edge gets dull. This can be dangerous.

When turning the outside of a face-grain bowl, turn from the bottom to the top (sometimes described as uphill).

When you remove stock from the interior of a face-grain bowl, always begin at the rim and work toward the center (also described as downhill).

When in doubt, sharpen the tool. And, the best way to sharpen a tool for beginners is with jigs and fixtures; they all work, and they all provide excellent results. Hand-sharpening also works after you learn what you are doing, but the jigs and fixtures will provide consistent results each and every time.

Be sure to touch up your edge on the grinder before making your final cut. A dull tool will pull or tear at the fibers, leaving a surface that you can't sand smooth. This is especially true on end grain.

Each instructor will show you his or her favorite grind for the bowl gouge. They all work if you take the time to learn how to use them. It is more important that you learn to consistently reproduce the grind you are using than which profile you choose.

Grinding by hand is important to learn, but for the beginner, jigs and fixtures are a great help.

16 **Too much pressure.** Another common problem is applying too much pressure when cutting the surface. This will force the heel of the tool into the surface and bruise the fibers, leaving lines that remain invisible until you apply finish. Yikes!

These lines are almost impossible to sand away. You must recut the surface. Relax and let the cutting edge do the work rather than forcing it.

The right mount
A lot of bowl-turning problems begin with how the material is attached to the lathe. Because every new lathe is shipped with a faceplate, this is the obvious choice for the beginning woodturner.

A grinding jig helps many new turners repeat the same bevel on a lathe tool.

Stop! Don't do that!
17 **Wrong screws.** Trouble can begin at the first step when you screw the blank to the faceplate. Here, several problems can occur. It usually starts with drywall screws; they are too thin and too brittle. You exacerbate the problem when you draw up drywall screws with a power screwdriver, which pulls them up tight and snaps them.

Sheet metal screws are a better choice to attach turning stock to a faceplate. These screws are case-hardened and have deeper and sharper threads. Make sure you choose a length that is appropriate. Square-drive screws are also popular and are much easier to remove from hardwood.

For securing turning stock, one size does not fit all. For an 8"-diameter blank that is up to about 2" thick, I recommend #8×3/4" screws. For a 14×8" blank, secure with #14×1-1/2" hardened screws.

18 **Difficult grain.** You must also consider the material you will be putting the screws into. End grain requires larger and longer screws. Beware of punky or spalted woods; once the wood has started to decay, it is extremely difficult to get a screw to hold.

Sapwood does not hold screws as well as heartwood. To be on the safe side, bring up the tailstock with a live center for insurance. This will give additional support if the screws do not hold.

Choose turning stock that offers a better chance for success. Dale Nish says it best: "Life is too short to turn crappy wood!"

19 **Poor grip.** Once you get excited about turning, it probably won't be long before you purchase a 4-jaw scroll chuck, which I think holds material better on the lathe. However, this chuck has its own set of challenges.

I have had many instances where students have made tenons too small or the recesses too shallow. Either case can cause the blank to separate from the chuck.

Punky wood and sapwood present the same challenges and grain problems as noted above.

20 **Loose fit.** Green wood requires you to tighten the jaws of the chuck repeatedly as moisture is forced from the blank. Just as with the faceplate, remember to use the tailstock and center whenever possible.

Turn safely and have fun. But by all means, think about what you are doing and consider the risks involved. If you are unsure, ask someone with more experience. If it looks dangerous, it probably is.

"Stop, don't do that!"

A founding member of the AAW, **Nick Cook** *is a frequent contributor to* American Woodturner *and lives in Marietta, GA where he owns and operates his studio. Visit Nick at www.nickcookwoodturner.com.*

If you want your bowl to stay in the chuck, you'll learn the value of properly sizing the tenon. If the chuck loosens, the bowl will fly out off the lathe.

Sheet-metal screws should be your only choice for mounting turning stock to faceplates. You can see how a drywall screw can break off , which leads to huge safety issues.

Get a Grip

Start with the right grip and feel the wood through the tool

Probably the best way beginner or intermediate woodturners can improve their technical skills is to learn to feel the wood through the tool. When you are feeling that effortless sweet cut and the shavings are piling up, the act of turning just naturally makes you smile. To develop the sensitivity to feel, a lot of repetition and some consistencies are needed. You need consistently sharp tools; you need to put in some hours behind the machine; and you need to know some basic strong and flexible hand grips. With the advent of the third generation of sharpening jigs, keeping the tools sharp is a no-brainer. If you make objects in series, you'll learn to turn faster. And if you learn good, solid, basic hand grips, they will allow you to develop the sensitivity in tool handling needed to feel the cut. When the sensitivity has been developed, you can make anything you want. All tool control flows from your grip.

Grips are built on the tool rest. The tool rest consists of three sections: the bearing surface or top, the saddle or horizontal support, and the post. The turning tool rests on the top; the saddle provides a place for your anchor, and the post allows for positioning the height and rotational angle of the tool rest in the banjo (which mounts the rest to the lathe ways). Tool rests these days have a lot of different shapes, and for beginners that can be confusing. Let's use the KISS (keep it simple, stupid) principle and talk about only one tool-rest shape: the straight.

You should file the top of your rest free of any nicks or grooves that could alter the tool motion. A good sensitivity exercise is to lay a tool on one end of the top and look away while sliding the tool across the rest. Try to sense any unnatural areas; develop your ability to feel. The tool rest should allow the tool to be as close to the work as possible, and that usually means a small and sometimes rounded top. The rest should be small enough through the saddle to allow you to hook your control hand index finger under to provide an anchor while using the underhand grip, and wide enough through the saddle for a good seat for your control hand palm to provide an anchor for the overhand. Folks with small hands do better with small tool rests.

Since some folks are right-handed and some are left-handed and some use either hand, let's simplify things by saying that the hand that is in contact with the rest is the control hand and the hand that supports the tool is the support hand. I'll use this terminology in describing the grips.

The common thread that runs through all grips is the anchor. Your tool must be anchored to the tool rest by your control hand in some manner. You can pull it down on the rest in the underhand grip, or you can push it down on the rest in the overhand grip. When vibration starts to creep into your work, you usually need more anchor. Your anchor can also be your pivot point for horizontal movement or your fulcrum for vertical movement, depending on what type of cut you are taking. One

thing is certain, however you slice it, without an anchor you are going to be out of control, adrift, and probably headed for the rocks.

In a good grip the control hand and the support hand work together. The control hand provides your anchor, and it manipulates the tool. In the overhand grip you can push or pull the tool by extending or withdrawing (crabbing) the fingers of your control hand. In the underhand grip tool movement is controlled by pushing with the thumb or pulling with the fingers of the control hand. The control hand also provides power for the heavy cuts.

The support hand provides the finesse to keep heavy cuts tracking. The support hand also provides the leverage, rotates the tool to allow edge presentation, and raises and lowers the tool handle. Each hand is important. Train yourself to feel with both hands.

The overhand grip is generally the first grip folks are taught. It is natural feeling and suitable for both center- and facework. The overhand grip will get the job done. This grip works better if the lathe center height is a little below elbow height. With a lower lathe, the turner can easily lean forward and put a little body weight on their anchor. If the anchor is firmly set, it can be used as a pivot point to scoop out heavy cuts.

The edge of the control hand's palm is set into the saddle to provide the anchor, and all the fingers are laid overtop and along the far side of the tool shaft. The thumb of the control hand is pointing toward the turner

AW 13:2, p16

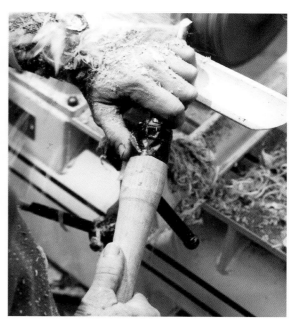

The overhead grip presses the tool down on the tool rest. The control hand moves the tool along the rest by extending or clenching the fingers and thumb. The support hand often is braced against the side of the body.

and laid on the tool shaft. The tool is held firmly in tension between the fingers and thumb. Do not put any part of your hand over the top of the tool rest, as friction from the workpiece will heat it in a hurry. I have lost a couple of patches of hide forgetting this rule.

In the overhand grip with a set anchor, you slide the tool along the top of the tool rest by either extending or clenching the fingers and thumb in short strokes while the anchor is held stationary. This grip is used primarily in hollowing, where the tool overhangs the rest a bit and a firm hold and precise control is needed. Sometimes the cut is only

an inch or two until a new anchor is needed. If you put some weight on your control hand and use the anchor as a pivot point and sweep the tool handle with your support hand, you can really hog some wood.

In the overhand sliding grip you move the tool by sliding the whole hand while maintaining even downward pressure into the saddle for a firm anchor. This grip is usually used for outside shaping and finish cutting in both face and center work. The sliding grip can be used pulling or pushing, just remember to increase or decrease your anchor in direct correlation with how heavy or light a cut you are taking. The support hand

holds the tool firmly with the fingers curled underneath and the thumb resting on top. Some folks like to hold the tool up around the ferrule for small tools and some like to hold it down around the butt for large tools. On long tools the support hand can tuck the tool into your hip and that helps your anchor. The support hand rotates the tool, raises and lowers the handle, and also pushes to advance and pulls to withdraw the tool. Concentrate on feeling with both hands. If the big V (vibration) starts in, put more pressure down on the rest and increase your anchor. Both these overhands have variations, depending on what you are turning.

The underhand grip begins with the control hand palm up, index finger extended under the tool rest. The tool is squeezed onto the rest between the thumb and index finger.

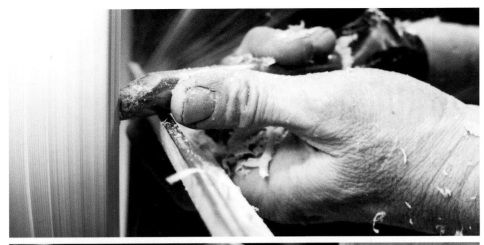

There is little danger of pinching the index finger of the control hand between the tool rest and the work. The author uses his finger, to find if there are flats remaining on the work.

The other basic woodturning grip is the underhand. I use the underhand grip a lot. I first learned it doing production centerwork, and I've found that it works great for facework, too, because of the flexibility it affords. With equal effort, you can hog or go light with this grip. I seem to be able to feel my tool edge slide through the wood a little better with the underhand, and I use it for almost all my finish cuts and detail work. Learn this grip—it's a good'n.

The underhand grip works well with the lathe centers at elbow height or a little above. Your anchor is dependent on the combination of using a little body weight and ability to squeeze the tool down on the rest between your thumb and index finger. You can see how developed the thumb muscle of my turning hand has become.

The underhand grip with a set anchor allows fine control in small centerwork, and you can power through the wood's tendency to throw the tool uphill by using your thumb on the tool-rest top as a stop. In hollowing open facework you might be able to cut in only an inch or two at a time before having to move your anchor but the grip is rock solid. As you gain experience, you'll be able to slide your index finger, grab an anchor, and hog some wood. The underhand works great with a set anchor or as a sliding grip.

To get an underhand grip you first extend your control hand and point your index finger at the lathe. Hook that finger underneath the saddle of the tool rest with your palm up. Lay the tool across the top of the rest and your open palm. Grasp the tool firmly with three fingers on one side and your thumb on the other

while pulling the tool down on the rest with your index finger. Rests that are small through the saddle are good for folks with small hands. Hold the tool in tension between your thumb on one side and your fingers on the other and pull up on the bottom of the saddle with your index finger: that pinches the tool and creates your anchor. By extending and pulling in your forefinger, you move in and out across the rest. Push with your thumb or pull with the opposite fingers to move the tool across the rest. Your support hand does the same job it does in the overhand: it raises, lowers, and rotates the turning tool.

Don't worry too much about getting your index finger of your control hand pinched between the wood and the rest. If the work hits your finger, it will throw it down and out. I commonly use my index finger to find if I have left any flats on the work. In one variation of this grip, for small diameter centerwork, your control hand index finger extends under the saddle and lightly touches the back side of the spinning work. In effect, your finger acts as a steady rest. Sharp tools, a steady hand, clean living, and you'll turn long skinny stuff with ease. The precise control I get from this grip makes it my favorite.

These two grips with their respective variations are some of the meat and potatoes of woodturning. When they are used properly, a good turner will flow from overhand to underhand and back to overhand without missing a lick. Take the time to practice and learn these grips. Concentrate on feeling the wood through the tool.

Rodger Jacobs is an artist, writer, and instructor in NC. He has worked with all types of natural materials, but the pleasure of working with wood led him to cabinet making, furniture building, and his true passion of turning.

How to Avoid a Catch

Smart tips keep you and your work safe

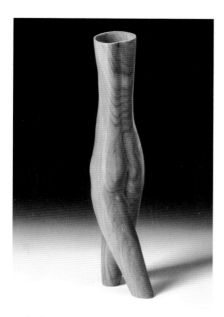

To hollow "Class Act" and similar sculptures, Lyle Jamieson uses a supported boring bar. "If you set up a supported system parallel to the floor, you can't get a catch.," he said. On his lathe, Lyle hollowed this 20×6×5" elm piece on three axes.

If you've been around the AAW for a decade or more, you may recall "Five Ways to Avoid a Catch," a well-read journal article Lyle Jamieson wrote in 1996. Lyle has revisited this topic with fresh drawings and thoughts to take you beyond the suffocating fear of catches.

It seems simple, but there are complicated forces taking place while you shape a revolving piece of wood with your turning tools. I want to simplify the process and put a language to catches. If you understand what causes a catch, you can eliminate the cause.

There are just four cuts in all of woodturning: push cut, pull cut, scrape, and shear scrape. Let's further break down these cuts into two groups:

- •The push and pull cuts require bevel support to prevent catches.
- •The scrape and shear scrape require that you don't violate the 90-degree rule. More about that later.

Start with sharp tools

A primary way to prevent catches is to turn with sharp tools. A sharp tool can shear off those end-grain fibers cleanly and smoothly. However, a dull tool will push, grab, and tear out end-grain fibers. You can have all the right techniques and still have trouble with catches if your tools are not sharpened properly and often. Sharp tools mean less sanding, and I don't like to sand. Who does?

When using gouges and doing the push and pull cuts, most catches come from allowing the gouge to cut while not being supported by the bevel. Without bevel support, the tool will dig in violently in a split second. Big chunks of wood are ripped away.

The bevel prevents the gouge from cutting too aggressively—it is a controlling factor.

Inside the bowl

Let's first focus on the inside of a bowl. This is where catches are most apt to occur because the inside of a bowl is where we are prone to lose bevel support.

The direction the gouge wants to cut is along a line from the heel of the bevel to the sharp point of the edge, as shown in **Drawing 1a**. The first approach is to relax and let the tool go where it wants. Relax the tool-rest hand and direct the cut by moving the handle hand. You can get pretty good at white knuckling your way through a cut, as shown in Drawing 1b, but the surface left behind will need a lot of sanding.

It is not much fun when a catch ruins the shape you intended. Relax, take a deep breath, and let your handle hand do the work.

AW 21:4, p60

How to hollow the inside of a bowl

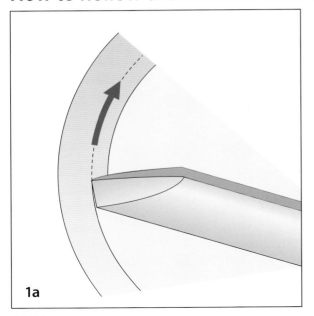

1a

SAFE

Note the arrow indicating the direction the tool wants to go. Swing the handle slowly toward your body to direct the bevel to travel the path indicated by the dashed line.

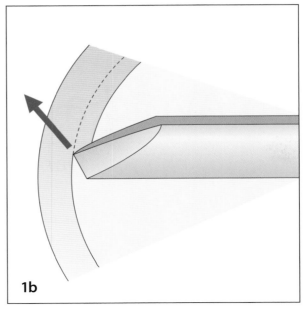

1b

RISKY

Note the arrow indicating the direction the tool wants to go. Swing the handle slowly toward your body to direct the bevel to travel the path indicated by the dashed line.

Find the sweet spot

You will hit the sweet spot for a clean cut with the flute pointing in the direction you want to travel with your cut. A twist of the tool will have the flute pointing at a 45-degree angle. Whenever possible, maintain this shearing cut to cleanly slice through each grain fiber as it spins past your tool. Your gouge cuts the shaving at the tip of the cutting edge, as shown in **Photo 2**.

This may help: Think of the motion of an ice cream scoop scooping out the inside of the bowl. You have one hand on the handle of the ice cream scoop and then follow the shape of the rounded scoop for your ice cream.

With the bowl gouge, you follow the little tip of the tool, or the bevel. Swing the tool handle to follow the contour of the vessel with the bevel.

"Ride the bevel" is the usual term to describe this, but it is a terrible term. You don't want to ride the bevel, you need to follow it gently. Riding the bevel too hard will cause a number of problems: It will burnish the surface, create vibrations, and bounce the bevel into any voids in the vessel. For me, a "bevel-supported cut" is better.

Bevel-supported cut

One of the hardest things to accomplish is to start a bevel-supported cut. The tool wants to skate in a spiraling manner across the face of the wood when you start at a 45-degree angle.

Note the arrow indicates the direction the wood is traveling past the tool. The 45-degree angled line shows the angle that will produce a clean slicing cut. To get this angle, twist the tool on its axis with your handle hand. The shaving comes off the right-hand side at the tip of the tool.

Starting a cut: Here's a safer way

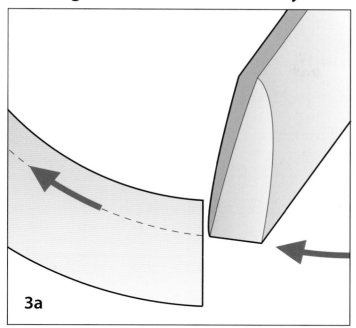

3a

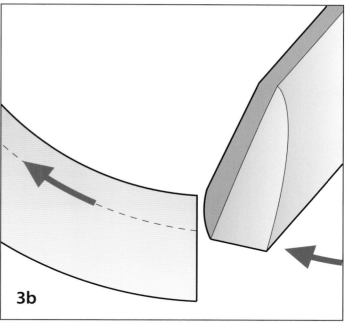

3b

SAFE

If your gouge is ground to the profile shown below, you get quick bevel support and reduce the chance for a catch. The red arrow indicates the cutting direction.

RISKY

A gouge with a hump at the tip cuts into the wood long before the bevel has a chance to give support. This can cause a catch or even blow up a thin-walled bowl or vessel.

wing corner

The wing (side) profile of Lyle Jamieson's favorite grind has a nearly straight line from the tip to the wing corner.

The bowl-gouge grind can make it easier to enter a cut. I reshape the Ellsworth grind slightly to make the entry into a cut easier for me, as shown in **Drawing 3a**. When I use a gouge with a slight hump near the tip, the tool attempts to grab the wood first before the bevel support has been established, as shown in **Drawing 3b**.

I prefer the sharpened edge that is almost straight from the top to the back corner of the wing—there is no hump when viewed from the side, as shown at left.

Hollowing systems

When setting up your supported hollowing system for boring out the interior of a hollow vessel, make sure the scraper cutting tip is parallel to the floor and on the centerline of the vessel, and you will never get a catch. This setup will be cutting right at 90 degrees. (You can err slightly with

the tool-rest position on the high side, but never have the cutter below center in a hollow form.)

If you choose to twist the cutter for a shear cut, keep this in mind: When you angle one side of the cutter down to shear scrape, the opposite side of the cutter is pointing up into the wood and will get grabby and produce a catch.

Scraper strategy

A scraper requires an entirely different process from a gouge. Whenever a cutting edge touches the wood without the bevel support, a catch can occur. (The exception is the edge touching the wood at less than a 90-degree angle, as shown in **Drawing 4a** and **4b**.) With a scraper positioned flat on the tool rest and parallel to the floor, the tool-rest height is critical. If the tool rest is high on the outside shape (like a spindle), it gets risky. If the tool rest

Scraper positions for spindles and hollow forms

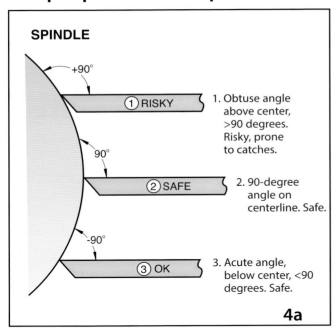

SPINDLE

+90°

① RISKY

1. Obtuse angle above center, >90 degrees. Risky, prone to catches.

90°

② SAFE

2. 90-degree angle on centerline. Safe.

-90°

③ OK

3. Acute angle, below center, <90 degrees. Safe.

4a

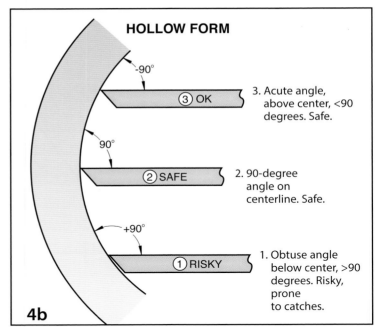

HOLLOW FORM

-90°

③ OK

3. Acute angle, above center, <90 degrees. Safe.

90°

② SAFE

2. 90-degree angle on centerline. Safe.

+90°

① RISKY

1. Obtuse angle below center, >90 degrees. Risky, prone to catches.

4b

is too low on the inside shape, like a hollow form, it gets risky, as shown in **Drawing 4b**.

This is why negative-rake scrapers came into vogue. The negative rake gives you extra insurance to not violate the 90-degree rule. With handheld scrapers, you can change the angle at which the tool touches the wood by raising or lowering the handle.

Move beyond fear

As I teach at chapters around the country, I meet many self-taught students. They settle for techniques that are difficult and demand considerable sanding, and some of the techniques are downright dangerous.

The fear generated from catches is suffocating. If you walk up to the lathe with catch butterflies, you are missing out on the true fun of woodturning. Do you worry about taking one more cut?

Woodturning enjoyment starts by being in control at the lathe. Taking "catch" out of your vocabulary will make turning a lot easier and more pleasurable.

You can watch others turn or read all the articles available and still have catch fear. I suggest getting some hands-on help. Take your turning job to the next level. It is not necessary to pay loads of money to get some woodturning instruction. All AAW chapters have good turners to mentor you—usually just for the asking.

Recently, I had a chance to speak with Michael Hosaluk, and he made a statement that summed up woodturning experience. He asked, "What is the difference between a beginner and an advanced turner?" And then he answered his own question with, "It is what you do with the basics."

I truly believe in this approach. Get the foundations right, and it

opens up possibilities of excellence rather than creating obstacles and settling for mediocrity.

Now, let's get over your fear of catches. The fun and creativity locked up inside you will take you places you never imagined.

Lyle Jamieson is a sculptor, instructor, and frequent contributor to American Woodturner. *Among his contributions to the craft is the boring bar and laser measuring system bearing his name. Visit Lyle at www. lylejamieson.com.*

Quick Guide for Avoiding Catches

Retaining tool control is key to preventing a common mistake

All catches start when you lose tool control. It's probably impossible to eliminate all catches, but you can minimize their frequency and severity. Here are a few guidelines.

Keep it sharp

A dull cutting edge or point on any tool will require more force, often resulting in loss of tool control. Sharpen often.

Maintain the toolrest

The toolrest supports the tool in your hands. Think of it as the interface between hand tool and machine. The tool needs to glide over the toolrest with a minimum of effort. File the toolrest to keep it smooth.

Watch out for different diameters

Whether you are working on the foot of a bowl or a handle of a mallet, the intersection of vastly different diameters is a place to be extra careful. A tool's cutting edge that straddles two different diameters is liable to catch.

Match the tool to the job

The long point of a skew chisel is the best tool for a V cut and a spindle gouge is ideal for cutting a cove. Generally it is best to use a large tool on a small turning, not vice versa.

Special care while using scrapers

In scraping and shear scraping, the bevel does not touch the wood and safe cutting takes place at the centerline on the exterior of a form and slightly above the centerline when working on the interior. Use only a portion of the cutting edge, and keep the edge trailing. Shear scraping presents less of the cutting edge than scraping, but take care to move the tool smoothly across the toolrest and take light cuts. Avoid using scrapers on flexible thin-walled bowls near the rim.

Practice cuts

With the lathe off, go through the motions before cutting a cove or a bead. Practice builds muscle memory, making the main event easier. Professional golfers and major league hitters practice regularly.

Maintain bevel contact

To develop confidence in controlling the cut, with the lathe running, keep the cutting edge clear of the surface while allowing just the bevel to touch the wood on a straight or slightly curved surface. Slowly engage the cutting edge to take a small shaving and then resume the safe position of just the bevel touching the wood. This is an excellent exercise for understanding how the bevel limits the cut and keeps it from running away.

Clearing the work

While helping a beginning woodturner, I noticed she removed the tool quickly while hollowing an endgrain box. It was a nervous response and a catch could easily have happened. Control includes safely clearing the cutting edge after making a cut.

Relax

Too firm a grip usually results in a more severe catch. Carl Ford III, a trusted friend and an excellent turner, gave me this advice, which I use when I challenge myself with a tricky cut: "Stop clenching your jaw or you'll bust a tooth."

AW 27:3, p51

The Complete Spindle Turner

Tips and techniques for honing a key skill

I zaac Walton's *The Compleat Angler*, published in 1653, is in its three hundredth printing. It is the third-most published book in the English language, after the Holy Bible and the works of Shakespeare. *The Compleat Angler* is an essay on the history, mental attitude, and skills required to be accomplished at fly fishing. For us woodturners there is also a history and set of skills to learn before we become accomplished woodturners. One of those skills is spindle turning.

There are many reasons why woodturners don't learn how to use spindle-turning tools: lack of interest because spindle turning is associated with beads, coves, and furniture parts; beginners have their eyes focused on bowls and want to turn them as soon as possible; and more than a few are afraid of the dreaded skew chisel. As a result, a generation of woodturners, expert and beginner alike, is missing half the experience and fun of turning wood. They are also missing an opportunity to

show off their turning and artistic skills. It doesn't have to be this way. Devoting a couple hours' time to learning a few skills will make you a better woodturner.

This article is an introduction to spindle turning without making beads and coves or learning how to use a skew chisel.

Those who have been around woodturning for a few years will recognize the candleholders in this article as being similar to those made famous by Rude Osolnik. I chose

AW 25:1, p38

Getting Started in Woodturning

this form as an introduction to the spindle because it is relatively easy to turn and it represents a historical art form that anyone would be proud to display. I could have just as easily featured a weed-pot, but sticking dried grass in a piece of wood went out of fashion in the 1970s, along with leisure suits. This elegant candleholder form is timeless.

Why spindles are important

The spindle teaches us how wood should be cut. After that, everything else about turning wood becomes easier. When good spindle-turning techniques are learned, a person can analyze what is going wrong when those "other" turning tools cause problems. This doesn't mean that turning can't be learned from using a bowl gouge; it's simply easier to learn cutting techniques when the action is right in front of us, not hidden inside a form or buried in shavings.

Tools

You will need a ¾" (20mm) spindle-roughing gouge and a parting tool. That's it.

I am going to show you how to transform your ¾" (20mm) spindle-roughing gouge into a continental-style spindle gouge *(Photo 1)*. This large tool can make a planing cut as smooth as a skew chisel. Its large radius will make long sweeping curves easier and smoother than with smaller fluted spindle gouges. It becomes a safer tool when those pesky corners are gone—they can't "catch" when they aren't there. (Changing the shape of the tool doesn't prevent it from being used for turning square wood to round.)

While the modification of the spindle-roughing gouge is recommended, you could also turn these candleholders with a continental-style spindle gouge from Sorby or the forged spindle gouge from Henry Taylor. The Taylor gouges

1 A ¾" (20mm) spindle-roughing gouge, modified into a continental-style spindle gouge.

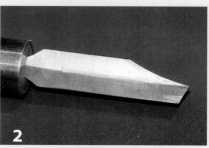

2 The author's 3/16" (5mm) parting tool, ground to make it easier to make a shearing cut.

are available from Craft Supplies (woodturnerscatalog.com) in ½" (13mm) and ⅝" (16mm) widths. There is also the German-style spindle gouge available from Packard Woodworks (packardwoodworks.com) in ¾" (20mm) and 1" (25mm) widths. A similar ¾" (20mm) spindle gouge by Sorby is sold in Woodcraft stores.

All of these tools share two common features with the modified ¾" (20mm) spindle-roughing gouge: they have a wide flute and a large radius across their cutting edge. This design makes them well suited for making the long shallow curves of these candleholders. (Smaller forged spindle gouges and conventional fluted spindle gouges are better suited to turning a form with tighter curves.) The modified gouge described in this article has the advantage of being heavier and stiffer, making it easier to use and control.

The other turning tool used in this article is a parting tool. Any type will do. I prefer a 3/16" (5mm)-wide diamond parting tool, ground to make it easier to make a shearing cut *(Photo 2)*. Any parting tool may be ground this way or it can be purchased with this profile from Craft Supplies.

The other items needed are a drill chuck, a 1" (25mm) Forstner bit,

a drive center, a live center for the tailstock, a pair of spring calipers, and a rule to measure diameters and lengths.

A pair of candle inserts will make it safer to have fire and wood together in the same place (inserts may be required by law in some places). Additionally, inserts make it easier to match the taper on the bottom of the candle. You can find these inserts at Craft Supplies and Packard Woodworks.

Lead shot will help keep the candleholders stable and it is available by the pound from gun and shooting supply stores. Five-minute epoxy will be used to hold the shot and a plug in the bottom of the candleholders. Of course, you will need sandpaper and your favorite finish.

Modifying a spindle-roughing gouge

The ¾" (20mm) spindle-roughing gouge comes with a straight-across traditional grind and a 45° bevel. It needs to be ground freehand because it won't fit in a Wolverine sharpening jig. Freehand grinding is easy if you follow three steps:

1. Begin to reshape the profile on the end of the tool by sweeping back the sides of the tool at 45°. This doesn't compromise the strength and stiffness of

Step one: To reshape a spindle-roughing gouge, grind across the top of the gouge, flute-side down.

The profile of the tip should look like a thumbnail when viewed from the top. The tool is ready for step two.

Step two: To create the cutting edge, grind the bevel to meet the edge of the profile just created. Start in the middle of the tool's bevel.

Continuing in step two, roll the tool on the platform, changing directions so that both sides of the bevel are ground equally.

Make sure that the upper part of the cutting edge has a straight-to-slightly convex line in profile.

the U-shape. To accomplish this, grind across the end of the tool (Photo 3), with the tool held flute-side down on the grinding wheel. The profile of the tip should look like a thumbnail when viewed from the top (Photo 4). From the sides, the profile should be either a straight line or slightly convex. You have just established what will become the cutting edge of the tool and are ready for step two.

2. Set the grinder platform to grind a 40°–45° bevel, as measured between the bevel and the bottom of the flute. Grind the bevel to meet the previously determined cutting edge. Start with the center of the tool on the wheel (Photo 5). Grind the right half of the bevel with one smooth motion, swinging the tool handle to the right as you roll the tool on the platform (Photo 6). Now change hands and go in the other direction.

3. Remove the burr on the inside of the flute with a slipstone. Sharpen the tool again with the grinding wheel.

Make sure that the upper part of the cutting edge has a straight-to-slightly convex line in profile (Photo 7). That upper area of the tool can then be used for making a smooth cut.

The toolrest

An even, smooth surface on the wood depends on a smooth surface on the toolrest. Nicks and dings are telegraphed to the wood as the tool jerks and bounces when moved along the rough surface of a toolrest.

Use a flat mill file to remove any nicks in the toolrest. Clean the file with a file card or stiff wire brush. Hold it with the handle in your left hand and draw the file toward your body. Reverse the file and hold the

handle in the your right hand when pushing it away from you.

Polish the top of the toolrest with 400 or 600 grit paper and a few drops of light oil such as three-in-one or mineral oil. Wipe it clean and the toolrest is ready to use.

The formula of thirds

In this formula, everything is proportional to everything else by multiples of either 1/3 or 2/3. Applied to candleholders, here are the proportions:

- The thin waist divides the candleholder into two sections, with the bottom being 2/3 the total length and the top 1/3 the length.
- The diameter at the waist is 1/3 that of the base.
- The diameter at the top is 2/3 that of the base.

Using these proportions and their resulting dimensions makes it is easier to create an attractive form (Photo 8). Additionally, duplicate pairs can be achieved without a lot of measuring or trial-and-error turning.

Selecting the wood

Any hardwood can be used for turning, but bold grain patterns always look more stunning than straight-grained wood. There is a wide variety of species and color available from all of our wood

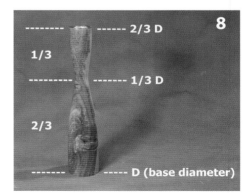

The formula of 1/3 is used to create this candleholder.

Getting Started in Woodturning

sources; finding a matching pair may be challenging, however.

Select two pieces that are 2" square and 10" long (50mm × 254mm) and as close to having the same grain pattern as possible. I am using a 10" (254mm) length because that seems to be the preferred length from wood dealers.

Determine which end of the blank will be the bottom and trim it square with the sides. Cut the blanks to 9" (230mm) long—that length is easily divided by three. The 1" (25mm) cut-off will be used later for a plug in the bottom.

Turning to round

Locate the center at both ends of the blank. Exact measuring to locate the center will result in the largest possible finished diameter. I always drill a small hole for the centers in each end using just the center spur of a Forstner bit. This makes a better hole than does forcing the points of the drive/live centers into the wood.

Mount the blank onto the lathe and turn it to a cylinder that is 1-7/8" (48mm) in diameter, because that number is easily divided by three.

Pushing a tool into a spinning, square piece of wood can be a frightening prospect for a beginner. Let me take you through the process. To begin with, adjust the toolrest to the proper height. With the lathe off, rotate the wood to where it is diagonal in the lathe—the corners will be in the 12, 3, 6, and 9 o'clock positions.

Put a pencil mark on the wood in the center of the diagonal facing you. With the toolrest loose and all the way down, hold the tool so the bevel is on the wood surface, the cutting edge is at the line (Photo 9), and the tool handle is held in a comfortable location at your waist or side. Depending on the height of the lathe, you may have to raise or lower the tool handle to achieve a comfortable position.

Raise the toolrest to support the tool in this position and clamp it in place. This is the height that the toolrest should be when starting to turn the square to round. A finer adjustment can be made later as the corners start to disappear. Also, move the toolrest closer to the wood as its diameter decreases.

Remove the tool and start the lathe. Select a speed that both you and the lathe are comfortable with. Something in the range of 1800rpm to 2200rpm is good.

Do the anchor-bevel-cut routine (ABC). Anchor the tool on the toolrest. Move the tool forward to where the wood is striking the bevel. Then, raise the handle to where the tool just starts to cut, and no more.

Slide the tool along the toolrest and you will be cutting wood.

Now, angle the tool about 30°–45° toward the direction of the cut. Roll the tool slightly so you are cutting near the center of the tool. You will be pushing the tool into the wood and making a clean shaving. Repeat the cuts until the wood is turned to a cylinder.

Layout

Locate the waist of the candleholder. This will be at 6" (155mm) from the base and 3" (75mm) from the top for a 9" (230mm) candleholder (Photo 10).

Set the calipers at ¾" (20mm), which is 1/3 of the base diameter plus 1/8" (3mm) for blending the top

9 To set the height of your toolrest, place the corners of the wood diagonal to bed of the lathe and mark a line in the center of one side. Position the cutting edge of the gouge at the line, then set the toolrest height so that the wood will be cut at or above that line.

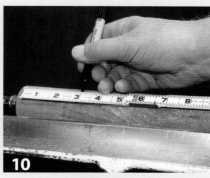

10 Locate the waist of the candleholder 3" (75mm) from the top for a 9" (230mm) candleholder.

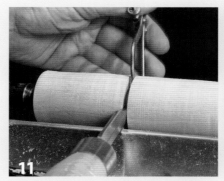

11 Set the calipers at ¾" (20mm), which is 1/3 of the base diameter, plus 1/8" (3mm) for blending the top and bottom curves.

12 Turn the wood down to 1¼" (38mm) diameter for the top section.

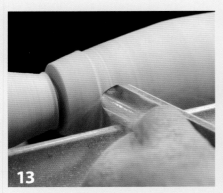

13
Turn two large ogee (lazy "S") shapes to connect the top and bottom sections with the waist. With spindle turning, cut from the large diameter to the smaller diameter.

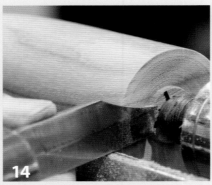

14
Make a light cut across the bottom and top using a parting tool to make sure both are square with the sides. Take care not to remove the drive and live center holes. Those will be used later for remounting the candleholders.

and bottom curves. Turn the waist down to ¾" (20mm) diameter with the parting tool *(Photo 11).*

Set the calipers to 1¼" (38mm) and turn the wood from the top down to this dimension *(Photo 12).*

Turn the shape

Now comes the fun part—turn two large ogee (lazy "S") shapes to connect the top and bottom diameters with the waist *(Photo 13).*

Run the lathe at 1800rpm to 2200rpm, and remember ABC. Begin cutting at either end and push the tool toward the waist with one long sweeping motion. Always cut downhill from the largest diameter to the smallest. This means cutting to the waist from both ends and meeting at the bottom of the curve.

The only criterion for the curves is that they do not end up interfering with the holes that will be drilled later in the top and bottom. That means the bottom will have a shallower curve for the first 2" (50mm) and the top for about 1" (25mm) before the curves sweep down to form the smallest diameter of the candleholder. Use the calipers

to check the diameters at these critical locations.

Make a light cut across the top and bottom using the parting tool to make sure both are square with the sides *(Photo 14).* Make a 1/8" (3mm) concave curve in the bottom by angling the parting tool. Part down to less than a 1" (25mm)-diameter with the trimming cut on each end.

Candleholders generally come in pairs, so make another that is the same as this one. Holding the finished candleholder alongside the one in the lathe will help you match the curves. The most important thing about a pair is that the waist be the same distance above the base. You may have to adjust the location of the waist so they will match. Close is close enough for everything else. Take them out of the lathe and stand them upright for a better comparison of their shapes.

Finishing

Sand and finish the candleholders before drilling the holes for the inserts and the lead shot. There are many ways to finish them. I sand to 600 grit followed by 0000-steel wool then apply a heavy brush-on coat of lacquer, wait two or three minutes, then wipe it all off, using new paper towels until the surface is dry. I buff it again with 0000-steel wood to get rid of extra lacquer and smooth out any rough spots. I apply lacquer again, wipe it off again, and let it dry for about fifteen minutes. The candleholder can now be handled for drilling the holes.

Drilling

The drilling may be a bit different from what you are used to doing, and it depends on the Forstner bit having a center spur. Insert a Jacobs chuck into the headstock and place a 1" (25mm)-diameter Forstner bit in it. Leave the live center in the tailstock. Hold the candleholder between the

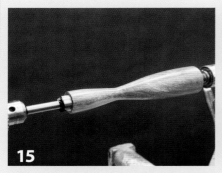

15
With a Jacobs chuck in the headstock and a 1" (25mm) Forstner drill bit inserted, mount the finished candleholder between the bit and the live center of the tailstock. Reduce the speed of your lathe to about 400rpm.

16
Using a small piece of leather, hold the rotating candle holder with one hand and advance the tailstock with the other hand to drill the hole. Swap ends and drill the hole in the bottom.

Getting Started in Woodturning

spur of the drill bit and the tailstock live center using the holes already there *(Photo 15)*.

Set the lathe speed at about 400rpm. Hold the candleholder with your left hand *(Photo 16)* to keep it from turning while advancing the wood into the drill with the tailstock. Use a small piece of leather to help grip the wood. Drill the hole in the top to 1" (25mm) deep, or what is required for your candle insert. Swap ends in the lathe and drill a 2" (50mm) deep hole in the bottom.

Completing the candleholders

Attach the cut-off piece of wood between centers of the lathe and turn it down so that there is a tight fit in the hole in the bottom of the candleholder *(Photo 17)*. Taper it slightly to get a tight fit and then part it off to where there is no more than ¼" (6mm) in the hole.

Fill the hole with the lead shot to within ¼" (6mm) of the top. Mix enough epoxy to cover the shot and have some left to glue in the plug. Mount the candleholder and glued-in plug between centers in the lathe, spin it by hand to see that it runs reasonably close to true, make any necessary adjustments, clamp it tight, and wait for the epoxy to cure *(Photo 18)*. Using a parting tool,

cut off the plug, but do not turn away the previously trimmed edge, which is square with the sides of the candleholder.

Sand the bottom of the base (this is optional). If you choose to do this, put a 2" (50mm)-diameter sanding mandrel and a 100-grit sanding disc in the Jacobs chuck in the headstock (or use your drillpress). Hold the candleholder so that the edge of the disc matches the recess in the bottom, and sand by rotating the candleholder *(Photo 19)*. Be careful not to cut away the wood at the edges of the base. Sand to as fine a grit as you wish. I usually stop at 220 grit.

Wipe on a coat of lacquer, wipe it off, and let it dry. Give the candleholders a good buffing with buffing wheels, using both abrasives and wax.

Install the candle inserts *(Photo 20)*. Some of these are held in with a screw, while others use an epoxy or silicone adhesive. Use whichever is appropriate.

You have now learned the basics of spindle turning without having to use a skew chisel, and you have a pair of candleholders to prove it. Display them with pride. I think Rude would approve.

Russ Fairfield, who passed in 2011, was a respected turner, instructor, and member of the Inland Northwest Woodturners and the INW Pen Turners Association.

17 Attach the cut-off piece of wood between centers and turn it down so that there is a tight fit in the hole in the bottom of the candleholder.

18 After filling the hole with lead shot and epoxy, insert the plug and mount the assembly between centers of the lathe. Clamp tight and wait for the epoxy to cure.

19 Sanding the bottom of the candleholder is made easy by attaching a sanding mandrel in the lathe's headstock.

20 Install the candle inserts.

20 Ways to Master Spindle Turning

Avoid common pitfalls on the journey to expertise

In the hands of an expert, turning a spindle looks effortless. But there are plenty of pitfalls to avoid on the journey to expertise. Here are 20 tips to help you become a spindle master.

Spindle turning may seem easy for production turners and others who have stood in front of a lathe for a few decades. Many of us simply turn on the machine, mount the blank between centers, and start cutting. Those who watch—either in demos or as students and even clients—are amazed at the speed and accuracy with which we perform what we consider the mundane task of turning spindles.

But for the beginner, there are so many things to think about!

Let's start with mounting the blank. Should we use a safety center or a spur-drive center? A two- or four-prong spur center? Should I use a mini-spur? Should it be spring-loaded or not?

See what I mean? This may be too much for the average student.

Most beginners don't really have to think about all that much. The lathe they just purchased came with a drive center and a four-prong spur center without a spring loaded center, and is large enough to drive most anything that will fit on it.

Here are some do's and don'ts to improve your spindle work.

Mount your stock

1 **Choose your turning stock carefully.** Avoid knots, checks, and other defects. Straight-grain blanks produce the best results. Poplar is inexpensive, easy to turn, and readily available. For projects requiring detail, maple is my favorite light-colored hardwood; walnut and cherry are ideal when dark woods are preferred.

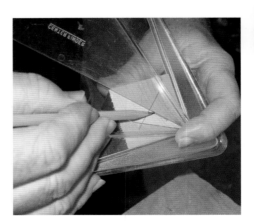

2 **Always use a centerfinder or a straightedge across the corners of the blank to find the center.** This is especially true if you are going to leave squares on the final turning. It is also necessary to make sure the blank is truly square when preparing the material. On fully rounded work, this is not as critical.

3 **Never mount the blank with the lathe running.** It is dangerous and can cause you harm. Don't do that!

Don't do that!

4 **Never drive the blank onto the spur center while it is mounted in the spindle.** This can damage the Morse taper and stress the lathe bearings.

Photos: Marisa Pruss

AW 21:4, p46

Tool-rest tips

Don't do that!

5 **Never drive the spur center into the blank with a steel-faced hammer.** This will damage the Morse taper, preventing it from fitting properly. Always drive the spur with a wooden mallet, dead blow, or other soft-faced hammer.

6 **Never apply excessive pressure on the blank with the tailstock.** Slide the tailstock forward, lock it in place, and run the live center into the end of the blank. Be sure to lock the quill in place once you've snugged up the tail center. At the tailstock, use a good-quality live or ball bearing center; one with interchangeable tips to accommodate different applications is worth the extra expense. A cup-shaped tip on the live center will be less likely to split smaller blanks.

7 **Maintain your tool rest.** All turning tools are harder steel than the tool rest. Nicks and dings in the tool rest will be reflected in the workpiece. Use a mill file to keep the tool rest smooth. Some turners even wax the tool rest with paraffin (sometimes called canning wax).

8 **Position the tool rest parallel to the blank and as close as possible**— 1/4" is adequate clearance. Be sure to lock the tool rest to the support and the support to the lathe bed. Always rotate the workpiece by hand before turning on the machine. No matter how many times you have seen it done in demos, never move the tool rest with the machine running. Always move the tool rest closer after removing the corners from the blank—excessive overhang of the tool will cause chatter.

Popular tailstock centers

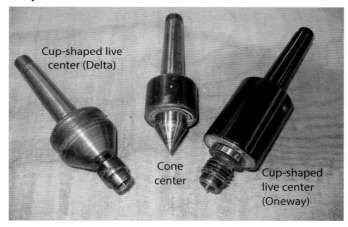

Cup-shaped live center (Delta)

Cone center

Cup-shaped live center (Oneway)

Popular drive centers

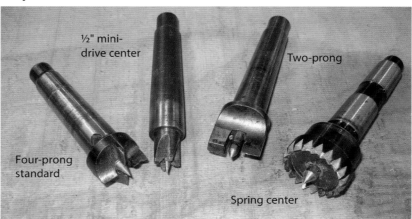

½" mini-drive center

Two-prong

Four-prong standard

Spring center

9 **Adjust the height of the tool rest to match the tool you are using.** You should cut above center for most lathe tools. If you switch from a thick tool (like a spindle roughing gouge) to a thinner tool (like a skew) you will need to raise the tool rest.

Turning tips

Uphill—No!

Downhill—Yes!

10 **Always cut downhill, from large diameter to small diameter on spindles.** Attempting to cut uphill on some woods will produce disastrous results—expect a lot of catches.

11 **Never work with dull turning tools.** If in doubt, sharpen the tool. The skew in particular needs to be razor sharp. Honing is required to maintain the edge of the skew; other tools may be used straight off the grinding wheel. Sharpening jigs or fixtures will ensure that you get a consistent bevel angle on your tools.

12 **Never turn on the lathe without first checking the speed.** Step pulleys are easy to check visually. Variable-speed lathes that utilize an adjustable pulley system do not allow you to change the speed without the machine running. Turn on the lathe before mounting the blank, adjust the speed, then turn it off and mount the workpiece. Some of the electronic lathes are equipped

with digital readouts so you can see the RPM as you make adjustments.

Here are speed guidelines (wood species and experience are key variables): For 1"- to 3"-diameter stock, I recommend roughing out at 1,200 rpm and moving up to 2,000 rpm for finishing cuts. For stock 5" in diameter or larger, rough out at 800; finish at 1,500.

13 **Use your body—not just your hands—as you move the tool along the tool rest.** This will provide more support and better control.

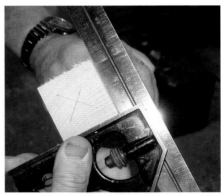

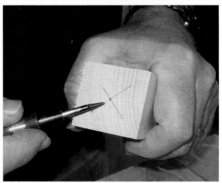

14 **When turning furniture parts or architectural elements with square ends or pommels,** make sure your blanks start out perfectly square. It is also critical that you accurately locate the centers on this type of work.

Master skills

15 Take your time; rushing through a project will probably create less than satisfactory results.

16 If duplicating two or more spindles, make a pencil gauge or story stick. Use your template to mark each blank once it is roughed out. The marks will identify where details are located along the spindles. Use a parting tool or bedan and a vernier scale to cut down to the appropriate diameters. Always measure from the same end to provide consistent results.

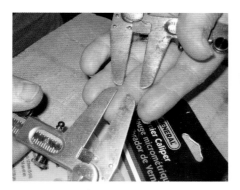

17 Vernier scales and spring calipers can get caught in the workpiece and snatched from your hands. Always round over the tips of your measuring tool before using them on spinning stock. Or even safer: Stop the machine to take measurements.

18 For additional support and better control of your spindle turning, wrap your index finger around the tool rest.

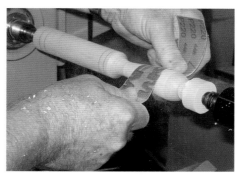

19 Remove the tool rest prior to sanding. It's too easy for fingers to get caught between the tool rest and the turning stock.

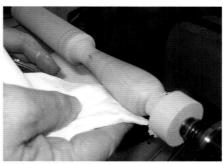

20 Never use cloth rags for applying finish, only paper towels. In an instant, the spinning lathe can grab a thread and your finger. It's false economy to use cast-off T-shirts if doing so leads to a trip to the emergency room.

Always think SAFETY!

Whatever you turn, keep two safety tips in mind:

- Always wear a proper dust mask while sanding.

- Never turn without proper eye protection.

Enough said.

*A founding member of the AAW, **Nick Cook** is a frequent contributor to* American Woodturner *and lives in Marietta, GA where he owns and operates his studio. Visit Nick at www.nickcookwoodturner.com.*

Wood: Kiln Dried, Green, or Air Dried

Making the best choice depends on the task at hand

There is one truth that all woodturners come to understand: When freshly cut, trees are full of water and the moisture-laden lumber is unstable as it dries. This fact determines much about the working properties of our raw material and dictates some processes woodturners employ.

To explain in simple terms, in freshly cut (green) wood, water occurs in two forms: *free* and *bound*. The free water resides in the cell cavities and is first to evaporate—or be slung about your shop while you are turning green wood. The loss of free water does not cause wood to change shape or crack.

The inside of a vacuum kiln (top has been removed) shows slab material that has been dried. This kiln at Berkshire Products in Sheffield, Massachusetts, can dry up to about 2,000 board feet of lumber in only a few days. Boards are layered in the kiln and separated by heated aluminum plates.

AW 28 :3, p20

Getting Started in Woodturning

Bound water exists within the cell walls and evaporates after the free water is gone. When the bound water begins to evaporate, the wood does most of its shrinking (as the cells collapse), causing the wood to change shape and possibly crack. Thus, high moisture content necessitates some form of drying process to stabilize wood, either before or after turning on the lathe.

Although wood is not alive after being cut, it may seem so because wood is hygroscopic—it continues to absorb and lose moisture as the relative humidity changes. Understanding the nature of wood will help you understand the options available for acquiring this material we enjoy turning.

Kiln-dried lumber

When you buy lumber from a lumberyard or hardwood dealer, most often it has been dried in a kiln. This is the fastest way to dry wood after it has been rough sawn. In as short as a week, depending on the type of wood and the kiln being used, dimensional lumber will be ready to turn. Kiln-dried lumber is dried to about 6 to 9 percent moisture content, which makes the wood stable. Even so, the wood might need to be acclimated to the humidity of your shop before working it.

Wood kilns operate much like a convection oven, making use of some type of heat source and a fan to move the air. There are a number of different types of kilns—vacuum, dehumidification, and solar—but the purpose is the same for all of them: to speed up the process of evaporation of bound water from the wood, thereby stabilizing it. For woodturners, the stability of dried wood—whether kiln-dried or air-dried—makes it suitable for all kinds of glue-ups prior to turning, such as in segmented work. Kiln-

Carl Ford, untitled (natural-edge bowl), 2003, Ash, 6½" × 12" (17 cm × 30 cm)

dried wood is also used for spindle work and for small projects, such as pens.

Some kiln operators also infuse water into the process, commonly when drying walnut. Doing so moves some of the dark color of the heartwood into the sapwood, thereby making the overall color of the board more uniform, which many furniture companies prefer. This process also increases the amount of wood that can be used. On the downside, the process tends to homogenize the wood, making it less interesting. Also, applying heat and steam changes the quality of the wood, making it harder and more brittle. This is why turning kiln-dried wood dulls tools faster and produces a "dusty" cut.

One key limitation of kiln-dried stock for woodturners is the thickness of the wood that can be dried: It is difficult to sufficiently dry timber much thicker than 4" (10cm). Kiln-dried lumber is well suited for woodworkers who use boards (planks or slabs) to make projects that do not require thicker material. But for turners, using kiln-dried lumber limits faceplate work to shallow bowls and platters (unless you glue up stock to make thicker turning blanks).

Carl Ford, untitled (beaded-rim big-mouth vase), 2009, Ash, 7" × 6" (18 cm × 15 cm)

Green wood

If you have not yet experienced the joys of turning green wood (freshly cut timber saturated with moisture), you are missing out on a fantastic experience. Many woodturning projects become fun by using green wood instead of dimensional lumber. For example, if you want to turn a large, deep bowl without laminating layers of boards together to create sizable turning blanks, using green wood is the answer. A natural-edge bowl with the bark remaining on the rim is best made from green wood. Turn it green, let it warp, and bask in the glory of your

3

I used the crotch grain in this black walnut log as a feature in a turned platter.

4

The finished platter, 2011, walnut, 1½" × 15"

5

A freshly sawn log shows natural wonders with great potential for a bowl!

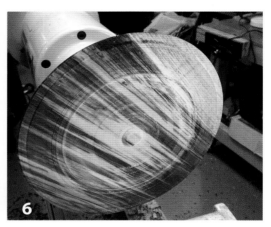

6

The dark streaks in this maple resulted from the unique mineral content of the soil.

family's compliments. They will truly wonder at your creative use of nature's bounty *(Photo 1)*.

The size and scope of hollow vessels would be severely limited if only kiln-dried wood were used. Woodturners can take a whole section of a green log, mount it directly to the lathe, shape the outside and remove the wood inside to create a hollow vessel *(Photo 2)*. With this process, the wood can usually move without cracking while drying. The small area of pith on the bottom can be treated with CA glue or drilled and plugged.

The process of turning green wood is easier on tools because the water in the wood lubricates the cut—shavings easily peel away, many in long ribbons. Cutting tools stay sharper longer and tools leave a smoother surface.

Working with green wood requires some investment of time, effort, and money up front. For example, you will need some means of cutting logs into usable pieces for turning, which means acquiring a chainsaw and a bandsaw. Portable bandsaw-type sawmills can be expensive. Also, woodturners require room to

process and store wood properly. If you live in an apartment or your neighborhood association has strict codes, chainsawing lumber on your driveway is probably not conducive to being neighborly. Ideally, processed spindle blanks and roughed-out bowls should be stored in a warm dry place for air-drying. Do you have the room to do so?

If you have the knowledge, space, and equipment, harvesting green wood can have significant benefits. Top on the list is the cost of wood. Kiln-dried lumber is relatively expensive. By the time you buy it, the wood has been handled many times: the tree felled, log rough sawn in a mill, and boards dried in a kiln, perhaps even planed to a uniform thickness. During this process, the wood likely has been transported several times, and that cost is built into the final price. Conversely, you can acquire freshly cut logs free, either from a local tree surgeon or from trees that have come down around your neighborhood. Even in urban settings, there will be tree pruning and removal periodically, so friendly communication with public works or botanical gardens personnel could prove beneficial.

When you learn to process your own turning stock from logs, you can choose which parts of a tree to harvest, such as crotch grain or a section that appears to have figure in it. Often, I am happily surprised with the interesting characteristics I find within the logs I harvest (*Photos 3, 4, 5, 6*). A maple log from a neighbor's tree may have beautiful ambrosia markings, mineral streaks from the soil, or spalting—qualities that generally are too unusual or cost-prohibitive for hardwood dealers to handle.

Harvesting and air-drying bowl stock

When you harvest wood from a log, it is best to do so as quickly as possible after cutting the log to length, before endgrain checking has had a chance to occur. First, locate the pith (*Photo 7*). This is the original strand within the stem or trunk around which the annual growth rings form. The pith is not necessarily located at the center of the tree—growth rings can form quite out of round. The wood closest to the pith tends to be unstable when the wood dries, and if not removed, that area can cause unnecessary cracking throughout the entire turning blank. Unless you

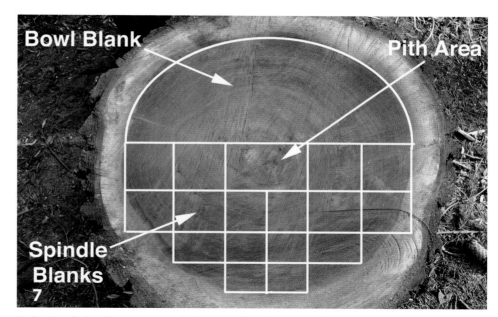

Bowl Blank **Pith Area** **Spindle Blanks** **7**

Endgrain of a log illustrates a typical approach to harvesting bowl and spindle-turning stock. To maximize the size of a bowl in this orientation, the log should be cut at least as long as its diameter. The pith and its surrounding area should be cut away since it is unstable during drying and often results in cracks.

8

The half logs of black walnut reveal a richly colored treasure. A small amount of pith can be seen in the upper part of the logs, but that will be cut away later.

9

A bowl blank can be rough-shaped with a chainsaw. The chalk mark represents the top of the bowl blank.

intend to incorporate the pith into a project for dramatic effect, it should be cut away, either during blank preparation or at the lathe.

Cut the log in half, at or near the pith, essentially splitting the log lengthwise (Photo 8). This can be accomplished with a typical chainsaw setup, but make sure you use a sharp chain. Special chains made for ripping along the grain can make this process easier. Another way to cut a log along the grain is with a portable bandsaw-type sawmill. (See AAW's recent

book, *Safety for Woodturners* for hints on how to safely rip wood with a chainsaw woodturner.org/products.)

To harvest bowl-blank material, mark a circle on a half log using chalk, and then rough-shape the bowl blank with a chainsaw (*Photo 9*). Alternatively, you can cut the log in half and form the bowl blank using a bandsaw if you have one with enough capacity (*Photo 10*).

Drying wood much thicker than 4" (10cm) thick is not feasible, so it is best to turn bowls right away

10

To rough shape a log using a bandsaw, start safely by initially cutting the log in half with the grain running vertically. Each half can then yield a bowl blank with the grain running horizontally, as in Photo 9.

11

Rough turning the outside of a maple bowl from green wood reveals mineral streaks and ambrosia markings.

12

After air-drying this walnut bowl blank for several months, it can be finish-turned.

from green blanks. To rough-turn a bowl, shape and hollow it, but leave the walls extra thick for safe, slow drying and to ensure there is enough wood left to re-turn the bowl round after the wood warps *(Photos 11, 12)*. The rule of thumb for wall thickness of a rough-turned bowl is 1" (2.5cm) per 10" (25cm) of rim diameter, so a 15"- (38cm-) diameter bowl, for example, would have walls that are 1½" (4cm) thick.

It is important to make the wall thickness as uniform as possible from rim to bottom so drying can occur evenly, which further reduces the chances of cracking. Immediately after rough turning, coat the bowl with a wax emulsion sealer, which will slow the drying process and even out moisture loss from endgrain and side grain wood—moisture loss is greater from endgrain than from side grain.

Set aside the bowl for several months to a year to air-dry, preferably in an environment that is not too hot and dry. As the wood loses moisture, the bowl will change shape and go out of round—wood shrinks more across the grain than along the grain. After the bowl blank is dry, remount it onto the lathe for final turning, sanding, and finishing. This is what is commonly called a twice-turned bowl.

It is also possible to turn a bowl from green wood directly to its final thickness. This is a lot of fun, but you need to work quickly so the wood does not dry and distort as you turn. It helps to keep wetting the wood as you go. The walls can be turned quite thin, so the wood will dry faster than for a rough-turned bowl. The bowl will also warp and change shape, often leaving a wavy rim.

Spindle-turning stock

To harvest spindle-turning stock, make additional rip cuts in the freshly cut half-log to create blanks of various dimensions *(see Photo 7)*. These rip cuts can be made with a chainsaw *(Photo 13)*, but are more easily accomplished on a bandsaw *(Photos 14, 15)*. Spindle blanks do not need to be cut exactly square— eventually they will be turned round when mounted between centers, so it is sufficient to make these rip cuts freehand. Seal the ends of spindle blanks with a wax emulsion to minimize endgrain checking, and set them aside for air-drying, stacking them so air circulates around each piece.

The rule of thumb for air-drying wood is one year for each inch of thickness, and this applies to both flat lumber (spindle stock) and roughed-out bowls. Drying times vary greatly, however, depending on the type of wood and the humidity level in which the wood is being dried. Ultimately, the goal is for the wood's moisture content to reach a point of equilibrium with the surrounding humidity. Then it will be relatively stable in that environment. If in doubt, a moisture meter can be used to verify moisture content.

Air-dried lumber is often of a much nicer quality, with a gentler cutting response, than kiln-dried stock. It has been dried slower and by a more natural process. For woodturners, kiln-dried lumber certainly has its uses, but if you have only turned kiln-dried wood, you may be missing out on some of the unique joys of harvesting and turning green wood.

Joshua Friend, a woodturner and writer, is a member of the Nutmeg Woodturners League, an AAW chapter that meets at the Brookfield Craft Center in Brookfield, Connecticut. See jfriendwoodworks.com for examples of his work and contact information.

Spindle stock can be cut using a chainsaw, but an easier option would be to rip the blanks using a bandsaw after cutting the log to a manageable dimension.

The Secrets of Sandpaper

Understanding the nitty-gritty is the key to a smooth finish

Who knew that P400 was the same as 320 grit? That's just one of many facts I learned from my research on sandpaper. After thirty-eight years of woodworking, I thought I knew about sandpaper. Turns out I didn't.

When I took up woodturning, I found that there was a lot I did not know. For instance, I was not getting the results I wanted when sanding and if I talked to three different woodturners, I got three different answers.

I decided to undertake a study of sandpaper. I began by emailing questions to my suppliers. One replied, "I don't envy your task. The subject has always confused me."

From Rockler Woodworking I received an email that said, "Sorry that I don't have an answer for this. It looks like you have already done more research on this topic than any information I know. I'd be interested in hearing more, though, on any details your further research digs up." What I learned may astound him. It did me.

We are not using our grandfathers' sandpaper. Today's sandpaper does not contain sand and at times does not include paper. Sandpaper is not properly called sandpaper but should technically be called *coated abrasive* or *abrasive sandpaper* or *abrasive paper*. And, identical grits rated under different standards do not have the same abrasive particle size.

Some artists can work wonders with materials, while individuals with less talent struggle. Perhaps your sanding results are suitable, but if you are like me and see room for improvement, try the progression recommended in the comparing methods section.

The ideal is, of course, to improve tool use and control in order to minimize the amount of sanding that is required. But if sanding is what is called for, additional knowledge and a few hints will improve results.

U.S. and European standards: What's the difference?

There are two different standards used to specify the average abrasive particle size in the abrasive sandpapers we use in the United States. The Coated Abrasives Manufacturers Institute (CAMI) governs grit scaling in the Unites States. The Federation of European Producers of Abrasives (FEPA) provides the standard for the European scale.

The letter *P* in front of the grit number indicates that the abrasive particle size falls under the European classification for coated abrasives.

In this article, when you see a grit number alone, the number is classified under the U.S. standard. If the grit number has a *P* in front of it, its abrasive particle size is classified under the European standard.

Grit refers to the grit number printed on the backing of the abrasive sandpaper.

Simply put, it is the number of abrasive particles that will fit in one square inch. A larger number indicates a finer grit because more of the smaller abrasive particles will fit in one square inch.

Manufacturers determine the grit size by passing the abrasives through a series of sieves for the larger particle sizes. The smaller abrasive particles (from 230/P230 and finer) are selected by sedimentation and measured with a photosedimentometer.

There is a range of abrasive particle sizes that is permitted within each grit size. The European system allows a smaller variation in particle size, so their papers will produce a finer scratch pattern than the U.S. ones.

The future of grading systems

In email and telephone exchanges, both Ted Mullins of Keystone Abrasives and Coleman Fourshee of Klingspor Abrasives agree that the U.S. grading system is gradually going by the wayside and the FEPA (European) grading system will eventually become the only system used.

It was difficult to find all the grits I needed when looking for the CAMI-based abrasive sheets for the evaluations for my study. The hardware stores did have all the grits, although some were in an abrasive material other than aluminum oxide. Some grits were only offered in garnet, others only in silicon carbide, emery, or even flint. Not all of these materials will give us the results we strive for.

Not so with the European system. All grades are easily available,

AW 25:05, p25

% Change in particle size for same grit between CAMI & FEPA				
USA		European		% increase from USA to EUROPEAN standard for the same grit
CAMI-grit	average particle size in microns	FEPA-grit	average particle size in microns	
80	188	P80	201	6.9%
100	148	P100	162	9.5%
120	116	P120	127	9.5%
150	92	P150	100	8.7%
180	78	P180	78	0.0%
220	66	P220	68	3.0%
240	51.8	P240	58.5	12.9%
280	42.3	P280	52.2	23.4%
320	34.3	P320	46.2	34.7%
400	22.1	P400	35	58.4%
600	14.5	P600	25.8	77.9%
800	12.2	P800	21.8	78.7%
1000	9.2	P1000	18.3	98.9%

Table 1 *(Above)*. The difference in average abrasive particle size between the two main standards used in the United States.

Table 2 *(Right)*. Grits for both classifications (U.S. and European). (Grits are listed according to their average abrasive particle size in descending order from the coarsest to the finest. The sizes are in microns. One micron equals one millionth of a meter, or a thousandth of a millimeter.)

Ranking the grits by particle size		
average particle size in microns	CAMI (USA)	FEPA (Europe)
201		P80
188	80	
162		P100
148	100	
127		P120
116	120	
100		P150
92	150	
78	180	P180
68		P220
66	220	
58.5		P240
51.8	240	
52.2		P280
46.2		P320
42.3	280	
34.3	320	
35		P400
25.8		P600
22.1	400	
21.8		P800
18.3		P1000
14.5	600	
15.3		P1200
12.6		P1500
12.2	800	
9.2	1000	
6.5	1200	

but the main problem is that the catalogs rarely list any grits with the *P*, even though they are actually European. Klingspor, a German company, only carries the European grades. In major home-improvement stores, the *P* is omitted on some of the packages, but it is present on the back of the sheets. This can lead to the false assumption that the grits from both systems are equal, which they are definitely not, especially in the higher grit numbers (see Table 1).

Selecting based on abrasive particle size instead of grit number

Notice in Table 1 and Table 2 that the abrasive particle sizes classified under the FEPA and the CAMI systems are only identical at grit 180/P180. For all the other grits listed, the particle sizes of the European grits are larger than the U.S. particle size for the same grit number.

For 320 grit (U.S.), the average abrasive particle size is 34.3 microns, while for P400 (European) it is 35 microns. This difference is only 2%. The difference in abrasive particle size between 320 and P320, however, is 34.7%! In U.S. workshops, 320 grit should be thought of as equal to P400.

In my study, I used the endpoint for the CAMI system as 320, while for the European system I used P400. The endpoint for both, then, is a comparable abrasive particle size.

But what about P600? Its equivalent CAMI grit would be 380, which is slightly smaller than the critical 400 grit. The P600 can be used to get a super-smooth finish.

Ted Mullins of Keystone Abrasives noted that when you sand much above 400 grit, there is the danger of burnishing the pores closed during the sanding process, which means that stains and colored finishes may not be evenly absorbed into the wood, resulting in a blotchy look. For wood that will not receive a color or stain, however, sanding to a very fine grit is generally not a problem.

Progressively sanding

One recommended method of progressively sanding through the range of grits is to use each available grit. Some authors, however, recommend an abbreviated version. Most experts recommend

USA progression with 1.5 factor (Method # 1-US)			European progression with 1.5 factor (Method # 1-EU)		
CAMI-grit (USA)	average particle size in microns	% reduction between grits	FEPA-grit (Europe)	average particle size in microns	% reduction between grits
80	188		P80	201	
		38.3%			36.8%
120	116		P120	127	
		32.8%			38.6%
180	78		P180	78	
		33.6%			25.0%
240	51.8		P240	58.5	
		33.8%			21.0%
320	34.3		P320	46.2	
		35.6%			24.2%
400	22.1		P400	35	
		34.4%			26.3%
600	14.5		P600	25.8	

Table 3. Comparing the U.S. and European systems when increasing the grit number by 50% (increasing each grit by a factor of 1.5)

(This method results in a more uniform change for the U.S. sequence with an average change between each grit of 34.8%. But for the European system, an extra grit is added to achieve a similar abrasive particle size for the endpoint of each system [320 vs. P400)].)

Uniform change with USA standard (Method # 2-US)			Uniform change with European standard (Method # 2-EU)		
CAMI-grit (USA)	average particle size in microns	% reduction between grits	FEPA-grit (Europe)	average particle size in microns	% reduction between grits
80	188		P80	201	
					19.4%
		38.3%	P100	162	
					21.6%
120	116		P120	127	
					21.3%
		32.8%	P150	100	
					22.0%
180	78		P180	78	
		33.6%			25.0%
240	51.8		P240	58.5	
		33.8%			21.0%
320	34.3		P320	46.2	
		35.6%			24.2%
400	22.1		P400	35	
		34.4%			26.3%
600	14.5		P600	25.8	

Table 4. Grit selection based on getting a uniform change in particle size from one grit to the next.

not skipping more than one grit in any progression. An article in *AW* (vol 13, no 3, Fall 1998) suggests a sequence of 80, 120, 180, 220, 280, and ending at 320. Which method should you use? Should you use a selection of grit sizes based on a different method?

If you apply the theory of using all available grits, the sequence you use for the CAMI standards (80 through 320) would involve nine different grits. With the European sequence (P80 through P400) you would be using ten grits of abrasive sandpaper. This increase of one grit number is because of the slower progression of the abrasive particle sizes in the European system.

I have found it isn't necessary to use all available grits to achieve superior results. Using fewer grits saves money and time.

You might never sand beyond 220/P220 or 320/P400 grit in your shop. That is okay, but keep in mind that the P400 grit has almost the exact same abrasive particle size as 320 (320 = 34.3 microns while P400 = 35 microns).

Comparing methods

Method 1

Method 1 is based on increasing the grit number by 50%. Here, you are increasing each grit size by 50% (multiply the grit by 1.5) beginning with 80-grit abrasive.

Running through the grits using the 1.5 method will result in the following progression in the U.S. system.

$80 \times 1.5 = 120$ and a 38.3% reduction in particle size
$120 \times 1.5 = 180$ and a 32.8% reduction in particle size
$180 \times 1.5 = 270$

At this point, we must make our first decision since 270 is not an available grit. Should you select 320, 280, 240, or 220? Since 280 is not available in aluminum oxide from the suppliers I most frequently use, the choice is either 220 (15.4% reduction), 240 (33.6% reduction), 280 (45.8% reduction) or 320 (56% reduction).

Attempting to keep the percentage change between the grits similar, I selected the 240-grit abrasive.

$240 \times 1.5 = 360$, and I chose the 320 grit for similar reasons.

I applied the same process to the European classification and compared the two systems (see Table 3). A major difference in particle size can be seen between P320 and P400. In the European sequence, this means you use one additional paper. Remember, it is more important

Mahogany cylinder prepared with an oval skew chisel. As in all cylinders, the first section on the left will be finished to 320 grit with Method 1 & 2-US. (Note: Methods 1 and 2-US are identical and are referred to as Method 1 & 2-US.) The middle section will be finished to P400 grit with Method 1-EU. The section on the right will be finished with Method 2-EU, which has the extra two grits added (P100 and P150).

Cherry cylinder prepared with an oval skew prior to using any abrasives.

Ash cylinder prepared by scraping with a dull bowl gouge to produce torn grain and tool marks.

Ash: Close-up view of the first section of the cylinder in *Photo 3*, before applying any abrasives.

The various woods used, left to right: Maple, ash, cherry, mahogany, yellow poplar. The top section of each cylinder has been finished with Method 1 & 2-US to 320 grit. The middle sections are all finished with Method 1-EU to P400 grit. The bottom sections are all finished with Method 2-EU to P400 grit. Method 2-EU included grits P100 and P150, which were not used in any of the other sections.

to compare particle size than grit number to accurately compare grit to grit.

Method 2

Method 2 is based on selecting a uniform change in particle size. The goal is to develop a progression through the grits that comes as close as possible to a uniform percentage change between each of the grits used in the sequence. This is based on the assumption that if there is a consistent percentage change between grits, a superior, smooth, scratch-free finish can be achieved faster.

With the U.S. system (see Table 4, Method 2-US) the average change in particle size is 34.6% (32.8% to 38.3%) and a progression of 80, 120, 180, 240, 320, for a total of five grit numbers. This sequence of grits is identical to Method 1-US where each grit number is increased by 50%.

For the European system (Method 2-EU), you can achieve a change in particle size from grit to grit for an average change of 22% and a progression of P80, P100, P120, P150, P180, P240, P320, and P400 for a total of eight grit numbers (see Table 4). This method results in an increase of two grit numbers over the 1.5 method and a percentage change between grits that is more consistent. The grit sequences for all of the methods are compared in Table 5.

Setting up the evaluation

I used abrasive sheets rather than discs for my study because there are more operator variables using a power sander or a Sandmaster-type tool, and not all grits may be available in the various disc systems. However, the basic principles used will still apply regardless of the system you use in your shop.

In an attempt to keep as many variables as possible out of my evaluations, I made several

decisions, the primary one being to use a spindle-turned cylinder for my test studies. I chose not to use bowls in this evaluation because of the variables introduced by the many different designs as well as the occasional need to reverse the lathe in order to smooth stubborn endgrain. Granted, it will take longer to smooth the endgrain encountered in the bowls as compared to the face grain of spindles, but the progression I use should apply to all projects. Here is how I set up the evaluations:

- I turned a cylinder for a consistent, smooth surface. (Bulk reduction with a ¾" [20 mm] roughing gouge and finish with a 1" [25 mm] oval skew.) *(Photos 1, 2)*
- I also compared the progressions on cylinders with a rough finish achieved with a dull ½" (13 mm) bowl gouge held off the bevel resulting in tool marks and torn grain. *(Photos 3, 4)*
- I used abrasive sheets applied by hand to minimize pressure variables.
- I used abrasive paper cut into strips that were 1" (25 mm) wide.
- I used each strip only once on a section before throwing it away.
- I kept the strips in constant motion when touching the wood.
- I applied firm pressure but not enough to result in feeling any warmth in my fingertips.
- I cut each wood sample to be 9" (23 cm) in length, divided it into three 3" (8 cm) sections.
- I sanded each section separately even if two adjacent sections called for the same grit number.
- I used kiln-dried wood.

I used a variety of hardwoods, with pores that went from ring-porous and open to diffuse-porous and small. The hardness range was from the medium-hard maple and ash down to yellow poplar, one of the softer hardwoods *(Photo 5)*.

CAMI progression with 1.5 factor is the same as uniform % change between grits (Method #1-US=Method #2-US)			FEPA progression with 1.5 factor (Method #1-EU)			European progression with uniform change in % reduction between grits (Method #2-EU)		
CAMI-grit (USA)	average particle size in microns	% reduction between grits	FEPA-grit (Europe)	average particle size in microns	% reduction between grits	FEPA-grit (Europe)	average particle size in microns	% reduction between grits
80	188		P80	201		P80	201	
								19.4%
		38.3%			36.8%	P100	162	
								21.6%
120	116		P120	127		P120	127	
								21.3%
		32.8%			38.6%	P150	100	
								22.0%
180	78		P180	78		P180	78	
		33.6%			25.0%			25.0%
240	51.8		P240	58.5		P240	58.5	
		33.8%			21.0%			21.0%
320	34.3		P320	46.2		P320	46.2	
		35.6%			24.2%			24.2%
400	22.1		P400	35		P400	35	
		34.4%			26.3%			26.3%
600	14.5		P600	25.8		P600	25.8	

Table 5. Comparison of selection methods. (U.S. grit choices based on Method 1 and 2 are on the left. The grit sequence is identical for the two U.S. methods.) European grit choices in the middle column are based on the 1.5 method. European progression in right column is based on a uniform percent change between grits.)

I kept the lathe's speed consistently at about 500 rpm, as I do when sanding in my shop. There are several reasons for using a slower speed for sanding:
- The heat produced with pressure and high speeds can result in cracks occurring in the wood.
- If there are resins present, they can be brought to the surface by the heat, which causes burns resulting in wood discoloration.
- High lathe speed, combined with coarser grits, can change the shape of the turning, although not as evenly as with steel tools.
- Most bowls are slightly out-of-round by the time the sanding process happens—when sanding at a high speed, the abrasive will be primarily hitting the high spots (rather like hydroplaning), leaving the lower areas untouched by the abrasive paper.

When the abrasive paper meets the wood

I always started each sequence with 80/P80 grit (Photo 6). Whichever number you begin with, the goal is a uniform surface before moving to the next grit. The rougher the tool finish, the more time should be spent on the very first grit. The objective of the first grit used is to remove torn grain and tool marks.

For the cylinders with a smooth tool finish, I used the 80/P80 grits for one minute on each section, then all the other grits in the sequence for 30 seconds each. Although I begin with a finer grit for my own turning, for testing purposes I started with 80 grit because in some of the progressions I tested I am comparing several grits that I would have skipped had I begun at 240/P240. I wanted to be consistent and use all of the grits in a progression

regardless of the tool finish to ensure more accurate results.

On the cylinders with a rough finish, I used the 80/P80 grits for two minutes on each section, then 30 seconds for the remainder of the grits.

The European abrasive paper was the cloth-backed J-flex from Klingspor. For the U.S. system, I used GatorGrit for 80-120-180. Then I switched to the multipack abrasive rolls for pen finishing from Craft Supplies, USA, for the 240 and 320 grits. I used these rolls because, even after checking catalogs, local hardware stores, and the major home-improvement stores, I could not find all the grits I needed under the U.S. classification from the same manufacturer.

In the photos, the first section on the left is always the U.S.-grit sequences. Method 1-US and Method 2-US have identical

Maple: The first section is finished to 80 grit and the other two sections were finished with P80.

grit sequences, so the first section represents both US-methods. The middle section is the same sequence of grits as the first section but with the European-graded papers. The last section on the right is the European graded papers with the extra grits added (P100 and P150).

Comparing results

I found that the sequence of P80, P120, P180, P240, P320, P400 consistently produced the most acceptable finish with all five woods, regardless of whether the initial tool finish was smooth or rough.

Adding two extra grits (P100 and P150) to the sequence did not make any difference in the surface finish at P180 when compared with the sequence that left these two grits out *(Photo 7)*.

Finishing to a P600 grit left an extremely smooth surface.

All methods passed the feel test; they all felt smooth. The *P* grade finishes were a little smoother in all sequences.

The sight test was a little different. After each sequence was completely finished and I looked at the cylinders when they were in a horizontal position while still on the lathe, it appeared as though all three sections of each sample were scratch-free *(Photos 8, 9, 10)*. When I removed the cylinders from the lathe and placed each one at a 45° angle, however, I saw scratch marks in all of the five cylinders in the sections finished with the U.S.-grade paper *(Photos 11, 12, 13)*.

I noticed that for each grit from 80/P80 to 180/P180, the U.S. grit felt smoother than the other two columns where the European grits were used.

At 240/P240 all three sections felt the same. Then at 320/P400 the European grit felt slightly smoother and markedly smoother at the 320/P600 level.

It also appears that having a consistent change in abrasive particle size from one grit to the next is not essential. The best sequence (Method 1-EU) had a change in particle size

in the upper 30% range for grits P80, P120, and P180. Then the percentage change dropped to the low to mid 20% range for the remainder of the grits *(Photo 14)*.

Substituting between the European and U.S. systems

If you have abrasive papers from both systems in your shop and run out of one grit number, Table 6 will help you find a replacement grit in the other system with the closest average abrasive particle size.

From 80/P80 to 220/P220, the best replacement is the identical grit. For those numbers higher than 220/P220, the replacement grit will be a different grit number. For P240, you could go either way: 220 = change of 12.8% or 240 = a change of 11.5%.

Choosing abrasive materials

Selection of an abrasive material is based on the friability of the particles—how easily the particles fracture under use.

There are a number of abrasive materials available. The following three are the ones most often used by woodturners.

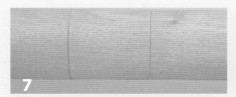

Cherry: The left section is finished with Method 1 & 2-US. The middle section is finished with Method 1-EU. The right section is finished with Method 2-EU.

The maple cylinder, viewed horizontally. The same section, viewed at an angle in *Photo 11*, reveals some scratches that are not evident in this photograph.

Cherry: At this viewing angle, no scratches are visible. Scratches become obvious when viewed at an angle, as in *Photo 12*.

Poplar: The apparently smooth finish actually has abrasive scratches, which become noticeable when viewed at an angle, as in *Photo 13*.

Maple: The same cylinder in *Photo 8,* but viewed at an angle to reveal scratches.

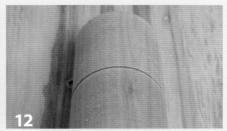

Cherry: The abrasive scratches are revealed when the cylinder in *Photo 9* is viewed at an angle.

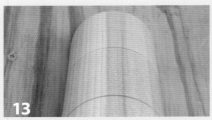

Poplar is the softest of the hardwoods used for this article. Scratches are present, but are not as evident as in the other woods.

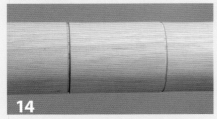

Ash: This is the same cylinder in *Photos 3 and 4*. The three sections, left/middle/right, have been finished to 320 (Method 1 & 2-US); P400 (Method 1-EU); P400 (Method 2-EU). Two additional grits (P100 and P150) were used in Method 2-EU that were not included in the other sections.

If missing a grit in one system, what is the closest replacement in the other system and at how large a difference in particle size?				
USA grit	particle size	European grit	particle size	% change in grit from USA to European
80	188	P80	201	6.5%
100	148	P100	162	8.6%
120	116	P120	127	8.7%
180	78	P180	78	0.0%
220	66	P220	65	1.5%
		P240	58.5	
240	51.8	P280	52.2	0.8%
280	42.3	P320	46.2	8.4%
320	34.3	P400	35	2.0%
		P600	25.8	
400	22.1	P800	21.8	1.4%
		P1000	18.3	
600	14.5	P1200	15.3	5.2%
800	12.2	P1500	12.6	3.2%
1000	9.2	P2500	8.4	8.7%

Table 6. Nearest comparable grit from one system to the next. (From 80/P80 through 220/P220, the nearest grit is the same grit. After 220/P220 the average abrasive particle sizes begin to separate and best choice will be a different grit number.)

Aluminum oxide

- the workhorse
- available with paper, cloth, or a synthetic backing
- abrasive particles are easily broken down as the paper is used, resulting in the creation of new, sharp edges; in effect, renewing the surface and extending the life of the abrasive
- most common abrasive in woodworking catalogs

Garnet

- softer abrasive than aluminum oxide and wears out more quickly
- produces a finer, softer scratch pattern on wood
- recommended by some as the last few grits because it will result in a much smoother final finish. I have found I do not have to use garnet to achieve a super-smooth finish.

Silicon dioxide

- often called wet/dry sandpaper and usually has a waterproof paper backing
- hard material not easily broken down on wood, is very aggressive
- usually used on metals
- too aggressive to use as a primary abrasive on wood

Reviewing backing material

The *backing* is the material used to hold the abrasive particles. Backings include paper, cloth and synthetic materials like Mylar. Some can be waterproofed.

Waterproof backing allows the paper to be used with water to rinse off dust that tends to clog the abrasive, or to finish sand with oil instead of using steel wool.

Papers are graded from A through F, with A being the most pliable. Coarser grits will have a heavier, stiffer grade of paper. Grade F is the stiffest and is used for sanding belts. The paper grade, if listed, will follow the grit number, for instance 800A or P60C. The paper grade is not always included with the grit number.

In the manufacturing process for coated abrasives, the backing is first coated with a resin that will hold the grit. As the paper is passed over and slightly above the abrasive particles, an electrostatic charge is introduced, resulting in the abrasive particles moving up and into the resin. The larger part of the particle embeds in the soft resin with the smaller, sharper end exposed. The resin with the embedded particles is then dried. A second coat of resin is applied over the exposed particles to extend the life of the abrasive.

This somewhat scientific approach to sandpaper selection has provided me with an understanding of the abrasive particle size used in the various grits, which has greatly improved the finishing portion of my turnings. I hope it will do the same for you.

Art Scott turns with a Powermatic 3420B in Folsom, LA, and is a member of the Bayou Woodturners. They meet monthly in Harahan, LA and can be reached at *bayouwoodturner.org*.

Guide to Finishing

Follow these five easy steps for foolproof results

There may be nearly as many ways to finish a turning as there are turners, since it is such an important and individual component to the process. Finishing also is a large part of the work—accounting for anything up to one-third of the time spent on a piece.

Over the years, I have experimented with various methods and would like to discuss the approach I have come to use on just about all of my work. It is relatively straight-forward, general, and usually effective. I hasten to add that although this isn't the only way to finish a turning, many turners use variations of this approach. I would be happy if this article stimulates a discussion on finishing and other turners write about their successful techniques.

I use a five-step process: sand, seal, sand, oil, and buff. Everyone sands and oils, but I believe the key is the sealing step. Sealing the wood prior to final sanding provides three major advantages: It exposes rough grain and tool marks; it stiffens the grain so sanding is more effective; and it fills the surface pores—more or less—to produce a smoother surface for the final sanding and finish coats.

Step 1: Initial sanding

Often called "rough sanding," the idea is to finalize the surface shape and get it to a preliminary smoothness. Power-sanding works best for me; I use 3" Powerlock sanding disks in an electric drill (Photos A and B). The spin of the disk against the revolving piece on the lathe reduces swirl lines. Grits 80 and/or 100 are hard and aggressive. Some subtle shaping of the curves is possible, but the emphasis is on cleaning up tool marks and preparing the surface for sealing. Many turners use foam-backed pads with 5" or 6" PSA disks rather than the stiff resin paper of Powerlocks. If you are not after subtleness, I believe foam disks are unnecessary.

I use a five-step process: sand, seal, sand, oil, and buff. Everyone sands and oils, but I believe the key is the sealing step.

Power-sand your turnings with 3" disks.

AW 19:2, p38

A couple of observations: The lathe speed should be slow to avoid the sandpaper skating over the surface. In addition, power-sand carefully at the edges so you don't sand them too sharp or blunt the details with too coarse of an action. Some turners progress through finer grits and move to the oil finish, but I recommend the next step of sealing the wood.

Step 2: Sealing

Apply a liberal coat of sealer (Photo C), then wipe off the excess. If you've overlooked tool marks, rough areas, nicks or bumps, they're certain to reveal themselves. I prefer this to wiping with solvent because sealer doesn't disappear immediately.

Of all the sealers on the market, I prefer shellac. I've also had good luck with lacquer-based sealers such as Deft, which dries quickly and penetrates well.

The disadvantage of shellac as a sealer is that it can be gummy when sanding off and seems superficial in its penetration. I have tried water-based sealers and like the advantage of raising the grain of the wood. One disadvantage of a water-based sealer is that it requires extra drying time.

Step 3: Final power-sanding

After about 30 minutes or when the sealer is dry, it's time to remove it by more power sanding. I first use some 100-grit sheets of paper, cut into quarters, to remove most of the sealer by hand sanding (Photo D), which rapidly clogs the sandpaper. I then switch to Powerlock disks (100 or 150 grit), even if they quickly become filled. One trick is to lightly coat the disks with blackboard chalk before sanding the surface; the chalk makes it easier to remove the gunk with an abrasive cleaner.

Concentrate on the tool marks and rough grain, removing most blemishes and feathering in the sanding with the rest of the surface. This is done with the piece fixed in place with the lathe index pin (if available), and moving the piece round notch by index notch, and working each area. If you sense you've reached bare wood, reseal and repeat. Finally, turn on the lathe and sand the piece all over with 150-grit paper. Use chalk and sanding cleaner to keep the disk surface fresh.

Step 4: Oiling

After the 150-grit power disks, the surface should be almost bare wood—but it is sealed bare wood! The difference is at once apparent with the next step when you apply finishing oil (Photo E). The sealed surface comes up smooth and easy, whereas unsealed wood will soak up oil and look patchy.

I am a great fan of Danish oils. I'm sure many of the other oils out there will do. It is easy to mix your own penetrating oil varnish from 1 cup of any brand of poly-urethane varnish, 1 cup of naphtha solvent, and 1/3 cup boiled linseed oil. Mix and store in a plastic squeeze bottle (e.g. shampoo).

Don't worry about building up a finish since the sealer has gone some way to make this unnecessary. However, there is more sanding required by hand—first with 150-grit, then 220- and 400- or 600-grit paper (Photo F). The oil acts as a lubricant, thus is applied liberally. The sandpaper sheets quickly clog up with mud, which is wiped off the wood.

These oils are amber colored in general and give a rich glow to darker woods. On light woods—

Even on the interior, 3" disks are nimble.

With shellac, seal the grain.

After the shellac dries, sand again.

particularly maple—the oils often give an unsatisfactory grayish tinge to the wood.

I have recently experimented with water-based polyacrylic finishes at this stage. These dry quickly and are crystal clear, and leave the wood pale. Water-based finishes, which do seem to be improving all the time, are a viable alternative for some woods, although the "mud" is missing (water evaporates). This finish also works at the sealing stage.

After the 600-grit paper, the wood surface should be sensually smooth. Stroke it and feel for yourself. Inspect the piece under a bright light and look for the telltale scratch marks. You can usually remove these with lots of oil, 220-grit paper, and a circular action. You can feather out anything really bad with the power sander and 150-grit disks, although the oil and mud will make this only effective in small areas. Follow this with 220 and then 400 grit to match the rest of the surface. Part the bowl and finish the foot with the same look as the rest of it, then polish the whole piece at one time.

Step 5: Polishing & buffing

The oil takes about 1 week to dry. After a day or two, you can rub a second coat of oil into the wood if there are any dry patches (on end grain usually). Now is the time to hand-sand and touch-up if required. When dry, the wood has a nice smooth matte finish, which might be suitable for some pieces. In the Winter 1996 issue of American Woodturner, Alan Hollar discusses film finishes and why gloss is not always advisable on large spreading bowls (the reflecting light over-emphasizes the different surface planes).

However, for many bowls, hollow vessels, and small pieces, polishing is the mark of distinction. Polish—so hard to get right, so easily lost—indicates additional preparation whether it is on shoes, nails, or silverplate.

A coat of gloss varnish is rarely satisfactory. First, it is hard to get an even coat on the work piece since the varnish will run and sag on the slopes. Some turners would agree that it's the gloss varnish that looks artificial on a small object. From my observations, a gloss coat seems to obscure the wood grain and texture.

Polyurethane (oil- or water-based) makes a great tough film on tables and floors, but on turnings it looks like plastic (see Hollar's article). Some finishers recommend using a gloss varnish for its clarity, and then "knocking down the gloss" with fine steel wool and a lubricant (such as Murphy's oil soap) to produce a more subtle sheen.

Carnauba wax—widely used in furniture polishing—is a hard natural wax from the South American carnauba palm. Although not very serviceable as a work surface, the shine it produces is much admired.

Experienced turners often suggest that a wax polish be applied to the work while it is turning, using the lathe rotation for buffing. This works fine for spindles, but the problem with applying wax—or any finish—to a bowl while still on the lathe is that the polish can't reach the area of the parting cuts.

The popular Hut Polish, a mixture of wax and fine abrasives, is applied while the work is rotating, and then pressing a cloth against the spinning piece brings up the shine. This makes it superb for pen barrels, but since it does not reach the cut-off areas, not for other turnings. Moreover, any oil finish will not be dry and will disturb the final surface. So rather than apply one fine shine over 90 percent of the piece and complete the remainder a week later, leave the final polishing until later when the oil is dry.

E

Apply the oil finish directly to the piece.

F

Use oil as a lubricant with sandpaper.

For final polishing, the Beall System attracts many turners, and is my favorite. It includes three separate cloth wheels on a 1,750 rpm motor for three specialized polishes. The first polish is tripoli, a fine grit, which produces a dull shine. Next is white-diamond—a finer polish on a softer wheel. The third buffing—solid carnauba wax on a cotton wheel—is the final act. The heat of the turning melts the wax to a uniform film. The carnauba produces a semi-gloss surface with a deep shine that brings out the best of the wood. To restore the luster, rebuff the wax.

Conclusions

So there we have it—both the practice and the theory. Although by no means the only approach, these five steps produce predictable and satisfying results. I continue to follow this process after many years and several flirtations with alternatives.

Peter Smith is a 14-year AAW member who lives in Princeton, NJ.

The science of sanding and polishing

Shine on a surface comes from reflected light, and light is reflected from a uniform, smooth surface. Non-uniformity breaks up the light and disperses the light rays; light rays lose their coherence and thus the reflection diminishes.

A gloss varnish will cover a smooth surface with an even smoother film that is highly reflective when dry. To make that varnish matte, finely ground sand is added to the gloss base, which is what we stir from the bottom of the can, and the fine particles disperse the light rays. (These particles are much finer than can be sensed by touch.)

Sanding from 100 to 150 to 220 to 400 grit produces increasingly finer surface scratch marks that go beyond tactile sensations and provide increasingly uniform light reflections. This is why sanding down to these levels is so critical: No amounts of gloss varnish will coverup a poorly finished surface. But even 600-grit sandpaper is not enough for an unaided gloss. The Micro-mesh ultra-grits (6,000 and 12,000) add enough uniformity to the surface to provide shine.

Polishing goes beyond sandpaper by using finely ground minerals—rouge (iron oxide), diatomaceous earth (microscopic sea shells), ground pumice stone, and rottenstone (fine dust). These abrasives are by definition harder than the surface they abrade. They progressively produce a smoother and smoother surface to reflect light. The finest of these powders can gloss up a matte surface by reducing all non-uniformity and leaving scratch marks so fine they do not interfere with light rays.
Often these powders are managed in a liquid medium to provide lubrication and ease of use. Cream polishes, for example, suspend the abrasive in a wax/water emulsion.

Food-Safe Finishes

Understand finishes that play well with food

I doubt any issue has crippled woodturners as much as the controversy over food safety—that is, which finishes are safe to use on salad bowls and other objects that will come in contact with food.

So much confusion has been sown that many woodturners choose to "play it safe" and use walnut oil, mineral oil, or some form of raw linseed oil on their turnings, even though these finishes perform poorly because they don't cure well—or don't cure at all.

The shame is that this controversy ever got started in the first place. There has never been any evidence of a food-safety problem with any clear finish sold to woodworkers or woodturners. Only the widespread poor understanding of wood finishes in general has made this controversy possible.

Food-safe finishes
I believe the topic got off on the wrong path almost 30 years ago in *Fine Woodworking* magazine and is fueled by continued comments and cautions in much of the woodworking literature, especially articles written by and for woodturners. The existence of several brands of salad-bowl finishes also serves to perpetuate the controversy because these finishes are marketed as "food safe," implying that other finishes aren't.

Amazingly, the only legitimate issue in the entire food-safety discussion is the instructions on the cans of salad-bowl finish, which claim the finish is safe to eat off of before it has had time to cure adequately. More about that later.

Most likely you are familiar with the controversy over food safety. You may have even seen or heard my name cited as an advocate for all finishes being food safe (a lonely position even though it seems so obvious to me).

History lesson
To fully understand the issue surrounding food safety and finishes, you need to know a little history.

As you may remember, the 1970s was a time not only of explosive growth in woodworking but also of increased attention given to all sorts of environmental issues. In fact, the Environmental Protection Agency (EPA) was established in 1971.

One of the environmental issues concerned the existence of lead in paint. Lead compounds make pigments perform better, and many of the most effective pigments contained a large percentage of lead. The dust from these pigments,

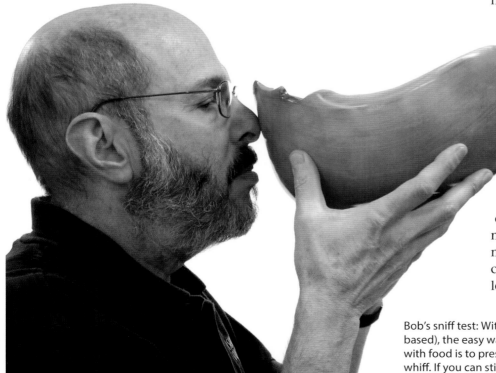

Bob's sniff test: With any solvent-based finish (not water-based), the easy way to tell if the finish is cured enough to use with food is to press your nose against the finish and take a whiff. If you can still smell solvent, the finish isn't cured. If you can't smell anything, the finish is cured and safe.

AW 23:1, p36

which resembles finely ground earth in its consistency, would settle on floors, get on children's hands, and then into their mouths. Some children chewed on paint chips containing the sweet-tasting lead pigments.

When ingested, lead causes mental and developmental problems in humans, especially in children whose brains are still maturing. So there was a widespread interest in removing lead from paint pigments.

Lead compounds were also used in very small amounts (usually less than half of 1 percent of the total solids) as a drier in oils, varnishes, and oil paints. (Driers are catalysts that speed the introduction of oxygen and thus the curing of these coatings.) This amount of lead wasn't enough to be a major concern like lead in pigments, but lead in driers was included in the efforts to remove all lead from consumer coatings.

The Consumer Products Safety Commission (CPSC) officially accomplished this in 1978, though most paint manufacturers had removed the lead from products several decades earlier.

You can read the CPSC directive on the Web by going to the AAW website and following the link to woodturner.org/foodsafe.pdf.

With the exceptions noted in this directive, including certain artists' paints, some industrial and agricultural coatings, and coatings on the backs of mirrors, paints and clear finishes no longer contain lead, or at least not more than a trace, .06 percent, or .0006 of the total solids, being the upper limit permitted The specialized coatings that still contain lead in greater amounts are required to state this on the label.

Thus, since 1978 there has been no reason to avoid using any oil or varnish finish (or consumer oil-based paint, for that matter) because of fear of lead.

All clear finishes are safe to use on objects that come in contact with food. The finish on this bowl is wiping varnish—varnish thinned about 50 percent with mineral spirits to make it easy to apply. Several coats of wiping varnish produce a very nice sheen, slight yellowing, and excellent water and scratch resistance.

The finish on this hand-carved spoon is walnut oil, a finish that is popular with woodworkers who have been led to believe there is a food-safety issue. Walnut oil doesn't cure well so it leaves the spoon looking dull.

Nonlead driers

Oils, varnishes, and oil paints continued, and continue now, to contain other metal driers because these are necessary for the coatings to cure within a reasonable time. These driers include salts of cobalt, manganese, and zirconium—bad-sounding stuff. And the bad "sound," rather than any serious research or thought, was and is responsible for creating the controversy about food-safe finishes.

It's too easy for someone without any technical knowledge to sound credible making statements such as, "I wouldn't eat off a finish that contains cobalt!" Or, "Why take the chance? You never know what we might learn about these substances in the future."

In fact, the U.S. Food and Drug Administration (FDA) considers these and other nonlead driers to be safe for food contact when used in coatings. Not only is the amount of drier in a coating tiny compared to the amount of pigment in paint, but also the drier is totally encased in the crosslinked finish once it has cured. Even if you were to eat a chip of a clear finish, it would simply pass through your system like any other plastic material, without causing any harm.

You can read the FDA regulations for coatings by Googling "21CFR175.300" and clicking on the current top link. For the approved driers, scroll to page 168 and then to (xxii). You'll find all the driers, which are salts of the various metals, commonly used in consumer finishes.

Keep in mind that the FDA lists the ingredients that can be used safely in food-contact coatings, but it does not "approve" the coatings themselves. Manufacturers are

Both of these brands of salad-bowl finish are regular alkyd varnish thinned about 50 percent with mineral spirits. They contain metal driers from the same FDA list as do all varnishes (otherwise, they wouldn't dry). For almost three decades woodworking books and magazines have cautioned against using varnishes (and also boiled linseed oil) because of the included toxic driers, while simultaneously recommending the use of these salad bowl finishes as safe. This contradiction alone should make you question the validity of the food-safety issue in choosing a finish.

responsible for formulating these coatings so they cure properly.

But salad-bowl finishes are simply thinned varnish, what I call a wiping varnish. They contain driers from the same FDA list, as do all varnishes on the market.

In the early 1990s, when I was researching my book on woodworking finishes, I called Behlen, the principal manufacturer of salad-bowl finish at the time, to ask how the company could market their finish as food safe when it must contain driers. The discussion went something like this:

"Of course, Bob, our Salad Bowl Finish contains driers. How else would it cure?"

"But... but," I stammered, "how can you call it 'food safe?'"

"Because it is. All varnishes are food safe. It's just a marketing situation. There's a big market for food-safe varnishes, so we simply label our varnish as such. We sell lots of this finish."

Obviously, marketing worked. But here's the most incredible assertion of all. The two national

brands of salad-bowl finish currently available, Behlen and General Finishes, both claim on their containers that the finish is safe to eat off of after 72 hours—three days.

Bob's sniff test

I suggest a simple test. Apply one or two coats of either product to wood and let the finish cure for three days in a warm room. Then put your nose against the finish and take a whiff.

Would you really eat off this surface? There's still paint thinner coming out! The finish isn't cured. At the very least, it will affect the taste of the food.

Wait until you can't smell any finish anymore. Then it's safe.

Remember, the FDA regulation requires not only that the ingredients used come from their list but that the finish also must be cured.

Conclusion

It's not possible to prove a negative. You can't prove, for example, that milk doesn't cause any sort of health problem and is totally safe (beyond a doubt). You can only assume it

doesn't because there is absolutely no evidence it does.

The same is true for wood finishes that have fully cured. You can't prove that no harm can come from eating off them. But here again, there's absolutely no evidence that harm does come.

Until someone can actually produce evidence beyond the gratuitous "play-it-safe" warnings that a commercially available clear finish causes some type of harm, let's choose a finish for salad bowls and other eating utensils the same way we choose a finish for other wood objects: for water and scratch resistance, color, and ease of application.

Let's put the issue of food safety to rest and move on.

Bob Flexner, *considered woodworking's premier finishing expert, is the author of the best seller,* Understanding Wood Finishing. *His most recent book is* Wood Finishing 101. *He currently resides in Norman, OK.*

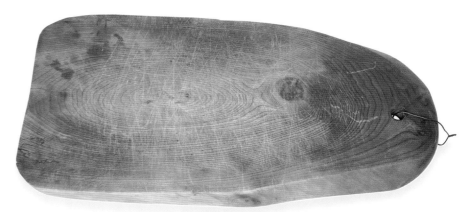

Cutting boards are cut on, of course, which defeats the purpose of using any finish to make them look nicer. In my opinion it's best to leave them unfinished unless you are selling them and find you can improve sales with a finish. Don't make the cutting boards look too nice, though, or people won't buy them because they won't want to mess them up.

Nice Turners Finish Last

Expert finishing advice from a seasoned turner

When it comes to the magic moment of applying a finish to a turned piece of wood, most turners reach for an oil-based product. Oil-based finishes are well suited for turnings because they are relatively forgiving in their behavior and the first coat can often be applied while the piece is on the lathe. Oil finishes enhance grain contrast and bring depth and warmth to wood, contributing to the aesthetic gratification we all get from the medium. But narrow your choices down to an "oil-based finish" and you will still be faced with a bewildering number of options. Add in the abundance of misleading information from finish manufacturers, and it is no wonder many turners settle on one or two options and use those without a lot of further thought. If a perfect finish existed, we would all be using it. The choice of finish is almost always a compromise, and it is good to know the tradeoffs you are accepting.

Types of oils

To be suitable for finishing, oil should cure after it is applied to wood. Curing is a chemical reaction mediated by oxygen that results in the cross-linking of fatty acids in the oil. The result is a change in state from fluid to a solid polymer of interlinked molecules. But not all oils cure. In fact, oils can be classified into one of three groups: non-curing, semi-curing, and curing.

Non-curing oils include mineral oil, peanut oil, and olive oil. Applied to wood, these oils remain viscous and can transfer to other surfaces (hands, tablecloth, furniture), will limit options for repair (they inhibit glue adhesion), and in the case of natural oils, potentially turn rancid and impart undesirable odors or flavors. Because they never harden, they provide no protection from physical damage.

Semi-curing oils include corn, sesame, soybean, safflower, and sometimes walnut oil. In their raw form, these oils partially cure and remain soft. Manufacturers incorporate some of these oils into wood finishes with the addition of drying agents, thinners, resins, or heat treatment, all of which speed curing and help produce a harder finish. This is also our first opportunity for confusion. Walnut oil is sometimes semi-curing and sometimes a curing oil. This is probably because the concentration of the polyunsaturated fats that moderate curing may vary depending on growing conditions and processing. Walnut oil for finishing should contain enough of the fats to make it a curing oil. When these oils are destined for the grocery store, manufacturers include additives to inhibit curing to extend shelf life. Purchasing from the grocery store moves these oils into the non-curing category.

Curing oils include linseed, tung, and walnut oil. Applied to a porous surface, all of these oils cure to a matte finish. They also remain relatively soft in comparison with other finish options such as varnish.

Types of oil finishes

Raw oil

Raw oil is rarely applied to woodturnings because it cures slowly—on a time scale of days-(walnut, tung) to-months (linseed). Raw oils do not build a film surface on the wood, and therefore offer negligible protection against physical damage. Linseed oil imparts a yellow tone and will continue to yellow with age. Tung oil imparts some color to wood but less than linseed oil, and its color changes little with age. Walnut oil imparts the least color and it is non-yellowing. Tung oil provides some water resistance after about six coats; walnut oil offers little water resistance; linseed oil offers the least. These characteristics tend to accompany these oils as they are combined with other products or are processed to improve their application and finishing qualities. The greatest utility for these oils in the turner's shop is that they constitute the basic ingredient for creating your own finish.

Thinned oils

Thinning linseed, tung, or walnut oil with solvent makes an easily applied wipe- or brush-on finish that cures quickly. This approach to finishing is simple, inexpensive, and produces a matte finish *(Photo*

AW 29:1, p42

1). Successive coats are easy to apply, and waiting about a day between coats assures adequate curing between applications. This is my preference for production pieces, and I often apply only one coat of finish with the understanding the user will soon need to oil the piece if the object is used for food service.

The first coat of thinned oil can be applied on the lathe. A shop towel held against the rotating work will generate heat to speed the rate of curing. I often follow the oil with a paste wax. This provides luster and modest protection for the piece as it is handled in a gallery or craft show. Be aware that wax can trap moisture and encourage mold.

Boiled linseed oil

Once upon a time, linseed oil was boiled to hasten its curing rate. These days, manufacturers blend linseed oil with metallic driers to achieve the same objective, retaining the name despite the absence of boiling. More coats can be applied in a far shorter time, but the result is still a soft finish that offers negligible water resistance.

Polymerized oil

The curing process can be hastened by heating raw oil to about 500°F (260°C) in the absence of oxygen to produce polymerized oil. So modified, these oils look and behave more like varnish than raw oil. Polymerized oil cures quickly, can be thinned for easier application, will build a surface film, and is well suited for turned objects. Mahoney's Utility Finish is a walnut oil product that appears to be at least partially polymerized during the manufacturing process, improving its curing rate. Lee Valley

Oil finishes are forgiving to apply: pour (or wipe) them on and remove the excess oil before the finish begins to cure.

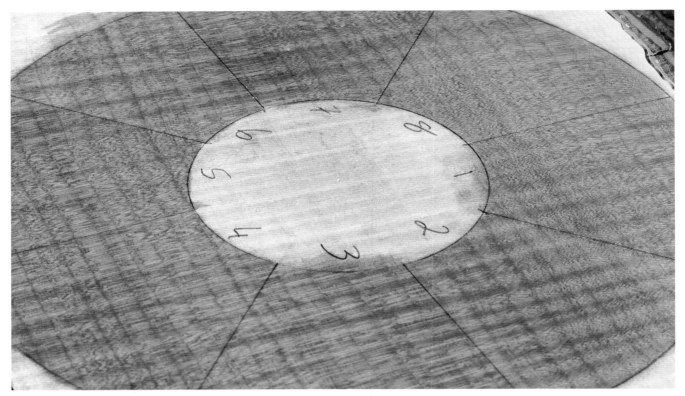

Six coats of eight finishes applied to curly maple. (1) Boiled linseed oil (3) walnut oil and (6) Watco Danish Oil show little or no build and a matte surface. (2) Thinned tung oil and (4) polymerized tung oil are beginning to build a semi-gloss sheen. (7) Minwax Antique Oil Finish and (8) Formby's Tung Oil Finish show a semi-gloss surface. (5) The shopmade thinned oil/varnish blend shows the most surface build and a gloss surface.

markets polymerized tung oil as well as raw walnut oil, and provides directions for heating the latter prior to application to speed curing.

Oil/varnish blend

Manufacturers create varnish by heating oil combined with a synthetic resin. The resulting product is no longer oil, but a new substance with its own properties that make it one of the most durable finishes, but also challenging to apply well. Manufacturers blend oil with varnish to capture some of the beneficial properties of each. Minwax's Antique Oil Finish, Tung Oil Finish, and Watco's and Deft's Danish Oil finishes are four readily available oil/varnish blends.

Most of these products allow subsequent applications in 8 to 24 hours. Each gives a slightly different appearance to the finished wood, probably due to the quantity of resins in the varnish, and the type of oil each manufacturer uses. Some of these products will build a surface film after numerous applications, while others show little or no build after five applications. Imaginative marketing creates a lot of confusion in this and the wiping-varnish categories. Danish oil contains no Danes, but is a blend of linseed oil and varnish. Lax regulation permits a product to be labeled "tung oil finish" (for example), yet contain no tung oil at all.

Wiping varnish

Finish guru Bob Flexner defined this category of finish to distinguish products combining varnish and thinner. The products are not truly oils, but are often marketed as such. Products in this category include Formby's Tung Oil Finish, Waterlox Original Formula, and General Finishes Salad Bowl Finish. These finishes build a surface film, creating a satin or glossy surface. If you wish to achieve a varnished look, this is a good way to go. While glossy surfaces may attract buyers, they create a maintenance challenge for non-woodworkers when the film surface becomes worn or damaged, and worn items may get relegated to the next yard sale.

The manufacturers' goal here, as with oil/varnish blends, is to make these products easier than varnish alone to apply. On non-horizontal surfaces, these finishes need a thin application to prevent sags or drips, thus requiring more applications to build depth. These finishes are dust magnets before they cure, and invariably result in

After ten years and about a dozen maintenance coats of thinned tung oil, my fruitwood rolling pin remains a pleasure to use.

Five coats of an oil/varnish blend and a surface film has begun to build a semi-gloss surface on this quilted-walnut bowl.

captured dust and lint. Sanding lightly between applications with 320-grit abrasive smoothes the surface, but the last finish application must be kept dust-free until it cures.

Choosing an oil finish

I have developed a decision-making process that helps me narrow finish options before I start work on a piece. I first consider how the piece will be used—is it utilitarian or decorative? For utility ware, I stick with one or two coats of thinned oil and a coat of paste wax. Buyers will readily understand that basic care requirements come with owning treenware. A thinned-oil finish is easily maintained by a non-woodworker.

Because decorative pieces will receive no exposure to water and only an occasional dusting, any oil-based finish will work, so other factors come into play. What sort of surface appearance do I want to achieve? Thinned oil produces a matte finish, polymerized oil and some oil/varnish finishes can build a film surface that is generally in the semi-gloss range, and wiping varnish can build to a glossy finish

with noticeable depth, but may also leave wood looking like plastic.

Will there be voids in the completed piece (typical of burls), or natural bark inclusions or a bark rim? Does the wood contain spalt that will soak up finish at a different rate? Does the wood have large pores like oak? Getting an even finish on a porous surface is a challenge, especially with a film-building finish. I tend to reach for an oil/varnish blend in this situation for a little more luster than thinned oil and easy application over bark or in voids. Spalted wood can turn a sickly yellow color when finished with oil; many turners reach for an alternative, including buffing with wax, applying a water-based finish, or oiling only the solid wood surrounding the spalt.

How much time can I invest in this piece? If I am making a piece for market, I consider the potential return on my investment in time and materials—the quicker the finish, the greater the return on investment. But this must be balanced against visual appeal for the buyer and my own sense of aesthetics. In increasing order of time and expense required, oil-

based finishes go from thinned oil, to oil/varnish and polymerized oil, to wiping varnish.

Domestic or tropical hardwood? Many tropical hardwoods contain non-curing oils that foil our finishes, inhibiting curing and leaving the wood surface gummy. The best alternative may be no applied finish. Many of these species can be brought to a beautiful natural finish simply by buffing. A coat of paste wax will offer some additional protection. Another trick for oily timbers is to first apply naphtha or acetone to remove the natural oils from the surface of the wood, and immediately follow up with an application of finish. I tend to reach for an oil/varnish blend or polymerized oil in this situation— both cure fairly quickly, and I hope before those natural oils rise to the surface again!

Finally, I recommend two exercises to improve understanding of finishing options. If you are curious about how a finish will cure, take a piece of glass or a metal lid and apply a few drops of finish. Do this with several different finishes on the same surface (label them), and then give them a few days to cure. The cured drops can be tested with a nail to see how hard they have become. Another trick is to create a finished surface on a turning before reaching the final dimensions. To this surface, I apply a few of my finish options in strips that go all the way around the form. This lets me evaluate how each finish will look on both sidegrain and endgrain. After making a decision, I carry on with turning, removing the treated fibers.

Applying an oil-based finish

Application of oil-based finishes is simple and forgiving, which is a big part of their appeal. Most manufacturers recommend a wipe-on/wipe-off process with a specified waiting period before recoating. The idea is to liberally coat the surface of the piece, allow five to 10 minutes for the liquid to enter wood pores and saturate fibers, and

remove the excess before it becomes gummy. The curing piece should be checked periodically and any oil bleeding out of the pores should be wiped away. Multiple coats increase build and any protective qualities the finish offers.

Food safety

This is another arena in which misleading marketing and myth rule supreme. All finishes are safe for food contact after they have cured, which occurs in 30 days or less. To determine if a finish has cured, plant your nose against the finished surface and inhale. If you can smell the finish, it has not cured. The Food and Drug Administration (FDA) thoroughly addresses food safety and finishes in a bulletin that is worth printing and keeping on hand, especially if you market your work (www. accessdata.fda.gov/scripts/

cdrh/cfdocs/cfcfr/CFRSearch. cfm?FR=175.300).

A related topic is the concern over the potential allergenic properties of nut oils. Again, this concern is covered under the FDA's consideration of food safety. Proteins in nuts can cause an allergic response. These proteins are fairly delicate and exposure to high heat or organic solvents will modify them. The cross-linking that occurs during curing is the decisive step. Cross-linking changes the fundamental nature of the proteins, making them unavailable to react with other molecules, including the receptors in the human body that spark allergies.

Shop safety

Linseed, tung, and walnut oils, limonene, and mineral spirits are all relatively mild oils or solvents. Basic handling precautions are still warranted because these

The magic moment—when the first coat of finish pops the grain and all the promises of beauty are fulfilled.

products are concentrated, and sensitization can come from cumulative exposure. Solvent-resistant gloves, eye protection, and a fresh air supply are minimum requirements. Applying commercial finishes containing stronger solvents should include a respirator that filters organic vapors.

Oils, solvents, and waxes are flammable. Take extra care disposing of oil-soaked rags as rapid oxidation can cause spontaneous combustion. Deposit oiled rags in a water-filled can or lay them out flat to cure before discarding.

Don McIvor is a full-time turner and artist living in Washington. He can be reached through his website, mcivorwoodworks.com.

Shopmade finishes

Blending my own finishes allows me to use ingredients that are relatively benign, minimizing exposure to harsh chemicals. I can control the ratio of the components, affecting the rate of curing or surface build of the finish. My personal preference is for tung oil (water resistance, durability, ready availability). For a solvent I use limonene (or citrus solvent, *not* citra solve—a finish stripper), which is pressed from orange peels. Experiment by substituting raw walnut or linseed oil, or use mineral spirits or turpentine instead of limonene.

Thinned oil
1 part raw oil
1 part solvent

This is a great finish for treenware. With tung oil as a base I also use it on wood trim, floors, natural tile, and concrete countertops. It is versatile! The shelf life is at least six months, although I never keep it on hand that long. Label the container.

Thinned oil/varnish
1 part raw oil
1 part solvent
1 part satin or gloss varnish

This finish is easily applied with a shop towel, cloth, or varnish brush, and readily builds a surface film. The oil/varnish ratio can be altered to change application qualities or build properties. My biggest challenges are keeping dust out of the finish before it cures, and the short shelf life. I mix only what I can use in 24 hours.

Paste wax
2oz (59ml) raw oil
0.07oz (2g) carnauba wax
0.6oz (17g) beeswax
2oz (59ml) solvent

This recipe requires heating flammable ingredients! Use low heat and a double boiler in the **absence of a flame** and do not leave the pot unattended. Gently heat the wax and oil in a sacrificial pot until the wax has melted; remove from heat and stir in the solvent. Pour this mixture into a small, large-mouth container (a cosmetics jar works well) and let cool. Label the jar. Varying the ratio of waxes to oil/ solvent changes the consistency of the product. Shelf life is about four months.

Section 4: Practical Projects

Show us a man who never makes a mistake and we will show you a man who never makes anything. —Herman Lincoln Wayland

Learning how to turn wood is like acquiring most skills: you need to practice. And what better way to practice than to make stuff—especially things you can use or give as gifts, such as bowls, doorknobs, and Christmas ornaments? Each of the projects in this section is designed to introduce new skills while developing the ones you've already acquired. By tackling each one, you'll learn the best methods, among others, to hold your work onto the lathe, how to master the art of center drilling and precise turning, and how to turn multiples to improve your design eye and tool control. In the end, no matter what you make, every turning project will build your skills at the lathe. But, while you'll surely make mistakes, you'll definitely have a lot of fun. So start turning, and turn some more.

Honey Dipper is a Perfect First Project

Develop key skills as you turn a handsome kitchen classic

Here's a sweet way to introduce turning skills to students.

Because so many young woodturners like to see quick results for their efforts, the honey dipper is a favorite first-time project. Your novice woodturner will learn how to mount the material, basic tool usage, and a little about sanding and finishing. It also allows the turner a fair amount of creativity in the design of the project. With success practically guaranteed, your student will beg to complete another project.

These how-to instructions include additional comments you may direct to a new woodturner regarding safety measures and good turning habits.

Get started

For lathe tools, you'll need a ¾" or 1¼" spindle roughing gouge, a thin (¹⁄₁₆") parting tool, and a ⅜" spindle gouge. A centerfinder, mini-drive center, and cup center are all helpful but not necessary.

For turning stock, choose a close-grain hardwood that takes detail well with little or no tear-out. The honey dippers shown on these pages were turned from 8"-long squares of 5/4 (1¹⁄₁₆" thick) hard maple (also known as sugar maple). The 5/4 stock gives you a little more room for design opportunities.

Mount the turning square

Use a centerfinder to locate and mark the center on each end of the blank.

Put a dimple at the center of each end with an awl or centerpunch.

Remove the drive center from the spindle and use a mallet or dead blow mallet to drive the center into one end of the stock. Return the drive center, with the blank attached, to the spindle. Bring up the tailstock with live center to the opposite end of the blank. Lock the tailstock in place and advance the quill to engage the blank. Lock the quill in place.

Adjust the tool rest to a position just below the centerline and about ¼" away from the corners of the blank. Always rotate the workpiece by hand before starting the machine to check for proper clearance. Never move the tool rest with the lathe running.

Adjust turning speed

Let's assume students will be turning at a mini-lathe with step pulleys. You should always stop the machine, unplug it, and move the belt to the proper pulley, then plug in the machine and proceed with the turning project.

You can safely turn this project at about 1800 rpm. With experience, you can turn a spindle this size at up to 3000 rpm. It is best to start out slowly and gain confidence before increasing the speed.

Rough out the blank

Begin turning with a spindle roughing gouge. Place the gouge on

AW 21:2, p38

the tool rest near the tailstock with the bevel above the workpiece. Lift the handle until the bevel comes into contact with the workpiece. Once the cutting edge engages the workpiece, roll the tool to the right to cut the corners off the end of the square stock while maintaining bevel contact.

Repeat the process several more times, each time beginning further to the left of the previous initial cut, until only 1" or 2" of the left end of the block is untouched.

Next, start at the left end of the workpiece and repeat the cutting process, rolling the tool to the left with each cut until the workpiece is fully rounded. Make a light pass in each direction the length of the

tool rest to leave a relatively smooth cylinder. Stop the machine and check that all flat surfaces of the square have been removed.

Cut grooves

With a thin parting tool, make grooves in the right end of the workpiece. Start about ¾" from the end of the workpiece and make five evenly spaced grooves to hold honey. The grooves should be approximately ¼" deep.

As with all turning tools, first place the parting tool on the tool rest with the bevel above the workpiece. Gently lift the handle to engage the cutting edge and push forward to make the grooves ¼" deep. Remember to keep the parting tool in a vertical position

and perpendicular to the axis of the lathe.

Design the handle

After cutting the grooves, you can return to the spindle roughing gouge to finish shaping your honey dipper. Add a little shape to the working end of your dipper and start thinning the handle end. The smallest diameter should be just to the left of the grooves. Thin the area down to the desired diameter, working first from the right and then from the left. Remember to always cut downhill (from large diameter to small diameter) on spindle work. Continue with the spindle roughing gouge and shape the rest of the handle.

Pare down and part off

Starting at the tailstock end of the workpiece, use a 3/8" spindle gouge

to pare down the ends of the honey dipper. Turn the gouge to 90 degrees with the flute facing the direction of the cut. Lift the handle and push the cutting edge into the workpiece. Rotate the tool to the opposite direction and repeat until the stock is reduced to about ¼" diameter. Move to the other end of the workpiece and pare it down to ¼".

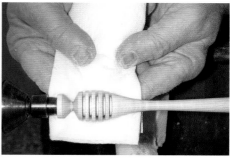

Sand and finish

You must sand the honey dipper before separating it from the lathe. Start with 150 grit and finish with 220-grit sandpaper.

Use paper towels to apply a coat of mineral oil and burnish it into the wood. At the lathe, I never use rags. A single thread from a rag can wrap around your finger in a split second, causing serious injury.

Add a light coat of beeswax and buff with paper towels.

Separate the ends

After buffing, continue to pare down each end of the honey dipper with the 3/8" spindle gouge. Reduce both ends down to just under 1/8", then cut through the right end while cradling the honey dipper in the left hand. Reach under your left forearm and separate the left end from

the lathe.

Sand and finish the tiny nibs on each end of the honey dipper and find yourself a pot of honey and a fresh, warm biscuit.

Egg Cup Introduces End-Grain Hollowing

Mastering this daunting skill is easier than you think

Humpty Dumpty sat on a wall,
Humpty Dumpty had a great fall...NOT!
If only Humpty Dumpty
had been in an egg cup,
this never would
have happened!

Photo: John Hetherington

The egg cup is an ideal project to develop turning skills and have a little fun at the same time.

During the past 25-plus years, The Great Egg Cup Race at the Utah Woodturning Symposium has become a spectacle of sorts for woodturners from all over the world. The event matches individuals and duos of woodturners against each other and the clock to see who or what team can out-turn the rest. Richard Raffan holds the record—an amazing 18 seconds.

According to English turner Bill Jones, "You can watch heaps of really good wood being totally ruined by some of the world's finest woodturners!"

I have always avoided the temptation of this event. I just hate to ruin good wood! Most of the end products just barely resemble what we know as an egg cup, but everyone seems to enjoy watching world-class turners make fools of themselves.

An egg cup is a worthy project for both beginners and intermediate turners. In addition to incorporating spindle technique into a practical project, it introduces end-grain turning without the pressure of turning a lid (as many boxes require).

Many new woodturning students enjoy choosing a profile or coming up with their own design. Several profiles are shown.

How to photos: Cathy Wike-Cook

AW 21:2, p40

Get started

This project requires three lathe tools: a ¾" or 1¼" spindle roughing gouge, a ⅜" spindle gouge, and a parting tool. In the Youth Turning Room, we'll turn with the smaller ¾" spindle roughing gouge.

You may also prefer to make finishing cuts with a roundnose scraper. You will also need a scroll chuck to hold the blank for end-grain hollowing.

For turning stock, select a 4½"-long piece of 2½"-square soft maple.

Prepare the blanks

With a straightedge or center-finder, locate the centers on each end of the blank. Use an awl or centerpunch to make a dimple at each center. With a mallet, tap the drive center into one end of the blank and place the drive center into the spindle of the lathe.

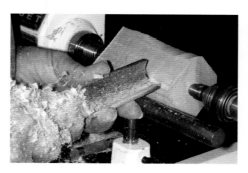

What about lefties?

It's believed that about 10% of the population is left-handed. Even though many right-handed turners learn to become ambidextrous at the lathe (and certainly capable of working to the left and right), there's always a little fear the first time you assist a left-handed student. Buck up!

Here are three suggestions:

- Teach students to use the right hand as the back hand.

- Assure the leftie student that he or she is a step ahead of right-handed students because of the ambidextrous skills most lefties acquire in this right-handed world.

- Remind all your students that turning is about control—not strength

—*Nick Cook*

Bring up the tailstock with the live center to the other end of the blank. Lock the tailstock in place and turn the hand wheel to apply pressure to the end of the blank. Lock the quill in place.

Place the tool rest parallel to the blank, about ¼" from the corners and just below the centerline. Lock the tool rest in place and rotate the spindle by hand before turning on the lathe.

Turn the egg cup

Set the lathe speed at 1000 rpm and turn on the machine. Use a spindle roughing gouge to turn the square down to a cylinder, as shown above. With a parting tool, turn a ¼×21/8"

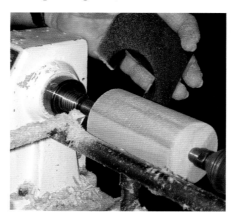

tenon at one end of the blank. A gauge like the one shown *below* will speed the sizing. Remove the blank from between centers and remove the drive center from the spindle. Slide the tailstock to the right end of the bed and remove the live center.

Mount the blank in the chuck and screw the chuck onto the spindle. Position the tool rest parallel to the blank, ¼" away and just below the centerline.

Lock the tool rest in place and rotate the spindle by hand to ensure clearance.

Turn on the lathe and make a peeling cut across the end of the blank with the spindle gouge.

Stop the lathe, measure from the right end back to 4", and make a mark. Make another mark at 2". Start the lathe and make a ¼"-deep parting cut at each mark.

The center mark defines where the bowl meets the stem, and the left mark defines the bottom of the finished egg cup.

Now, shape the outside of the egg-cup bowl. Use the spindle gouge to create your own details at the rim of the bowl and at the base of the bowl. Leave enough stock at

the bottom of the bowl to support hollowing the interior. *On the facing page* are 10 profiles for idea starters.

Experience end grain

Stop the lathe and position the tool rest across the end of the blank and about ¼" below the center. Hold the spindle gouge level and perpendicular to the end of the blank and push the tip of the tool about ¼" into the end grain.

Next, rotate the flute of the gouge to about 45 degrees to the left and push the handle to the right. This will push the tip of the tool toward the rim of the blank. Work to within ¼" of the rim (about 1½" inside diameter). Repeat until you reach a depth of 1½" to 1¾". If necessary, refine the surface with a roundnose scraper. Aim for a uniform wall thickness of ¼".

Reposition the tool rest to fine-tune the outside of the egg cup. Use the parting tool to reduce the top of the stem down to the finished diameter. Create transition details with the ⅜" spindle gouge.

Continue turning with the spindle gouge to reduce the rest of

the stem to the desired diameter and detail the foot of the egg cup.

Sand and finish

Before parting the egg cup from the chuck, sand and finish all exposed surfaces.

Always remove the tool rest before sanding at the lathe. Start with 150-grit sandpaper and finish with 220 grit. Remove all sanding dust with a paper towel.

With the lathe turned off, apply urethane oil with a paper towel to all exposed surfaces. Allow the oil to penetrate for 5 to 10 minutes, then wipe off the excess. Turn on the lathe and burnish the surfaces with a clean, dry paper towel.

Use the parting tool to separate the egg cup from the waste in the chuck. Make the cut slightly angled toward the top of the cup to create a hollow in the bottom.

Sand the bottom by hand and apply oil.

---

*A founding member of the AAW, **Nick Cook** is a frequent contributor to* American Woodturner *and lives in Marietta, GA where he owns and operates his studio. Visit Nick at www.nickcookwoodturner.com.*

Take the fear out of catches

Part of the woodturning learning curve is experiencing catches and learning tool control to avoid them. You can help your turning student overcome the fear of catches by selecting a cup drive (also known as a dead cup center or safe driver) for spindle projects. And it's not just for beginners!

Instead of a nasty catch, a cup drive—when coupled with light tailstock pressure—will stop the spindle. This method also minimizes damage to the turning stock.

The cup drive allows the turner to take a piece on and off the lathe without centering problems and reduces the probability of a piece being thrown off the lathe.

Letter Opener: A Skill-Builder that Makes a Fine Gift

Lend a personal touch to an old office standby

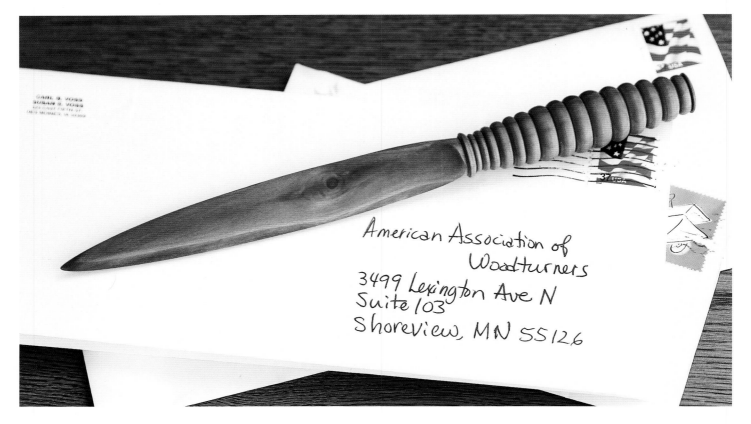

A letter opener is a favorite project in beginner classes I teach. And because it's an ideal project to develop skew skills, I encourage turners to detail the entire beaded handle using only a skew chisel.

For turning stock, I look for a closed grain wood that takes a good edge. Hard maple (plain, birdseye, or curly), cherry, apple, pear, plum, Osage orange and dogwood make good choices from domestic stock. Among exotic woods, fine options include cocobolo, boxwood, goncalo alves, tulipwood, and kingwood.

The size is somewhat a design question of proportions as well as a preference for what would feel good in the hand of the user. Turn several prototypes to work out the balance, look, and feel. I have settled on a 9" overall length and ⅞" at its greatest diameter. The rough blank should be slightly larger in diameter and about 10" in length.

Turn the opener

After making a cylinder (using either a roughing gouge or skew chisel), determine the handle length. I normally fit it to my hand, so the handle in this case was about 4" long. The handle detailing is what moves this project from simple to challenging.

Design the handle with an arching form—probably with a bead at the blade end and some finishing detail for the end of the handle. For added handle detail, try adding a series of beads or coves with either a ⅜" detailing gouge or ½" skew chisel. It is often more interesting to vary the size of these details rather than making them all exactly the same.

Finalize the handle area by sanding to at least 220 grit. For the blade area, I usually turn with a greater diameter in the middle and taper towards the handle and the tip, which adds visual interest.

AW 19:2, p34

Getting Started in Woodturning

Shape the blade

Rather than rough-shape the blade on a bandsaw, I prefer the safer route of sanding the blade into its final shape using the lathe. A small disc sander works quite well for this operation. A 5" ply-wood disc mounted on a faceplate or in a chuck makes for a quick sanding system, as does a 5" hard rubber disc mounted in a Jacobs-style chuck in the headstock.

I initially shape the blade with 80 grit, followed by 100, 120, 150, 180, and 220 grits. The basic shape is one of being thicker in the centerline of the blade and tapering to the two cutting edges. Strive for a sharp edge but one that is not so fragile and prone to chipping. The end of the blade needs to taper to a point that is easy to insert into the end of an envelope. Complete the final sanding by hand.

Now, apply finish

Again, several options are possible depending on the desired look and level of durability. For a film-type finish, pre-catalyzed lacquer (sold as melamine in turning-supply catalogues) produces a tough finish.

With a ½" skew, roll large beads with the short point and ¼" or smaller beads with the long point.

To shape the blade, the lathe becomes a sander. Mount a 5"-diameter plywood disc in a chuck or on a faceplate.

If using this finish, apply to the handle area on the lathe, then finish the blade by hand after the forming and sanding process.

For an oil finish, be sure and choose one that dries thoroughly. Good choices include pure tung oil, Watco, Deftoil, and Nordic oil. I recommend avoiding these oil finishes on light-colored woods unless you don't mind the amber color that the finish imparts.

On the Osage orange opener shown, I applied a coat of 100 percent pure tung oil every other day until I had completed four coats

(light coats, short soaking time, dried off completely, and sanded with 320 grit between coats). After about one week, I lightly buffed the opener with a cotton wheel on a lathe arbor.

A past President of the AAW and an Honorary Lifetime Member, **Alan Lacer** *has spent four decades as a turner, instructor, and contributing editor to* American Woodturner. *Visit Alan at www.woodturninglearn.net.*

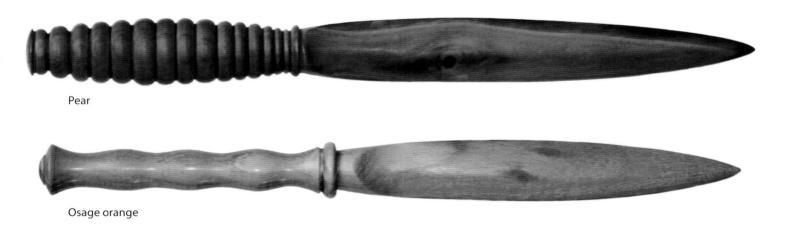

Pear

Osage orange

Basic Wooden Bowl

Learn these simple techniques for unlimited possibilities

A friend recently asked me for a bowl-turning lesson, but first wanted to understand the complete process. She wanted to know what equipment she might need to add to her basic turning setup, and what expenditures she could postpone or avoid. In particular, did she really have to spring for a scroll chuck before she had even tried bowl turning? I went digging through my woodturning literature but came up dry. I asked Ted Rasmussen, a retired technology teacher from rural Pennsylvania where shop class still matters, for a beginner lesson in turning a bowl without a big investment in special gear.

The shining path, Ted explained, would produce a bowl with no visible trace of its making (*Photo 1*) by using a pair of faceplates, glueblocks, and a shopmade jam chuck (*Photo 2*). For this lesson, we will skip finishing since that is an entire topic on its own. Here is the sequence Ted used:

- Lay out the blank, bandsaw it round, and screw a faceplate onto what will be the top of the bowl.
- Thread the faceplate onto the headstock spindle. Use your choice of scrapers and bowl gouges to flatten the foot and shape the outside of the bowl. Sand the outside.
- Glue a small disk of wood onto the foot and screw a faceplate onto this glueblock.
- Remount the blank on the lathe so you can excavate and sand the inside of the bowl.
- Turn a jam chuck to fit the rim of the bowl.

1

You, too, can turn a beautiful bowl like this with a few tools and a pair of low-tech faceplates on a midi-lathe—no need for a scroll chuck or a big bowl-turning lathe.

2

The jam chuck is a disk of softwood turned to fit the rim of the bowl. To mount a jam chuck or glueblock onto a faceplate, use substantial wood screws such as No. 14. Avoid thin drywall screws, as they will not hold and might break.

3

(L to R) A spearpoint tool and three scrapers, large and small bowl gouges, and a parting tool.

AW 29:4, p36

- Reverse the bowl one more time by fitting it over the jam chuck so you can turn away the glueblock and complete the base.

Lathe and turning tools

The cherry block Ted used (*Photo 1*) measured 9" (23cm) square by 4" (10cm) thick and weighed 13 lbs. The midi-lathe can handle a 12" (30cm) disk, but the blank for this bowl was about the largest it could drive without vibrating and stalling. You could not manage this much wood on a pen turner's mini lathe.

Ted explained that in the old days, students would begin with a sharp spearpoint tool and a scraper, which do not require much skill. Nowadays, you would begin with bowl gouges, which require more skill. We decided to show both methods in this article (*Photo 3*), along with two half-round scrapers for finishing cuts.

Choosing wood

"Are we going to use green wood or dry?" Ted wanted to know. That's because the moisture content of the wood illuminates the path to success. Seasoned wood like our cherry square is stable and therefore predictable. Plus, you can create a useful bowl that you can finish and use right away. Green (unseasoned) wood is easier to turn but requires

drying time and may seriously distort in the process. It also would require different holding methods than we have shown here.

To reduce the risk of cracking, be sure the center, or pith, of the tree does not run through the blank.

Preparing the blank

Decide which face of the blank will be the top of the bowl. Draw diagonals to find the center of the block and use a compass to draw a circle on that surface. To help envision the profile of your bowl, sketch shapes onto the side or end of the blank (*Photo 4*), although those surfaces will be cut away in the next step. At the bandsaw, cut out your bowl blank (*Photo 5*). If you do not have access to a bandsaw, use whatever sawing technology you have to cut the corners off the blank; an octagon is close enough.

Find the center of the disk (*see sidebar*) and draw a faceplate-sized circle for centering the faceplate on what will be the top of the bowl. Mark the screw locations, drill pilot holes, and screw the faceplate onto the wood (*Photo 6*). Use substantial wood screws (not brittle drywall screws) long enough to penetrate an inch into the blank. Since this surface will be the top, or rim, of the bowl, the screw holes will be turned away later.

True the blank

Thread the faceplate carrying the blank onto the lathe's headstock spindle and bring up the tailstock for added support. A level scraper cuts on center and its bevel does not rub, so set the toolrest the scraper's thickness below center and about ¼" (6mm) away from the circumference of the disk. Rotate the blank by hand to be sure it clears the toolrest.

The bandsawn blank is not going to be perfectly round and the faceplate might not be perfectly centered on the blank. Therefore, set the lathe to its slowest speed. Stand to the side when you turn it on and pay attention to undue noise or vibration; there should not be any. If there is, stop and figure out why. You might have to balance the blank by sawing off more wood. When the lathe runs smoothly, increase the speed (but not to the point where you introduce vibration) and prepare to take the first leveling cut.

Hold the small roundnose scraper horizontally on the toolrest. If you are right handed, your right hand grips the handle and powers the cut, while the left hand holds the tool down tight on the toolrest and steers it across the wood. Because the wood is irregular, the first cuts will be intermittent, as you will see if

Ted studies the block and decides to follow the wood's annual rings to sketch the shape of the bowl. He is trying for a catenary curve, the shape of a hanging chain and also of the St. Louis Arch.

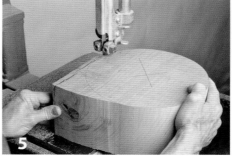

Bandsawing the blank into a disk removes 25% of the original mass. Cutting a thick blank like this requires a sharp blade with no more than 3 or 4 teeth per inch.

Use hefty screws to attach the faceplate to your bowl blank. Drill pilot holes for the screws.

(7) Ted trues up the circumference of the bowl blank.

(8) The small round-nose scraper flattens the face of the blank. The left hand holds the tool down tight on the toolrest and guides the traverse by sliding along the toolrest. The right hand steadies the tool and powers the cut. The scraper is level and its direction of cut is from right to left (center to outside edge). Ted used the tailstock for support but removed it to make the final truing cuts on the face.

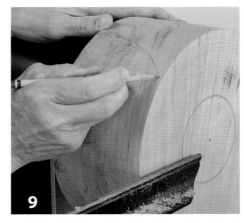

With the blank trued level and round, Ted stops the lathe to outline the bowl's foot. He also sketches the profile on the disk to help visualize the wood to remove.

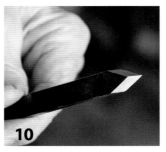

Spearpoint scraper, bottom view.

To begin shaping the outside of the bowl, Ted cuts with the left edge of the spearpoint scraper, rapidly forming a series of grooves he then skims off with the tool's edge. He pulls the tool's handle toward the headstock of the lathe, dragging the edge from right to left.

With its flute rotated 45° and handle swung 45° to the wood surface, the bowl gouge peels off a ribbon of wood with a bevel-rubbing cut. Shape the outside of the bowl, cutting with the grain, from the foot toward the rim.

you stop the lathe to check. Take small bites and repeatedly traverse the wood to smooth and level the entire surface (*Photo 7*).

Switch the lathe off so you can move the toolrest to the face of the blank. Rotate by hand to make sure the wood does not contact the toolrest, restart the lathe, and true the blank's face in the same way you trued its circumference (*Photo 8*). Now, with the lathe switched off again, draw the foot of the bowl onto the edge of the blank and try to visualize where you will remove wood (*Photo 9*).

Shape the outside

There is a lot of wood to remove, but it can be done safely and efficiently with good technique. Ted realigns the toolrest to the outside edge of the bowl blank and just below center. He brings up the tailstock for safety and support and begins with the spearpoint tool (*Photo 10*), a kind of scraper. With the tool firmly planted on the toolrest, he pushes the point into the wood to cut a series of grooves through its tough structure. Then he pulls the edge of the spearpoint smoothly along the toolrest to remove the loosened chips (*Photo 11*). The chips really fly as each sequence of cuts skins off a layer of wood.

As an alternative to scraping, Ted demonstrates the bowl gouge,

sharpened with sweptback wings visible in *Photos 12* and *14*. Ted takes a comfortable, wide-footed stance that allows him to traverse the surface by swaying from the ankles, rather than shuffling his feet sideways (*Photo 13*). He holds the gouge down on the toolrest with an overhand grip and rotates the tool so its flute is about 45°. He swings the handle so the shaft meets the wood at about 45°, also. The gouge's bevel below the sharpened edge rides on the just-cut surface, stabilizing the cut and reducing grain tearout. When Ted presses the edge of the tool into the wood and sweeps it across the surface, the gouge peels off ribbons of shavings up to ¹⁄₁₆" (1.6mm) thick (*Photo 12*).

As the outside of the bowl takes shape, Ted takes increasingly thinner shavings (*Photo 14*) and pauses often to sharpen the tool: the smoother the wood, the less sanding. Nonetheless, he begins sanding with coarse 60-grit abrasive and continues until there are no visible grooves, divots, or torn grain. Then he moves through the grit sequence—60, 100, 150, and 220—which leaves the wood smooth and gleaming. Finally, he removes the tailstock and turns his attention to flattening the bowl's foot.

14

The large bowl gouge makes finishing cuts. To control the action, Ted eyeballs the top silhouette of the spinning wood.

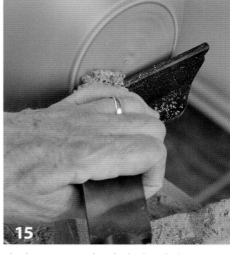

15

The large scraper levels the bowl's bottom.

13

Ted takes a comfortable, wide-footed stance. To traverse the surface with the tool, he sways from the ankles while rotating his right shoulder and elbow.

16

The straightedge reveals deviations in the flatness of the bowl's bottom.

17

Spread glue on both surfaces and use the tailstock to center and clamp the block to the bowl. Let the glue cure thoroughly before proceeding.

Gluing the block

The faceplate-and-glueblock technique allows you to turn a bowl with a very low foot, whereas a scroll chuck uses more of your valuable bowl wood to grab onto. But the low foot does need to be perfectly flat to achieve a good glue joint. With the tailstock out of the way, Ted pulls the large scraper across the foot (*Photo 15*). He checks with a straightedge (*Photo 16*) and repeats the cut until the wood is flat and smooth. Then he removes the bowl from the lathe and sets it aside, leaving it screwed onto its faceplate.

The glueblock is a flat disk of ¾"- (19mm-) thick wood bandsawn a bit bigger than the bowl's foot. Ted mounts it onto a faceplate and uses the roundnose scraper to true its face and edge and shave it to the exact size of the bowl's foot. Then he removes the glueblock, along with its faceplate, from the lathe and remounts the bowl onto the headstock spindle.

With a small brush, he spreads yellow wood glue onto the foot of the bowl and also the face of the glueblock. Then he uses the tailstock of the lathe with a live center that just fits the bore of the faceplate to press the faceplate and glue block into position on the bowl. Press gently at first and rotate the assembly by hand to be sure it is centered (*Photo 17*).

Excavate the inside

Once the glue has dried, Ted removes the bowl from the lathe and removes the faceplate that has held it thus far. He threads the glueblock faceplate onto the headstock (so the top of the bowl faces out) and brings up the tailstock (*Photo 18*). Then he uses the spearpoint, roundnose scraper, and bowl gouge to remove wood as before (*Photo 19*).

Ted plans to excavate the interior in stages. He will keep the tailstock in place as long as possible but soon it is in the way and needs to be removed (*Photo 20*). Using a small bowl gouge, Ted removes the post of wood where the tailstock was (*Photo 21*). He will go down an inch or so, refining and smoothing the bowl

Faceplate management

In this era of the scroll chuck, beginning turners are not always taught how to work with a faceplate. Here are some tips.

An ordinary framing square (*Photo a*), or the square corner of a piece of wood, can help you find the center of a bandsawn bowl blank. Put the corner of the square anywhere on the edge of the circle and mark where its arms cross the edges. A line connecting those two points is the diameter passing through the center. Shift the square to draw several diameters and you will find the center where they intersect.

To center the faceplate on the blank, you could just eyeball it or use a compass to draw a faceplate-sized circle. Or you could use a shopmade centering mandrel. To make the mandrel, install a finishing nail into the end of a cylinder turned to fit the hole in the center of your faceplate. The nail serves as a marking point. Drill a hole into the cylinder while it is still on the lathe (*Photo b*) and cut the head off the nail before you tap it in.

To use the mandrel, first mark the center of your bowl blank at the intersecting diameter lines. Press the nail point into

this center mark and slide the faceplate over the mandrel (*Photos c, d*). Mark the screw locations with a pencil and punch them with a scratch awl.

You want a tight and secure hold on your bowl blank, so bore pilot holes for substantial screws (No. 12 or 14) long enough to protrude ¾" to 1" (19mm to 25mm) beyond the faceplate. To gauge the depth, wrap a piece of masking tape on the drill bit (*Photos e, f*). To make the screws easier to drive, scrape a little paraffin wax onto their threads.

A

With the square's corner at the edge of the blank, mark the points where the square's arms cross the edges. Geometrically, these two points lie on a diameter.

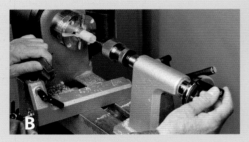

B

Bore the shopmade mandrel while it is still on the lathe. This guarantees a centered hole for the nail point.

C

D

A shopmade centering mandrel simplifies locating the faceplate on your bowl blank.

E

F

Wrap masking tape around the drill bit to indicate the hole depth when predrilling for faceplate screws.

wall before going any deeper. The mass of unturned wood stabilizes the thin wall and dampens vibration (*Photo 22*). He turns his attention momentarily to the rim of the bowl, shaping it to a gentle curve (*Photo 23*), and resumes excavating, but how deep to go? Ted uses a ruler to sight across the bowl and confirm it is 4" (10cm) thick. He wants a bottom about ½" (13mm) thick, so now he can

locate the ultimate bottom of the bowl by boring a hole 3½" (9cm) deep in its center (*Photo 24*). After placing a piece of masking tape around the ⅝" (16mm) Forstner bit shank exactly 3½" from its tip, he advances the tailstock quill in careful stages, eyeballing the tape's progress toward the plane of the rim and withdrawing the bit frequently to clear the chips.

Now he can continue hollowing until the drilled hole-bottom appears (*Photo 25*), alternating between the spearpoint and roundnose scrapers and the bowl gouge. He refines and smoothes the bowl wall as he goes. The heavy half-round scraper makes the final smoothing cuts that fair the bowl walls into the bottom (*Photo 26*). Then comes the complete sanding sequence

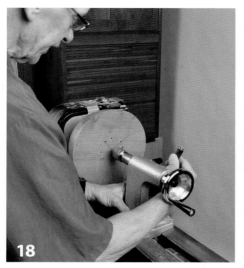

18

Remount the bowl by threading the glueblocked faceplate onto the spindle. For safety, bring up the tailstock for extra support.

19

The bowl gouge removes a lot of wood in a hurry, but soon it cannot reach the wall of the bowl because the tailstock is in the way.

20

With the tailstock out of the way, Ted can swing the bowl gouge handle wide over the ways of the lathe to pare wood off the bowl walls.

21

The small bowl gouge chews through the center nub of wood that had supported the tailstock.

22

Ted gauges wall thickness with his fingers and makes the bowl wall smooth with fine cuts before hollowing deeper.

23

The small bowl gouge shapes a gentle crest on the rim.

24

The tailstock quill advances the drill bit into the rotating wood. The process needs the steadying of one hand on the Jacobs chuck.

25

The depth of the hole indicates the inside bottom of the bowl. The toolrest is angled to be as close as possible to the cut.

26

The large scraper pares the wood and leaves a smooth surface. The scraper's mass helps dampen grain-tearing vibration.

27

Ted tears sheets of abrasive into strips and trifolds each strip to attain three fresh sanding surfaces. Switching the lathe direction from forward to reverse, he keeps the abrasive moving across the wood surface. The fold of paper towel backs up the abrasive and protects his fingers from frictional heat.

on the inside, from 60 grit through 220 (*Photo 27*). Sanding the wood takes as long as excavating it, maybe longer. Ted wears a dust mask while he patiently works through the full grit sequence.

Finishing the foot

The last step is to turn away the glueblock. But how can we hold this almost-completed bowl on the lathe without leaving any hint of how it was held? Ted makes a jam chuck. Center and screw a faceplate on a disk of 1"- (25mm-) thick softwood a bit larger than the inside diameter of the bowl's rim and mount it on the lathe. True the disk and cut a shoulder where the bowl rim will sit. Taper the shoulder a little at a time so you can sneak up on a good friction fit, to center and hold the bowl in this orientation (*Photos 28–30*). With the tailstock brought up for support, Ted turns away as much of the glueblock as possible (*Photo 31*), finally pulling the tailstock away and gingerly scraping the last traces of glueblock and glue off the lovely cherry wood.

Study project

Ted and I had planned to present this story as a study project with learning as the goal, never mind a finished

28

The jam chuck is a trued disk of softwood a bit bigger than the bowl's diameter.

30

Ted presses the bowl snugly onto the jam chuck.

bowl. We were going to saw the bowl in half and assess its cross-section; this exercise gives you valuable feedback about variations in wall and foot thickness. We still think you should do that, as you would learn a lot. But we have to confess: we chose not to (*Photo 32*). Cut it or keep it, you will always treasure your first bowl.

John Kelsey and *Ted Rasmussen*
are members of the Lancaster Area Woodturners, an AAW chapter.

29

Shape the edge of the jam chuck to fit the mouth of the bowl.

31

Turn the glue block off the foot of the bowl, leaving the tailstock in place as long as possible.

32

Ted's sample bowl was too nice to cut for cross-section examination.

Live-Edge Turnings

Preserve bark edges to lend your work a natural look

Turning a natural-edge bowl can be daunting. Even experienced turners may dread the process of splitting a log, locating the bark-side center, mounting the piece between centers, and removing a lot of wood to establish the outside shape and a tenon.

There is, however, a simple technique for making small, natural-edge bowls from green wood. It proceeds quickly with immediate and pleasing results, so new turners are not intimidated. Compared with the traditional method of making a natural-edge bowl, less wood has to be removed. A few cuts begin to reveal the bowl's emerging shape.

Instead of splitting a log, use a piece of tree limb, which is widely available from tree trimmings *(Photo 1)*. Bradford pear is perfect for this project, and limbs are usually plentiful following a windstorm.

For the photos, I used sweet gum, another tight-bark wood.

Process

Cut a 6"- (150mm-) long segment from a 4"- (100mm-) diameter limb. Drill a hole into the wood for a screw chuck *(Photo 2)*. Mount the log so the grain is perpendicular to the lathe axis, using a screw chuck and live center *(Photo 3)*. If you cannot find a 4" limb, cut a piece with a length

Mounting the wood

1 Cut a branch with the length one and a half to two times its diameter.

2 Drill a hole for the screw chuck.

3 Mount the limb onto a screw chuck, and use a live center for support. Spin the wood a few times to be sure it is centered and does not hit the toolrest.

AW 28:5, p38

that is one and one-half times the diameter.

Then, using a 3⁄8" (10mm) bowl gouge, turn the outside of the bowl. Take pull cuts, working from base to rim *(Photos 4, 5)*. After you have removed the bark on the base, establish a tenon *(Photo 6)*. Remove the tailstock so you can complete the foot. If necessary, use thin CA glue to stabilize the bark and the pith *(Photo 7)*.

Reverse the bowl and hold the tenon in a scroll chuck. Drill a depth hole to make hollowing easier and to avoid turning through the bottom *(Photo 8)*. To shape the inside, use push cuts from the rim to the center *(Photos 9, 10)*. Reverse the bowl again, holding it in a jam chuck, and remove the jaw marks from the foot.

Bingo! You have completed a neat natural-edge bowl in short order *(Photo 11)*.

Practice

Practice with a 2"- (5cm-) diameter branch about 4" (10cm) long, using a spindle gouge. You can produce a miniature bowl in little time. Then, it is just a matter of scale as you use larger limbs. Practice improves turning skills.

You can vary the shape of the bowl by changing the diameter-to-length ratio from 1:1.5 to 1:2 or to whatever pleases you. The pith remains in the bowl, but that has caused no problems and often adds character. Wrap your green-wood bowl in paper and allow it to dry, after which you can sand and finish it using your favorite method, or leave the wood unfinished.

Emmett Manley *is a retired medical scientist/professor who discovered he enjoyed woodturning in 2005. He studies and collects wood native to western Tennessee and turns wood to useful items. He may be contacted at emanley1@ comcast.net.*

Turning the outside

Begin turning the outside of the bowl.

A few cuts will begin to reveal the bowl's shape.

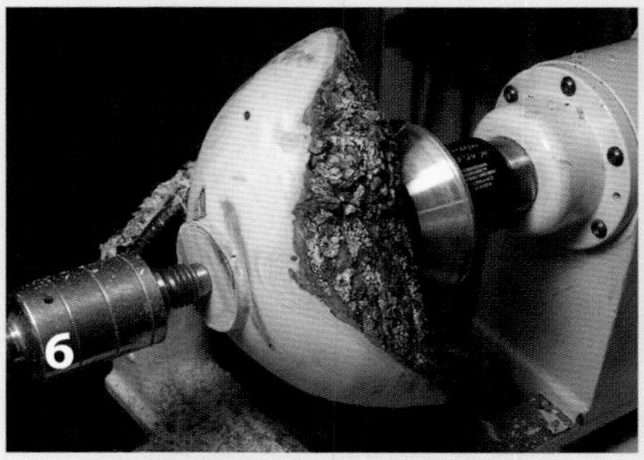

Complete the outside of the bowl and the tenon at the base. Remove the bark on the bottom and complete the foot.

If necessary, apply thin CA glue to stabilize the bark. Ensure the glue has cured before starting the lathe again.

Turning the inside

Grasp the tenon in a scroll chuck and drill a depth hole to begin hollowing the inside.

Take cuts from rim to base with a bowl gouge to hollow the inside.

Check your progress to be sure you do not turn through the bottom.

The inside is completed. The bowl can now be reversed in a jam chuck to finish the foot.

Ring Holders Make Great Gifts

Borrow production techniques for easy speed and precision

"**Y**ou need to find something small, inexpensive, and easy to make that everyone wants or needs." Those words of wisdom from Rude Osolnik, my mentor, were spoken more than 30 years ago. Rude was right: Production work is what it's all about.

For the past 20 years, I've adhered to Rude's wisdom by turning small production gift items that sell for less than $50. After getting started at crafts shows and then moving on to wholesale sales to gift shops and galleries, I have made a living turning everything from spinning tops, wine stoppers, baby rattles, letter openers, boxes, and ring holders.

Ring holders make great gifts for mothers, sisters, aunts, and friends. Ring holders are priced from $15 to $25 at craft shows.

You can turn ring holders from a single blank, as shown here, or by assembling the project from several pieces.

Get started

For turning tools, you'll need a ¾" spindle roughing gouge, a ⅜" bowl gouge, and a parting tool. You could turn this project with a faceplate, but a 4-jaw scroll chuck with #2 jaws will help you zip through the steps if you're turning several ring holders for gifts or sales.

For turning stock, select a 3×3×5½" hardwood blank. The ring holders shown on these pages are turned from canary wood, a dense, tight-grained hardwood from South America. As the name implies, its color is creamy yellow but it also has beautiful streaks of red running through it. It is relatively inexpensive and it turns and finishes well.

Easy turning steps

Locate and mark the centers on each end of the blank. Use a mallet to drive the drive center into one end of the blank. Mount the blank between centers on the lathe and lock the tailstock and quill in place.

Position the tool rest just below the blank's centerline, parallel to and approximately ¼" from the blank. Always rotate the blank by hand to ensure clearance with the tool rest.

Turn up the lathe to approximately 1,500 rpm and use the spindle roughing gouge to reduce the blank into a cylinder. Use the parting tool to turn a ¼"-long tenon on one end of the blank and sized to fit your scroll chuck (*Photo 1*). To ensure maximum holding strength, always keep the diameter of the tenon as close as possible to the fully closed size of the jaws. Also make sure the shoulder of the tenon is tight against the face of the chuck jaws for the same reason. (You will be turning at the end of the blank and

Photos: Marisa Pruss

AW 23:2, p50

a slight catch could pull the blank from the jaws of the chuck.)

Remove the blank from between centers and mount it in the scroll chuck. Position the tool rest, rotate the material by hand, and turn on the lathe. (You may continue to use the tailstock for greater security.)

Use the spindle roughing gouge, spindle gouge, or the bowl gouge for basic shaping of the ring holder. Reduce the end to slightly more than ½" diameter and start detailing on what will be the top of the ring holder (Photo 2). Remember to remove about ¼" off the overall length of the top to eliminate the hole left by either the drive or live center.

You have many options, among them: a ball, a point, an acorn or a series of beads. The important thing is to keep a ½" diameter so most rings will fit over the end of the ring holder (Photo 3). Now start working your way down the stem to create an attractive profile.

Once you are satisfied with the top and stem, shape the base. Options include bulbous, flat, or concave profiles to flow into the stem. If you wish, add a bead or a cove to fit in with your own design.

Depending on how much detail you add, you can use the spindle gouge (ideal for beads and coves) or the bowl gouge (bulbous) to shape the base. Stop the base abruptly or add a small bead or fillet at the bottom to give it more lift. Use your parting tool to make a cut to define the bottom of the ring holder (Photo 4). Do not cut it off the waste yet.

Almost everyone knows someone who has space for a turned wood ring holder to place near the sink or on the nightstand.

With a parting tool, create a ¼"-wide tenon that is sized for your 4-jaw scroll chuck.

With a ¾" spindle roughing gouge, turn the top of the ring holder to about ½" diameter.

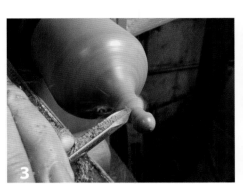
Use a spindle gouge to detail the top of the ring holder.

Define the bottom of the ring holder but don't yet part from the lathe.

Finishing details

Determine the location of the bottom and make a slight parting cut to define it. Sand the entire surface, starting with 150- or 180-grit sand-paper, and continue through 400 grit.

I prefer oil-based finishes for this type of project. Apply one to three coats of oil with light sanding in between coats. After the finish is completely dry, rub out the finish with 0000 steel wool and paste wax, and then buff to a sheen.

Continue the parting cut to separate the ring holder from the waste in the chuck. Aim the parting cut toward the upper end of the ring holder and undercut the bottom slightly to ensure it sits flat (Photo 5). Sand and finish the bottom by hand with the same finish as applied on the rest of the project.

After the finish has dried, use a parting tool to undercut the bottom.

*A founding member of the AAW, **Nick Cook** is a frequent contributor to American Woodturner and lives in Marietta, GA where he owns and operates his studio. Visit Nick at www.nickcookwoodturner.com.*

Classy Clocks

It's high time to test your turning skills

A

B

C

Detail tool: (A) spindle gouge; (B) spiral tool; (C) spindle gouge sharpened to razor point.

Years ago, Tom Gall and I spent a lot of weekends together as crafts show exhibitors, each of us trying to eke out a living and make names for ourselves.

One of Tom's bread-and-butter items was this mini clock design. A few years ago, Tom was in a car accident and suffered multiple broken bones. Today, after extensive physical therapy, Tom is doing much better than anyone ever imagined, and he continues to recover. With his permission, I'll show you how to turn one of his best-selling designs.

These clocks require minimal wood and just a few tools. The clock inserts are inexpensive. The 1½"-diameter clocks shown here require a ⁵⁄₁₆" recess.

Get started

For turning tools, you will need a ¾" spindle roughing gouge, ⅜" spindle gouge, and a parting tool. Optional tools include a ½" skew and

Sorby spiral texturing tool. At the lathe, you will need a 4-jaw chuck.

Select a 3×3" scrap about 1½" thick. The dimensions are not critical, but if the completed clock is too thin, it may not stand upright. It doesn't matter if you use end grain, side grain, or burl, but choose an attractive turning block.

Turn the clock

To make the best use of your blank, glue a round hardwood wasteblock to the back, centered. Grip the wasteblock with your 4-jaw chuck, and turn the blank to a 3" cylinder. Use a spindle roughing gouge on an end-grain blank or a spindle gouge on a side-grain blank.

With the blank turned to a cylinder, begin shaping the clock body. Don't remove too much material from the back of the blank *(Photo 1)* or it may fly off the lathe.

Install a Jacobs drill chuck into the tailstock quill, and chuck

a 1⅜" Forstner bit. For the clock insert, bore a ⁹⁄₁₆"-deep hole *(Photo 2)*. When withdrawing the bit, hang on to the chuck. If the bit binds in the hole, it could pop the drill-chuck taper out of the tailstock with ugly consequences.

Texturing adds interest

You may choose to cut a series of coves in the piece, texture it with a needle scaler, turn a series of beads, or simply sand the clock body. The goal is to have fun with this project and to come up with as many variations as you can.

I textured one version with a Sorby texturing tool. This tool produces nice swirl marks on the surface and excels on end grain. And if your cutting technique is good, you never have to pick up a piece of sandpaper.

AW 23:4, p30

To use the texturing tool, keep the speed of the lathe up (1,800 rpm or higher), angle the tool to about 45 degrees, and tip it down to keep the teeth from grabbing. Engage the tool in the wood at the edge of the movement hole and texture the front of the clock body *(Photo 3)*. Keep the tool moving. You can move it back and forth a bit.

To texture the entire clock, run the texturing tool to the widest diameter of the clock body and stop.

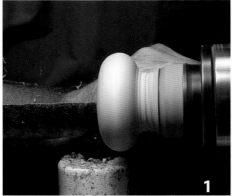

Leave a sturdy wasteblock on the back of the clock (1½" diameter shown above).

Complete the back

Continue to shape the back of the clock body and part it from the wasteblock. To hold the clock body for completing the back, measure a tenon diameter on the wasteblock for a friction fit of the clock-movement hole *(Photo 4)*. Instead of using the hardwood wasteblock from earlier steps, I recommend switching to pine because a softwood won't mar the turning stock.

Press the clock body onto the wasteblock tenon. The clock body should fit snugly and run true. Smooth the back *(Photo 5)*. Texture or sand the back to match the front.

To make the clock body stand up, cut an angled flat spot at the edge. To accomplish this, make a simple tablesaw jig *(Photo 6)*. Position the jam-chuck tenon so the edge of the clock body protrudes about ½" beyond the edge of the ¾" plywood.

Safety note: Do not attempt the tablesaw cut without the tenon.

Press the clock body onto the tenon, tilt your tablesaw blade 6 to 8 degrees, and make the cut *(Photo 7)*. I make two or three light cuts rather than one heavy cut. Sand the bottom and apply a finish.

If I'm in a hurry, I spray my clocks with Deft satin lacquer and then buff them. If I have a bit more time, I oil the clocks with Waterlox and buff the clocks on a 4"-diameter wheel. Finally, insert the clock movement.

Bob Rosand *(RRosand.com) is an* American Woodturner *contributing editor. He lives in Bloomsburg, PA.*

Advance the quill to bore a 9⁄16"-deep hole to accept the clock insert.

Engage the tool at the edge of the hole and move it toward the edge of the body.

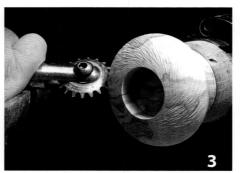

Use calipers to mark the clock diameter on the wasteblock that will become the tenon.

Use your spindle gouge to smooth the back of the clock body.

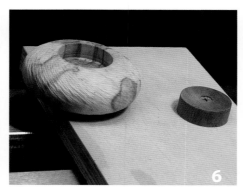

Part off a short length of the jam-chuck tenon and fasten it to a piece of plywood.

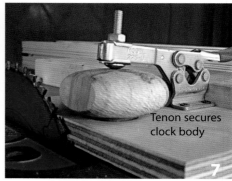

Tenon secures clock body

With the tablesaw blade tilted about 6 to 8 degrees, cut a flat spot on the clock body.

Turning Offset Handles Simplified

A simple chucking set-up is the key

AW 28:6, p26

Replacing the plastic handle of a 6-in-1 screwdriver *(Photo 1)* with a turned wooden one looks good, but its usefulness is limited because the slick round handle is difficult to grip tight enough to drive screws. Offset turning a handle changes its shape to provide a comfortable, powerful grip for attacking stubborn screws. You will be able to extend these offset-turning techniques to projects of your own design.

To transform a handle from ordinary to elegant, use highly figured, well-seasoned wood, and then follow these steps:

1. Disassemble a 6-in-1 screwdriver to retrieve the insert.
2. Prepare the blank.
3. Bore out the blank and install a ferrule and the insert.
4. Turn the basic round-handle shape.
5. Mark the handle with two circumference lines and three horizontal lines, 120 degrees apart.
6. Offset and turn the handle on three axes.
7. Remount at true center, trim up, sand, part off, clean up, and apply a finish.

Disassemble the screwdriver

To retrieve the metal insert that locks the bits into the handle, mount the screwdriver onto the lathe: The round butt end of the handle will fit snugly into the open end of the lathe's spindle. Use a cone center in the tailstock to hold the other end. Tighten the tailstock to provide a friction drive. Wearing a faceshield and dust protection, carefully turn away the plastic surrounding the insert. Typically, the plastic will start to break away before your gouge makes contact with the metal insert, so be careful *(Photo 2)*. Use a pair of pliers for the final extraction from the plastic.

Measure the insert to determine the diameter of hole needed for drilling into the wood handle. This turned out to be 9/16" (14mm) for the screwdriver in the photos, which might need to be enlarged slightly for harder woods. When the insert is driven into the wooden handle, it should have an interference fit to prevent turning in the hole. No glue should be needed.

To determine the length of the hole to be drilled into the handle blank, slip the insert over a screwdriver bit and snap it into place. Measure the length from the outside end of the insert to the tip of the inside bit, in this case, 3¾"

(95mm) *(Photo 3)*. If your insert is longer, increase the length of your handle accordingly.

Prepare the blank

Select a blank of wood 2" × 2" × 5½" (50mm × 50mm × 140mm). Sand one end smooth so it can be marked more easily. This will become the butt end of the handle. Find and mark the center points on each end. On the smooth-sanded end, use a compass and draw a 1" (25mm) circle using the marked center. This circle will be used later when doing the offset turning *(Photo 4)*.

Place the butt end of the blank into the jaws of a scroll chuck and loosely close the jaws. Bring up the tailstock and align the center of the blank with the live center *(Photo 5)*. Tighten the tailstock to help center and align the blank in the chuck. Tighten the chuck jaws.

Move the tailstock out of the way, turn on the lathe at a low speed, and verify the proper centering of the blank. Make any adjustments necessary. Using a pointed scraper or a skew chisel, turn a depression into the end of the blank to aid in starting a drill bit. Using a properly sized drill bit, drill a hole for the screwdriver insert *(Photo 6)*. For the screwdriver in this article: ⁹⁄₁₆" × 3¾" (14mm × 95mm) deep.

Ferrule and insert

Prepare a ferrule for mounting onto a tenon turned on the end of the handle. The ferrule should fit tightly. The ferrule will minimize splitting of the blank when the insert is driven into the handle. Using ¾"- (19mm-) ID copper tubing, or equivalent, cut off a ring about ⅜" (10mm) long. Remove any burrs with abrasives or a file. Nominally, the inside diameter will be ¾" (19mm), but measure it to verify. If desired, polish the ferrule.

Support the free end of the blank with a cone center mounted into

the tailstock. Turn a tenon on the tailstock end of the blank. Make it slightly longer than the ferrule and slightly larger in diameter *(Photo 7)*.

Carefully trim down the tenon to the point where the ferrule will just start to slide over the tenon. The tenon should have a slight taper from the end to the shoulder to achieve a tight fit. Test-fit the ferrule *(Photo 8)*.

Remove the blank from the lathe. Using a wooden mallet, drive the ferrule onto the tenon using a short piece of steel pipe or copper tubing positioned over the end of the tenon. Make sure the ferrule is tight against the shoulder. Sand the tenon flush with the end of the ferrule. If you turned the tenon too small for a snug fit, a small amount of thick CA glue may sufficiently adhere the ferrule.

Using a wooden mallet, drive the screwdriver insert into the hole. Verify that the screwdriver shaft and bits fit properly *(Photo 9)*.

Turn a round handle

Mount the blank between centers using a Stebcenter and a cone center. (A spur center can be used, but the spring-loaded Stebcenter pin causes less damage to the wood, which allows for easily remounting the blank later when doing offset turning.) The butt end will be at the headstock.

Leaving as much of the blank at the butt end as possible, turn the handle to a shape and size you like. The 1" (25mm) circle on the butt end and surrounding wood must remain *(Photo 10)*. Grasp the handle and test for comfort. Reshape as needed, but leave it a bit large at this point to allow for the offset turning.

Finish-sand the handle from the ferrule to its narrowest part. If not done previously, the ferrule can be polished, but be careful not to stain the wood next to it.

A 6-in-1 screwdriver provides parts for a custom-made screwdriver.

Mount the handle onto the lathe and carefully turn away the plastic to release the insert.

Mount the shaft and a bit into the insert and measure the length to determine the depth of the hole to drill in your new handle.

A block of Russian olive has the center marked and a 1" (25mm) circle drawn on one end. This will be the butt end of the handle.

Mount the blank onto the lathe using a cone center in the tailstock. The butt end is mounted into a four-jaw chuck.

After turning a small depression in the end to help center the drill bit, drill a hole for the insert.

7 Turn a tenon for the ferrule.

8 Test-fit the ferrule.

9 With the ferrule fitted onto the tenon, install the insert. Test-fit the screwdriver shaft.

10 Turn the handle round, leaving sufficient wood at the butt end.

Offset turning

First, draw *circumference* and *guidelines* onto the handle. Circumference lines establish the boundaries of the guidelines. Guidelines (1) help locate the different mounting points for offset turning and (2) provide depth guidance when offset turning *(Photo 11)*. The guidelines are drawn in between two circumference lines.

With the handle still mounted on the lathe, use a soft-lead pencil to draw two lines around the handle. One circumference line will be about 1" (25mm) from the ferrule and the other about ⅜" (10mm) from the butt end. (A pencil with hard lead will score the wood, which increases sanding time.)

Using the indexing feature of your lathe and the toolrest as a guide, draw three horizontal guidelines, 120 degrees apart, extending between the two circumference lines just drawn. Make sure the guidelines are reasonably dark and can be easily seen.

Lightly extend each line around the butt end of the blank to intersect the circle. Label the intersecting points A, B, and C. Use an awl to poke a hole into each point to help locate the center pin correctly. These points are mounting locations for offset turning.

Keeping the handle on the cone center, loosen the tailstock and move the handle so that point A is at the center pin *(Photo 12)*. This provides a ½" (13mm) offset at the butt (no offset on the other end). Retighten the tailstock and rotate the blank to check for clearance.

Turn on the lathe. You will see a shadow at the horizon of the blank. A piece of cardboard placed behind the lathe can help provide contrast to make it easier to observe the profile of the handle.

Start turning away the waste between the two circumference lines. When the shadow at the horizon is gone, you will have cut away the side

11 The guidelines help establish the mounting locations (A, B, and C) for offset turning.

12 Position the drive center at point A and you are ready for the first offset turning.

13 The offset cuts have been limited to the areas between the guidelines. The handle now has a triangular cross-section and is ready for sanding.

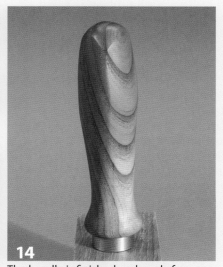

14 The handle is finished and ready for use.

of the handle down to two of the guidelines. Use light cuts and check your progress frequently. A roughing gouge with its large bevel seems to work better for this than a spindle gouge. Stop the lathe and examine the handle—the objective is to turn the wood down to two guidelines and no farther.

If cuts are not symmetrical between the two guidelines, then the most probable cause was an accuracy error when laying out the lines and the corresponding drive points A, B, and C. Discrepancies usually disappear during the sanding process.

The offset turning requires you to ride the bevel of the gouge. Using higher speeds helps, but do not run the lathe too fast or the out-of-balance blank could fly off. Ensure that the tailstock remains tight.

Repeat the previous step using point B, and then point C as the drive centers *(Photo 13)*. Hand-sand the handle to smooth out any irregularities.

Return the drive center to true center and clean up the shape of the handle at the butt end, removing as much waste as possible. Part off the handle. Erase any remaining pencil marks. Clean up the butt end using a rasp and abrasives.

Finish

An unfinished handle develops a patina through normal use and handling, but if you prefer to finish yours, an oil finish works well *(Photo 14)*.

Now that you have learned how to do basic offset turning to create a beautiful, utilitarian handle for a screwdriver, with a few simple alternative steps you can create other handles with a distinctive look and feel. Try different numbers or sizes of offsets. Or, offset both ends. Use your new skills to enhance other projects.

*After retiring from his engineering career, **John Giem** expanded his interest in woodturning into a second career. He is an active member of the Rocky Mountain Woodturners in northern Colorado. He can be contacted at jgiem@comcast.net.*

Drawing guidelines

When drawing guidelines on the handle, accuracy is important—guidelines influence the final shape, especially where they define the offset drive points A, B and C. When drawing a guideline, it must be lined up horizontally with the axis of rotation (i.e., it must be at the same height as the point of the drive center). Here are three methods:

Method one:

1. Draw two circumference lines on the handle, in between which guidelines will be drawn.

2. Remove the handle from the lathe and position the toolrest near the center pin of the drive center. With a pencil placed horizontally level on the toolrest, adjust the height of the toolrest so the pencil point is aligned with the drive center's pin.

3. Move the toolrest, remount the handle, and lock the spindle using the indexing feature of the lathe.

4. Without changing the height of the toolrest, position it (by moving the banjo) to draw a dark guideline along the length of the handle between the two circumference lines.

5. Relocate the toolrest and lightly extend the guideline onto the butt end, intersecting the circle to form point A.

6. Rotate the handle 120 degrees. Repeat steps 4 and 5 to draw a second guideline and establish point B. Repeat for point C.

Method two:

Guidelines can be drawn using a stiff piece of cardboard shaped to fit the handle profile, including around the butt end. Keep the template horizontally aligned with the axis of rotation. Use the pencil to trace along the edge to draw dark guidelines and lightly establish points A, B, and C *(Photo A)*.

Method three:

Perhaps the easiest method is to use a profile copy gauge *(Photo B)*. Push the gauge against the handle and allow the pins to adjust to the curves, including the butt end. Keeping the gauge horizontal, use a pencil to trace along the edge while drawing the guidelines and establishing the points.

Whichever method you use, one frequent source of error is not keeping the pencil, template, or gauge horizontal. An easy way to maintain horizontal is to use a small spirit level *(Photo C)*.

A A cardboard template can be used to draw guidelines.

B A profile copy gauge is an easy way to draw guidelines.

C A small spirit level keeps the cardboard template or copy gauge horizontal and aligned with the center pin.

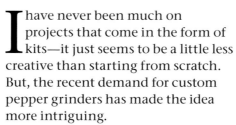

Perfecting the Pepper Mill

The ideal project for your daily grind

I have never been much on projects that come in the form of kits—it just seems to be a little less creative than starting from scratch. But, the recent demand for custom pepper grinders has made the idea more intriguing.

Once you figure out the sequence of steps to make them efficiently, pepper mills are really not that difficult. I've found that the 10" mills are a nice size to work with and everyone seems to prefer it to larger or smaller ones. You can, of course, vary the shape widely from the basic mill I describe here.

Before you start turning, order your mechanism. I have tried many manufacturers, but Chef Specialties makes my favorite reliable stainless-steel mechanism. It also sells a polycarbonate salt mill, which prevents corrosion. (Packard Woodworks and Crafts Supplies sell these as "deluxe" mechanisms in the $12 range.)

The following directions apply to the 10" Chef Specialties mill. Refer to the information sheet that is supplied with your mechanisms for specific requirements.

Prepare your stock

To get at least two blanks from each strip, I make my slabs about 24" long. I also turn the mills from solid cherry and hard maple. I purchase 3" x 3" x 36" blanks from a local supplier. (You can find them on the Internet at www.hardwoodweb.com.) The blanks for 10" mills—either laminated or solid—are cut to 12" lengths. This allows plenty of room for tenons at both ends and a parting cut to separate the top from the bottom.

For laminated pepper mills, glue up large slabs of a variety of 3" stock milled to random thicknesses. After the glue dries, make the first cut at a slight angle. Make the remaining cuts using the fence of either the tablesaw or a bandsaw. This is a technique I learned from Rude Osolnik when I assisted him in laminating and cutting of rolling pin blanks.

Locate and mark the center of each end of the blanks, then use an automatic centerpunch to make a dimple. Rough-turn the blanks to round cylinders with a tenon at each end. Size your tenon to fit the jaws of your scroll chuck. In addition to the tenon at each end, make a parting cut to separate the base portion from the cap of the mill (Photo A). For ease of drilling from both ends, add a tenon to the top of the base section; this eliminates the need for a drill-bit extension.

Make the base section 8" long plus a ⅜" tenon on each end; the cap will be approximately 2" long when completed.

Drill routine

Once separated, mount the top of the base section in a scroll chuck with the bottom facing the tail-stock. Drill the first recess in the bottom of the stock with a 1⅝" Forstner bit in a Jacobs chuck. The recess should be approximately ⅜" deep beyond the tenon. With a ¹¹/₁₆" bit, drill a second hole ⅝" beyond the first recess.

To drill the bottom of the base, tighten the base top in your scroll chuck. Mount an extra long 1" bit in the chuck and drill as deep as possible in the base of the mill. You must go slowly (lathe speed of 500 to 700 rpm) and back the bit out frequently to remove the shaving and prevent overheating.

Remove the base section from the chuck and re-chuck it with the top facing the tailstock. Make sure the blank is centered and make a finishing cut across the top end of the base section. Complete the 1" hole through the base (Photo B). Remove the base from the chuck and set aside.

Mount the cap section in the chuck using the tenon on the top end. Turn a 1" tenon approximately ½" long on the bottom end of the cap, then make a finishing cut from the perimeter toward the tenon. The tenon will fit into the 1" through hole in the base to align the two parts. It should fit without being too tight to turn freely. Next, drill a ⅛" recess in the end of the tenon with a ¾" Forstner bit; this step makes it easier to center the turnplate. Drill a ¼" hole all the way through the cap of the mill.

The next step is to remove the cap from the chuck and mount a waste block (I prefer poplar) to turn a jam chuck. The jam chuck should be 1⅝" diameter and about 1½" long. Make a finishing cut across the end so the stock fits squarely against the recess in the bottom of the base of the mill.

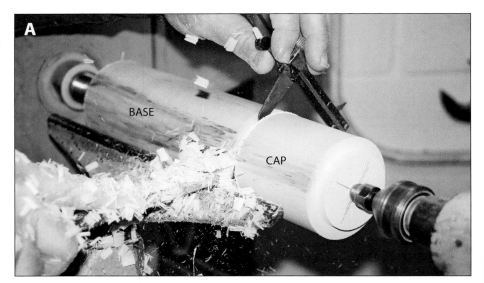

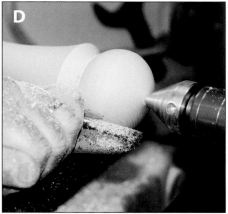

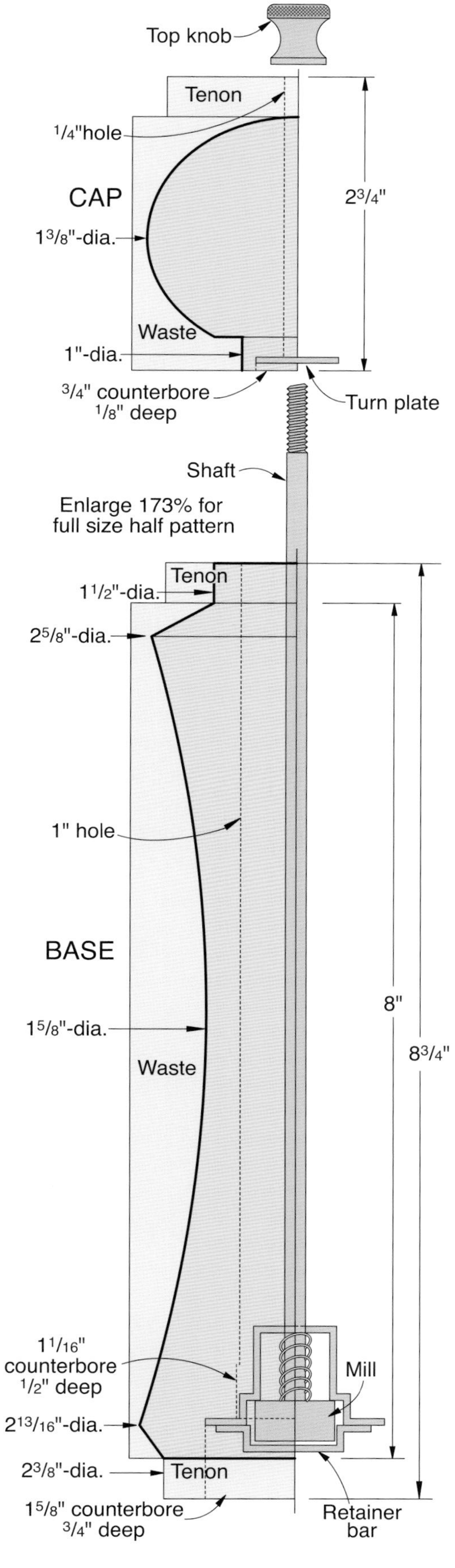

Diagram labels

Top knob

Tenon

1/4"hole

CAP

2 3/4"

1 3/8"-dia.

Waste

1"-dia.

3/4" counterbore
1/8" deep

Turn plate

Shaft

Enlarge 173% for
full size half pattern

1 1/2"-dia.

Tenon

2 5/8"-dia.

1" hole

BASE

8"

8 3/4"

1 5/8"-dia.

Waste

1 1/16"
counterbore
1/2" deep

Mill

2 13/16"-dia.

2 3/8"-dia.

Tenon

1 5/8" counterbore
3/4" deep

Retainer
bar

Illustration: Roxanne LeMoine

Before mounting the mill on the jam chuck, test and size the mechanism. I press the spring bar into the recess, and then insert the two halves of the mechanism and the shaft through the base of the mill (Photo C). While holding the parts in place, place the cap on the top of the base and make a mark on the cap at the center of the threaded portion of the shaft. This marks the finished length. Now, remove the mechanism.

Shape the mill

Depending on the final shape, you may wish to turn the cap and base separately. However, I find it faster and easier to turn the whole mill at once. Separate pieces require more turning time, but allow you better access for finishing the top of the cap.

Either way, cut off the tenon on the bottom end of the base. I do that with the mill mounted in the jam chuck with the cone center in the tailstock.

To turn them together, mount the base on the jam chuck, insert the tenon of the cap into the through hole of the base, and use a cone-shaped live center to hold the assembly together (Photo D).

To turn them separately, make a second jam chuck. This time, turn the chuck with a recess to fit the tenon on the bottom of the cap. Then press it into the chuck and turn to the desired shape.

Final dashes

After shaping the mill, sand with 150-, 180- and then 220-grits. My favorite finish for most utilitarian items is urethane oil. You can apply it right on the lathe and build it up to a high-gloss finish. For a satin sheen (my preference), cut back the gloss with steel wool.

After the finish dries, assemble the mechanism. Attach the turn-plate in the recess on the bottom of the cap. Press it in place, and drill 3/32" drill pilot holes to prevent the screws from splitting the wood. Screw the turnplate to the cap and set it aside.

Turn the base upside down and insert the spring bar in the recess in the bottom. Press the female portion of the grinder mechanism into the spring bar. Slide the male portion of the grinder onto the shaft and then the spring bar, and slide the shaft through the female mechanism and the spring bar.

Place the retainer bar over the assembled mechanism, line up the holes, drill pilot holes, and screw in place. Slide the cap over the top end of the shaft and screw on the top knob. Finally, tighten the knob to adjust the grind.

A founding member of the AAW, **Nick Cook** *is a frequent contributor to* American Woodturner *and lives in Marietta, GA where he owns and operates his studio. Visit Nick at www. nickcookwoodturner.com.*

Scoop for Ice Cream

Make a handy kitchen utensil that's built to last

Several years ago this article would have started with the following three steps: Drive to the nearest Wal-Mart or Target and buy an ice cream scoop with a plastic handle. Remove the handle by placing it on the lathe bed and striking it with a hammer to shatter or crack the plastic. Pick up plastic pieces flung far and wide across the shop.

For this effort you'd have been rewarded with a lightweight plated scoop with a skinny tang that was no match for a tub of hard ice cream.

Fortunately, you can now buy an unhandled solid-brass scoop with a confidence-inspiring tang. The kit includes a brass ferrule so you won't have to scrounge the Ace Hardware plumbing aisle. So skip the three steps and begin here.

Get started

At the lathe, you will need a 1¼" spindle roughing gouge, a parting tool, a ⅜" spindle gouge, and two 1" skews, one with the traditional straight grind and the other with a radius grind. You'll need a cup center (Oneway markets this as a safe driver) and a revolving cone center. In the event of a tool catch, the turning blank "stalls" on a cup center, preventing damage to the workpiece and possibly you.

For stock, select a 1¾×1¾×6½" dense, close-grained wood blank.

Prepare the blank

Mount the blank between centers. Turn the blank round with a spindle roughing gouge. Remove the blank and mount a drill chuck in the headstock. Chuck in a ⅜" brad-point bit and mark a 1¼" drilling depth by placing a piece of masking tape on the bit (¼" deeper than the length of the 1" scoop tang).

Remount the blank between centers using the drill bit as the headstock center. Advance the tailstock slightly while turning the blank by hand to start the drill bit into the wood. With the lathe set at a slow speed (about 500 rpm), turn on the lathe. To drill, stop the blank with your left hand and advance the tailstock quill with your right hand (Photo 1). If you need to clear chips from the hole, stop the lathe, back off the tailstock, and twist and pull the blank from the drill bit.

To mount the blank for turning, remove the drill chuck from the headstock and replace it with your cup center. Mount a revolving cone center in the tailstock and mount the blank between centers. The cone center fits into the drilled hole, and all subsequent turning centers on this hole. If you don't have a cone center, you can make a cone-shaped cover to fit over your revolving cup center (Photo 2). For a simpler but less permanent option, turn a cone that simply fits on the end of your cup (revolving) center (Photo 3).

Brass ferrule unites metal scoop and turned wooden handle.

Photo: John Hetherington

AW 23:4, p20

Getting Started in Woodturning

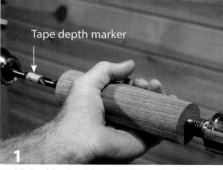

1

Hold the block with the left hand while advancing the quill with the right hand. To stop the drilling, remove your left hand.

2

If you don't have a cone center, turn shop-made cone-shaped covers to fit over your revolving cups.

3

One option: Turn a cone that fits on the end of your cup center. The cone should taper down to a diameter less than 3/8".

4

With a parting tool and calipers, size the tenon with the lathe running. Set the calipers to the outside diameter of the ferrule.

5

A small burnished area on the taper at the end of the tenon establishes the finished diameter of the tenon.

6

Use the skew as a scraper to size the tenon to match the diameter marked by the ferrule. Take light cuts and test the fit frequently.

Fit the ferrule

Mark the length of the ferrule on the blank. Begin sizing the ferrule tenon by setting calipers slightly larger than the inside diameter of the ferrule. Place the calipers on the spinning blank, and cut with a parting tool until the calipers slide over the tenon (Photo 4). Turn the remaining tenon length to this diameter. Make sure the caliper tips have been carefully rounded and smoothed at the ends. (Any small point or roughness could cause the calipers to catch and be thrown toward you.)

Fitting the ferrule is a process of trial and error, repeatedly cutting and testing until you reach the desired fit. Begin by cutting a small taper on the end of the tenon (Photo 5). Try to force the ferrule onto the taper using a twisting motion as though threading it on. This creates a mark close to the finished diameter of the tenon.

Using the parting tool, cut down to the mark. Cut and test until the ferrule fits snugly over the end of the tenon. Now use a skew chisel as a scraper to cut the entire length of the tenon to this diameter (Photo 6). Keep the tenon straight by sighting it over the ways of the lathe bed. Avoid undercutting the tenon.

I like to push and twist the ferrule all the way on. It should be a tight fit but not so tight you can't remove the ferrule to protect it during the upcoming sanding steps.

Before starting to form the handle, clean up the tenon shoulder using a skew chisel and a shoulder cut (Photo 7).

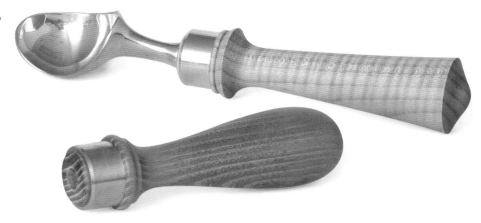

Photo: John Hetherington

Remove the ferrule, then take light cuts with a skew to clean up the shoulder on the ¾"-wide tenon.

With the long point of the skew, make a series of V-cuts to part the handle from the lathe.

Shape the handle

With the ferrule fitted, the rest of the project is all about design and spindle-turning skills. Turn the coves and beads with the ⅜" spindle gouge. Rough out the large gradual curves with a spindle roughing gouge and refine the contour with a radius skew and a planing cut. Rough out the rounded ends with a spindle gouge and refine the shape with a radius skew and a rolling cut.

Before sanding, I like to finish-turn the end of the handle so there is about ¼" of wood still driving the piece. On a project where all of the turning can be done with cutting tools, I'll start sanding with 180 grit, move to 220, and finish with 400 grit (400-grit paper actually burnishes the wood, which feels good and produces a low sheen).

Before sanding, reduce the lathe speed to about 500 rpm. Be careful to preserve your detail. If you can't remove the ferrule, cover it with masking tape. The best method I have found for sanding contours is to apply the sandpaper to a ½"-thick foam pad using 3M Spray 77 or Spray 90. (Both adhesives release when placed under a 100-watt bulb for a minute or so.)

The 1"-thick foam sanding blocks sold at paint stores are an ideal density for sanding curves, cylinders, and tight radii. Cut them to the size you need and apply sandpaper over the existing abrasive with one of the adhesives mentioned above.

After finish-sanding, slide on the ferrule and clean up any torn grain at the top of the ferrule with the skew chisel and a shoulder cut. If you're using a wood cone center, cut all the way to the cone.

For the final step, part the handle from the waste. First, back the pressure off between centers. Then, using the long point of a traditional skew, make a series of light V-cuts (Photo 8). If you're careful you can turn down the waste to less than ¹⁄₁₆".

Now make the final parting cut slightly beyond the end of the handle so that no fibers break off inside the handle. Put a hand under the handle to catch it as you part through. Finish-sand the end of the handle.

Assemble and finish

To secure the ferrule, place a small bead of epoxy around the inside bottom of the ferrule. Slide it on and use mineral spirits to clean up any squeeze-out. Then spread a generous amount of epoxy in the hole and push the scoop in until it seats. There should be a little bit of squeeze-out to clean up with mineral spirits. After the epoxy cures, apply an oil finish. (I use mineral oil.)

Buy ice cream. Scoop, eat, and enjoy.

A professional turner in OK, **Matthew Hill** *has pieces in private collections and the permanent collections of MN Institute of Art and Contemporary Museum of Honolulu. Visit Matthew at www. matthewhillstudio.com.*

A few words about design

Design involves form and function, and function includes comfort and strength. The handle should feel good in the hand and not break when applied to a pint of Häagen-Dazs Swiss Vanilla Almond. A simple cylinder would achieve this. But we're after more. We're on a quest for beauty! We want to transform the commonplace, the everyday object. We want the ice cream scoop to be a source of inspiration for generations to come, the distillation of a mature and profound aesthetic.

I generally work more efficiently and have fewer dogs if I spend some time sketching designs on paper. I make full-size sketches so I can use them to establish critical diameters when I begin turning. Although drawings help, good design evolves through the process of making lots of things and then critiquing them. Critiquing your own work and the work of others is essential to the development of ideas and the refinement of design.

If you are at a loss for ideas, then copy a profile that you like. You can learn a lot this way. Remember: Creating a series of coves and beads on a cylinder is an exercise, not a design. Coves and beads are elements of design, often used to accentuate areas of transition.

—*Matthew Hill*

Salt & Pepper Shakers

Spice up any meal with this handmade set

About 17 years ago, Rus Hurt wrote an American Woodturner article entitled "How to Make Your Lathe Shake and Pour." That article always intrigued me, and I pinned it on my shop wall with plans to complete the project.

Rus' shakers looked like a good design, potentially a good seller for craft shows and certainly a great gift item. Several additional things appealed to me: This project could be turned with scrapwood, it wasn't terribly complicated, and I could complete most of it on the lathe.

How time flies! Seventeen years later, I've finally started producing salt and pepper shakers à la Rus. The shape shown at right is similar to his original, but the size has changed and the technique is different. All and all, it's still a great project.

Get started

You will need a parting tool, a ⅜" spindle gouge, a ½" skew, a set of vernier calipers, and ⅝" and 1" Forstner bits. You will also need a spindle roughing gouge (SRG); I prefer the ½" width, but a ¾" SRG will do fine.

At the lathe, you'll need a 4-jaw scroll chuck with #2 jaws. For supplies, you'll also need a handful of 1" rubber bungs (stoppers).

For turning stock, you will need two 4½×2½" hardwood blanks. Some popular species include oak, maple, ash, walnut, and cherry. The shakers *below* are ambrosia maple with pyrography accents.

The shaker diameter I use isn't etched in stone. Feel free to modify the shape and size of these salt and pepper shakers as you see fit.

Turn the profile

First, place the hardwood turning stock between centers, then true or turn a cylinder. Turn a 2×¾" tenon—long enough for grasping in the #2 jaws of a 4-jaw scroll chuck. After tightening the scroll chuck, re-true the stock. The top of the shaker will be toward the headstock and the bottom will be toward the tailstock.

Ambrosia maple salt and pepper shakers feature pyrography accents.

Photo: John Hetherington

AW 22:1, p58

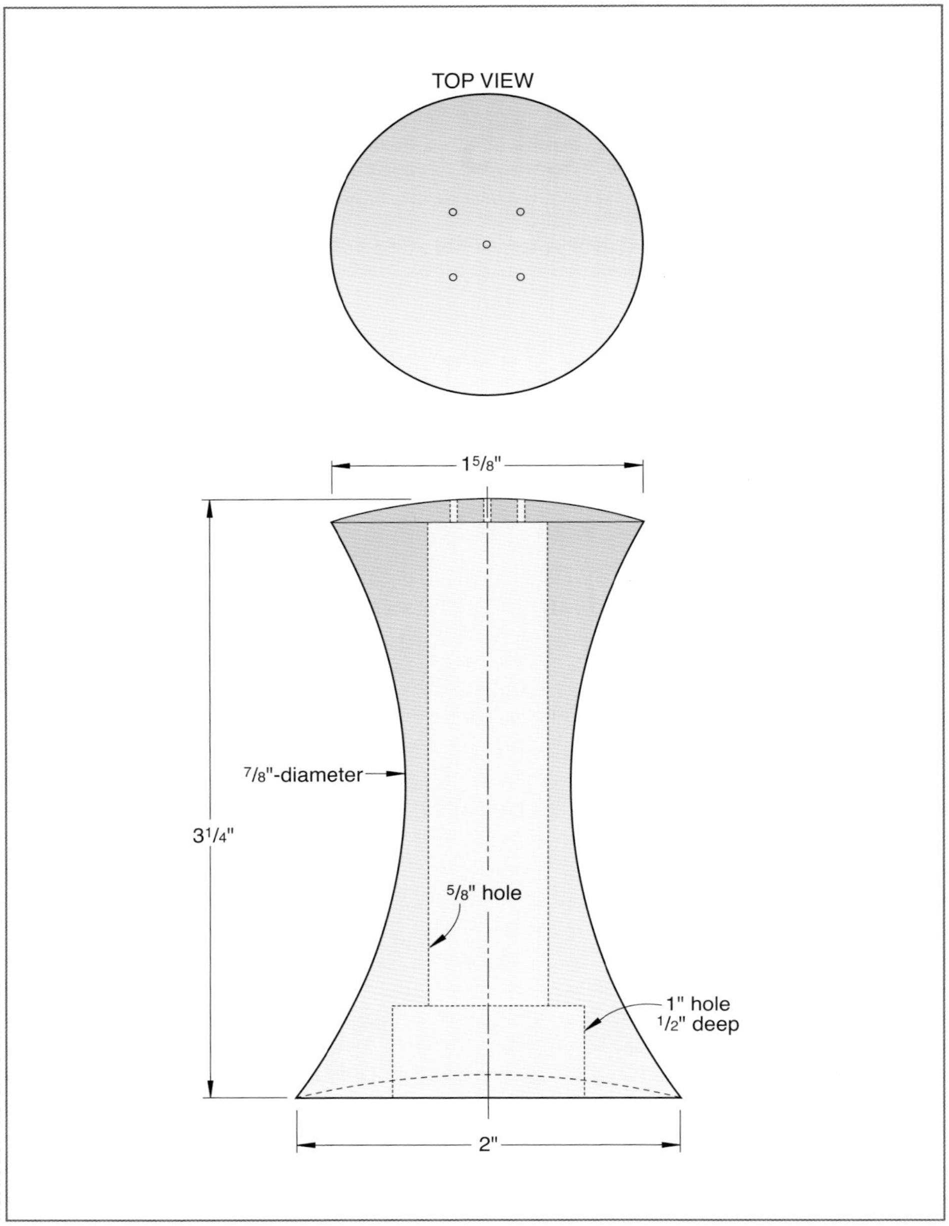
TOP VIEW
1 5/8"
7/8"-diameter
3 1/4"
5/8" hole
1" hole
1/2" deep
2"

Illustration: Roxanne LeMoine

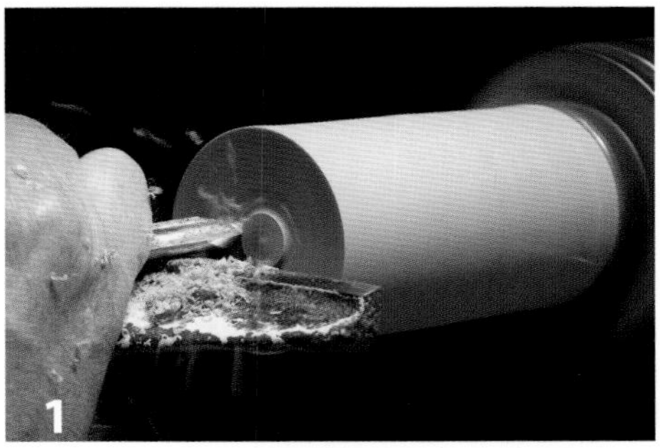
1

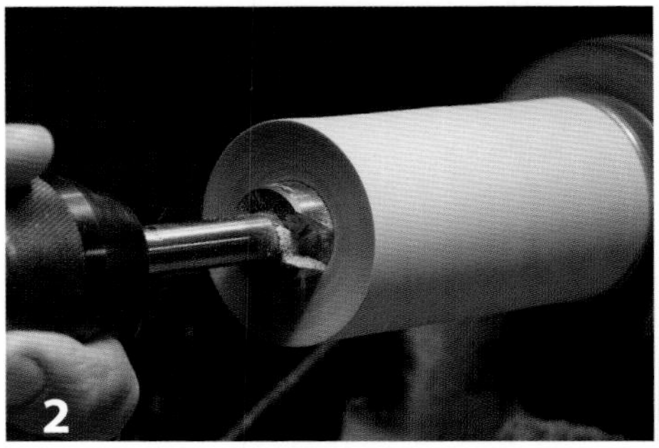
2

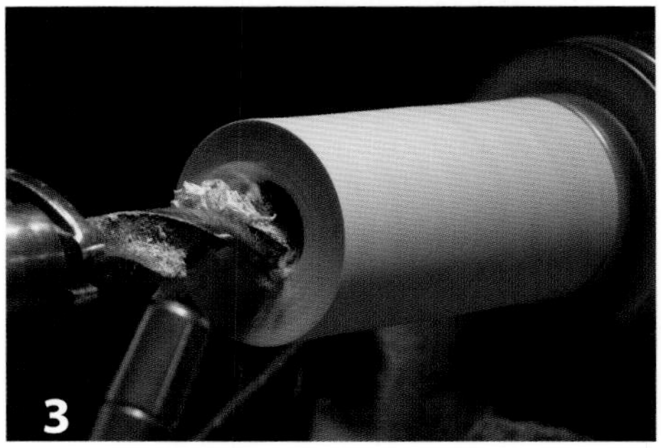
3

Using a spindle gouge, cut a curved recess in the bottom of the shaker, as shown in *Photo 1*. This recess needs to be deep enough that the shaker can sit flat when the rubber bung is inserted after the shaker is completed.

Next, drill a 1"-diameter hole in the bottom about ½" deep, as shown in *Photo 2*. The rubber bung will fit into this hole.

Then, drill a ⅝" hole about 3" deep, as shown in *Photo 3*. This will become the reservoir for the salt or pepper. A ⅝" Forstner bit will perform this job admirably, but I found a machinist's ⅝" drill bit with a #2 Morse taper that works even better. Additionally, you can regrind the drill bit's flutes to match the curve of the top of the shaker.

Be careful not to drill too deep at this point, or you may end up with some ugly napkin rings. (You can always remove a bit more from the interior prior to parting the piece from the lathe.)

Turn the exterior

Now, bring the tail center up to support the shaker while you turn the exterior. The cone centers on the Oneway live centers are ideal for this.

Next, set the parameters of the shaker. From the bottom, measure up 3¼" and part the stock about ½" deep. Using the SRG and calipers, turn the diameter of the shaker base down to about 2 1/16", as shown in *Photo 4*. Then turn the diameter of the shaker top down to about 1⅝".

Visually divide the shaker into thirds, with two-thirds on the bottom and one-third on the top. Using a combination of the spindle gouge and the SRG, turn a smooth curve that finishes with a diameter of about ⅞", as shown in Photo 5. But, don't go any further! Remember

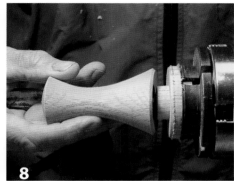

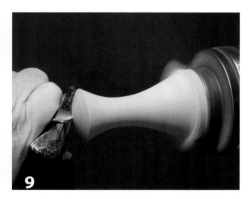

that you have a ⅝" hole through the entire shaker.

While the tail center is still in place, cut a small chamfer on the bottom of the shaker with the long point of the skew down. Then refine the curve on the top, as shown in *Photo 6*. Be sure to leave sufficient waste material to allow sanding after removal of the tailstock. If you are not confident in your skills with the skew, you can accomplish both of these cuts with a spindle gouge.

If you do remove too much supporting stock and the shaker wobbles, leave the tailstock in place for additional support.

Now, remove the tail center, slow down the lathe, and sand to about 600 grit. Before you part the shaker from the lathe, as shown

in *Photo 7*, inset the eraser end of a pencil in the ⅝" hole to check the thickness of the top. If it is too thick, the salt or pepper may clog the holes you drill in the next step. If necessary, enlarge the interior slightly or remove more from the top. (If you remove material from the top, do so with caution—you don't want to change the finished shape of the shaker.)

Using your skew or parting tool, turn a 1" tenon in scrapwood and friction-fit the bottom of the shaker to it, as shown in *Photo 8*. (The shaker bottom will now be near the headstock.) Finish turning the top with a spindle gouge, as shown in *Photo 9*. Sand the top to 600-grit smoothness.

Drill holes and finish

Finally, you'll need holes in the shaker tops. Use the pattern on *page 29* or create your own. A ¹/₁₆" or #55 bit mounted in your drill press is ideal for this task; give both a try.

Apply two or three coats of a penetrating oil finish (I use Waterlox Original Sealer & Finish). After buffing the finish, apply a protective liquid or paste wax.

*A previous member of the AAW Board of Directors, **Robert Rosand** is an instructor and frequent contributor to* American Woodturner. *Visit Robert at www.rrosand.com.*

Napkin Rings

Add a personal touch to your next meal

From top: 3/4" mahogany, 3/8" oak, 3/4" cherry, and 7/16" Osage orange.

In an evening, you can turn a variety of napkin rings to restock your family's gift inventory. With Jerry Hubschman's versatile expansion chuck, you'll have plenty of room for creativity in the ring designs.

Prepare the stock

The neat feature of this project is that it doesn't require thick turning stock. I treasure stock left over from furniture projects for these gift items. Boards of different thickness are ideal for rings of random widths.

With a compass, lay out circles roughly the intended diameter of your finished rings. An inside diameter of about 1¼" to 1⅜" seems fitting; I've settled on 1¼" for my rings because I have a good Forstner bit that size.

In order to produce a nice clean hole, drill a $^1/_{16}$" pilot hole through the center of the ring. Then break the surface with a Forstner bit on one side before reversing and entering the other side. The shallow pre-boring essentially scribes the back and prevents tear-out. If you pre-bore deeper than $^1/_{16}$", you will create a ridge where the borings meet, complicating internal finishing. After center boring, cut the blanks free and remove the corners with a bandsaw (Photo 1).

AW 19:2, p46

Make the expansion chuck

The essential feature of the mounting chuck is that it's a cylinder turned slightly undersize for the rings. The cylinder is then center-bored and cross-sawed with a bandsaw. Pressure applied by a live center in the tailstock will spread the quadrants enough to grip the previously bored stock as shown in the drawing directional.

The dimensions of the chuck will depend upon your lathe, the width of the rings, and your own turning style. Through several trials, I've found that the dimen-sions shown on page 48 work for me. The diameter of the headstock-mounting end should be large enough to provide a sturdy base. The body should be sufficiently long (shown as 6") to allow the gripping surface to expand when pressure is applied by the tailstock. The ring width dictates the diameter of the gripping surface. The ½" center bore works with a 60-degree x ¾" cone found on many live centers.

If you plan to reuse the chuck, select straight-grain hardwood; I chose ash because it is tough and flexible. Mount this stock on a small faceplate or in the jaws of a scroll chuck. I prefer the scroll chuck because I can easily re-center my expansion chuck with the tailstock live center in place before tightening the jaws.

Otherwise, this expansion chuck will require a dedicated faceplate for long-term use. If repeatedly remounted on a faceplate, it's unlikely that the gripping surface will run true. The snug fit at the business end of the wooden chuck does not lend itself to returning.

Turn the rings

The orientation of the grain suggests that you follow the traditional rule of faceplate turning. That is, use bowl-turning tools. In real life, the rings are small and spindle speeds high so that you can use any tool that you like (except a roughing gouge).

My plan starts with stock in the form of planks—not billets. If you are more comfortable with the spindle-turning techniques, then start with square stock bored end-grain. Everything else will follow the same procedures.

Mount the blank on the jaws of the expansion chuck (Photo 2). Bring the tailstock live center up to meet the chuck and apply pressure to expand the chuck quadrants (Photo 3).

I suggest roughing the blank to approximate finish size with a ⅜" bowl gouge (Photo 4). Turning the final shape is then up to you. I'm sure that you will quickly identify your own style and preferences. I favor napkin rings ½" to 1" wide. With relatively wide rings, I usually stop the lathe, release pressure by the tail center and move the ring so that it overhangs the end of the chuck. In this case, I reverse the ring on the chuck to finish the near side.

If you prefer narrower rings, make the bearing surface of your chuck narrower as well. This will allow you to turn with a very slight undercut on each side.

1

Maple stock in steps of preparation. Note the shallow pre-bore (about 1/16" deep) in the top row.

2

The rough blank is shown mounted on the expansion chuck.

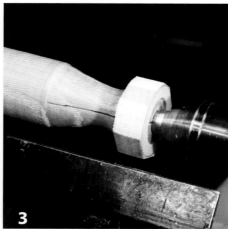

3

The tailstock live center, now snugged up, expands the chuck quadrants.

4

With a 3/8" bowl gouge, true up the napkin ring.

5

Rings dry on bent wire hooks after staining or slow-drying finish coat.

7/8" ash, left, and 7/8" ash with milk paint band, above.

Apply finish

The simple turning of napkin rings usually requires little sanding. A light touch with the finer grades works for me. Depending on how clean you bored with the Forstner bit, you may want to sand the inside surface with a spindle sander.

Your choice of wood species will influence the final finish. I finish my mahogany, Osage orange, and walnut rings with Mylands™ friction polish. (Some light colored stock such as white oak, ash, maple, or sassafras benefit from staining.)

For finishing, I reverse the ring on the chuck halfway through, allowing a deep overhang so I can polish the edge. Off the lathe, I apply the same finish to the inside using a cotton swab applicator. There is no need to polish the inside surface of the ring. When I anticipate heavy use, I apply a final coat of thinned satin polyurethane varnish.

For drying after staining or varnish, I hang the rings on shop-bent hooks made from coat hangers (Photo 5). Mine is an adjustable jig made from ¼"all-thread that I use for numerous applications around the shop.

Jerry Hubschman, a retired biologist, lives in Put In Bay and Yellow Springs, OH. He is a member of the Central Ohio Woodturners. Jerry teaches sign carving at the John C. Campbell Folk School.

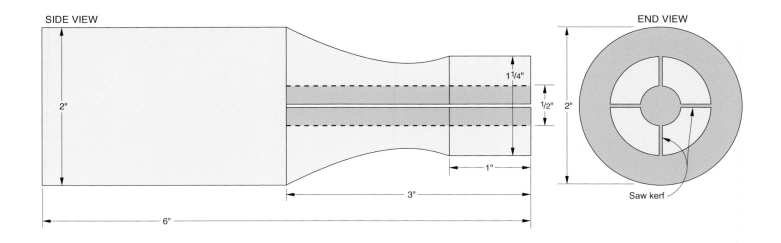

SIDE VIEW

2"

1¼"

1/2"

1"

3"

6"

END VIEW

2"

Saw kerf

Turning the Finger-Snap Top

These basic techniques allow for countless designs

I used to start my day by turning a finger-snap top before going off to my job. A salesperson at work—who was 110 percent Irish—heard about, then saw, my tops and dubbed them Top o' the Mornin.' She ordered 200 to pass out to the Big Brothers Big Sisters organization in her area.

Handmade tops are a great item to give to kids (and adults) or sell at craft fairs at low cost. They also represent a good exercise in product engineering and design. In this article I delve a little into the mechanics of tops and offer some tips to make your tops better. The focus will be one-piece finger-spin tops, but many of the principles provided are applicable to other types of tops as well.

Scale and ease of use

Finger-snap (or spin) tops are small tops that are propelled by a sharp twist of the thumb and first or middle fingers. Kids ages five and up already have the motor skills to spin these, unlike larger tops that are spun with a string or a whip. The tops described here are made from small scraps of wood and can be turned from start to finish in minutes. For demonstrations at shows, they are ideal.

Snap tops generally measure about 1" to 2" (25 to 50 mm) tall and 1" to 2" in diameter at the widest point, although larger tops

Medley of tops

are not uncommon. Wood is the traditional medium, but they can also be made from many readily available materials, such as plastic, aluminum, or brass, with ordinary woodturning tools. They can be painted, colored, grooved, or otherwise decorated from simple to very ornate, as in the collaborations of Bonnie Klein and Jacques Vesery.

Stem

The shaft or stem that drives the top is typically about ³⁄₁₆" (5 mm) in diameter. If the diameter is thicker or thinner than that, the top may become difficult to spin well. Thinner stems impart a faster spin, but the torque required to generate high speed with quick snapping of the fingers will also

AW 27:4, p20

Various tops *(top left clockwise)*: apple, bubinga, white oak, white oak, white oak, cocobolo

be higher. This is particularly noticeable for tops with heavy or large-diameter bodies.

Making the stem taller increases the probability of introducing wobble into the top. Shorter stems are easier to spin, with better performance. Make the stem no longer than half the overall length of the top. Good balancing also requires attention to the moisture content of the material. If your top was turned from green or semi-dry wood, there is a very good chance the stem will warp and make the top wobble.

I find that ornate features on the stem can often contribute to the beauty of tops. Plain shafts tend to look unimaginative if used for every design, whereas those with beads and graceful curves can greatly enhance the value of a top.

Top body
The larger the diameter of the body, the harder it will be to spin the top. Reducing the weight of a large-bodied top, however, can help. Use lighter wood for larger tops and denser wood for smaller tops. Heavy tops will generally spin longer but are harder to get up to full speed because of greater starting inertia. The top must accelerate to high speed in the brief time

that finger snapping imparts its force—less than a second! Keep the mass of the body (center of gravity) to the outer edge when possible for lighter tops to achieve longer spinning capability.

The choice of material for tops can be critical. For maximum performance, choose straight-grained wood free of knots and imperfections with an even density. Be cautious about using wood from branches or small trees. The ideal site for good top wood is about halfway from the center to the sapwood in a tree at least 8" (20 cm) in diameter. A large difference in the spacing of the growth rings will probably lead to instability of the top. Check that the grain lines are evenly spaced across the diameter of the body. Heartwood on one side of the top with sapwood on the other may create imbalance such that the top may not even spin. The grain should run the length of the top and not perpendicular to it. Make sure the outer edge of the body is perfectly smooth for better balance.

For easier spinning, locate the body somewhere in the lower half of the top. The higher the body on the spinning axis, the greater the chance of inducing a wobble in the top. For little kids, a shorter body that is low to the ground is easier to spin and is much more stable than one that rises halfway up the full height. Once you get a better feeling for the center of gravity and its effect on motion, you can experiment and make tops that prove harder to spin but have very interesting behaviors.

Tip of the top
The tip of the top requires a lot of attention. It needs to be in the very center of the bottom and smooth. An ultrasharp tip may actually be worse than one that is a bit rounded over. A sharp point may embed itself in the bearing surface and cause too much

Spalted maple, 1¾" × 1½" (44 mm × 38 mm), 45 second spin time, easy to spin with low center of gravity

Maple, 1½" × 1¾" (38 mm × 44 mm), maple, 65 second spin time, very easy to spin because of low center of gravity; tight sleeper, wakes up slowly

Troubleshooting structural problems with spin

If practice does not overcome spinning difficulties, the top itself may need tuning. First, make sure the tip is smooth. If you feel a burr, use very fine sandpaper to sand the tip perpendicular to the top's axis, but do so very lightly. If the point is off center, you may have to carefully remount the top in a jam or vacuum chuck to true the tip. You can also try to balance a wobbly top, but it takes a bit of an effort. It is obviously better to use uniform wood initially. My brother, a mechanical engineer, floats his tops in water. The heavy side will roll to the bottom. You can remove or add weight as you please to stop or retard the rolling. (A drop of dish soap will break down the water's surface tension.) With some persistence you can balance the top to very tight tolerances and make it spin a very long time, as well as go into a deep "sleep."

Experimentation with performance and design

Most of the rules of thumb offered up to this point apply to making basic tops that spin easily. Once you master these, you may sense that high performance isn't everything. For most people, attractive form and surface also matter. Such considerations, however, may conflict with optimum spin. You have to use your best judgment about which rules to break. For example, you may find it worthwhile to risk slight imbalance or shorter spin time by turning an urnlike silhouette or incorporating some striking sapwood. If the resulting top spins poorly, only a little time and very little material have been lost.

Strive to make your tops as elegant as possible. They will sell better and be much more interesting to look at. Also keep in mind the age and ability of your potential client

friction. It may also not allow the top to orient itself and stand straight up. While making the top, you can insert a round-headed brad into the wood point and then machine it to dead center. A metal tip will last longer than a wooden one, but a wooden tip that is not too pointed will hold up quite well.

Decoration, finish, and presentation

The surface of the top can be grooved with rings or textured, but don't create an imbalance in the process. Kids love to paint the tops and watch the colors change and meld as the top is spinning. If a natural finish is desired, coat with a simple product like Tung oil or buffing wax. Put finished tops in little velvet bags. They make perfect gifts to cherish forever. Consider making platters with slightly concave surfaces to spin the tops on.

Spinning technique

Finger-snap tops are spun by the rapid twisting of the stem between thumb and forefinger (middle finger works as well for some). Hold the top in a vertical position with the arm and hand held steady. The stem is allowed to roll between the two fingers as the snap progresses. Don't try for high speeds initially; that will come with a little practice. If snapped well, a good top in excellent balance should spin between 3,000 to 4,000 rpm and continue for about a minute or more, depending on the physical characteristics of the top, supporting surface, and initial snap speed. If the bearing surface is rough, friction will slow the top down sooner. If accelerated to speeds that it cannot handle, the top will wobble out of control.

An alternative method is to spin the top on the end of the stem rather than the tip. Just above a suitable surface, hold the inverted top vertically, body and tip up, between the first finger and thumb. Snap as before, but afterward quickly pull your hand away, allowing the top to fall free to the surface below. This requires a bit of practice. The top may hesitate a bit before righting itself on the end of the stem. Some tops spin better on the end of the stem than on the tip as designed. Go figure!

or audience, including the more sophisticated top lover. Experiment with different grains, densities, stem lengths, diameters, tip sharpness, and placement of the center of gravity. Surprisingly, you can make good spinning tops by doing everything "wrong." You never know until you try. I even keep many of my top "failures," since they are still lovely to look at. Some of the tops shown here have broken the rules in various ways. One of my very best spinners was cut from a 2"- (50 mm-) diameter maple branch with pith. On the other hand, if you want only a consistently good spinner, stick to the basics.

Top jargon

Along with tops comes a set of terms that you may want to use with your audiences. During spinning, a well-balanced top will come to a position where it appears to be actually standing still. This is called *going to sleep* or the top is *asleep*. At other times the top may have a secondary spinning axis called precession. This occurs when the axis of the top wobbles in a slow circle around the tip (just as the earth wobbles on its own axis, though much more gradually). As the top slows down, it will progressively tilt, which is called *waking up* (technically distinct from wobbling). Each top has its own sleeping and waking up pattern, which gives it a unique signature.

Games to play with the tops

Hold a contest to see which tops can spin the longest. Note that tops spun in a slightly concave dish will bang

Ebony, redheart, 2" × ¾" (50 mm × 19 mm), 20 second spin time, average spinner, less spin time because of its small size

Cocobolo, 2" × 1" (50 mm × 25 mm), 15 second spin time, difficult spinner because of its high center of gravity and narrow diameter

into each other; find out whose top is left standing at the end. Try spinning your tops on unusual surfaces such as the back or palm of your hand. Try to spin the top on the base of the stem instead of the pointed tip, as described earlier. Above all, have fun!

Roger Zimmerman *resides in Wausau, WI and is a writer, demonstrator, and member of the Wisconsin Valley Woodturners.*

Pen with a Wooden Grip

Start with a kit but then make it your own

Most pen kits I've seen use metal or plastic for the grip section, but I miss the beauty of a wooden-grip section. Metal grips add considerable weight to a pen. Weight isn't the most important factor in selecting a pen; in fact, many people prefer some heft. But to me, light weight is a bonus.

If you're ready to try a turned grip section from wood, the project on these pages shows you how to fabricate a closed-end fountain pen with a wooden grip. In a subsequent article, I will describe how to add a fully functional, flexible wood clip for the ultimate wood show pen. But for now, we will use the standard clips, simply replacing the stock metal finial with one turned from wood.

This project is based on parts from a Gentlemen's pen model. For the most part, you can apply these instructions to any other closed-end design. However, the grip section featured in this article is specifically for the Gentlemen's kit, the Statesman, and some of the other large kits from Crafts Supplies USA, such as the Emperor, the Lotus, or the Imperial. The sidebar details how to make a wood section for the El Grande, Churchill, or Ligero models.

In planning the design, there are some special considerations. When filling a fountain pen from a bottle, the end of the grip is inserted into ink. Because you don't want ink soaking into the end grain, it's important to completely seal all the wood surfaces. More about that later.

Get started

For turning tools, you'll need a ½" spindle gouge or skew, and a parting tool or square scraper. A diamond-point tool is handy for pen projects. For details on specialty penturning tools, see the photo, which includes a pen mill, shim tubes, Beall collet chuck, expansion mandrel, and other penturning tools.

Note: You can construct a shim tube by gluing a Slimline brass tube into a piece of scrap wood. The wood is then turned to just slip inside the larger brass tube used for this pen. This keeps the center shaft of the pen mill concentric with the barrel and the end perfectly square. Strictly speaking, for the pen body and cap, such shim tubes are not needed because the faces can be squared tight on the lathe.

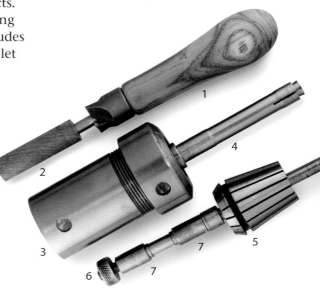

A pen mill (1) allows you to square the ends of the pen barrels. Make appropriate shim tubes (2) as needed. A Beall collet chuck (3) is the ultimate holding accessory, shown here with a homemade expansion mandrel (4). (A commercial version of this expansion mandrel is available from pen-supply catalogs.) At the bottom you see an industry-standard ER32 collet (5) holding a pen mandrel (6) with bushings (7). You need two sets of bushings: Gentlemen's bushings for the cap and Broker bushings for the grip section (shown).

The grip of each collet is 0.040"; make sure you have the right size collet. My homemade mandrel is 0.615" at the mounting end, so a 5/8" collet (a 16mm collet if you have a metric set) is right for me. Because each collet grips a range, it doesn't matter whether your collets are imperial or metric sizes.

This project requires more than a standard pen blank. You can turn the body and cap from one pen blank, but you'll need an extra piece for the grip section and the cap finial. If you are cutting your own pen blanks, this does not present a problem, but if you purchase blanks you will need the equivalent of 1½ blanks. Carefully choose blanks that have similar grain. The project shown uses *afzelia xylay*, one of my favorites.

The photo *above right* shows the components required from the Gentlemen's kit. Put the leftover body and cap finials into your spare parts box for another project.

Turn the pen body

Creating the closed-end body is relatively straightforward. Cut a 3" piece of pen blank, and use a 15/32" bit to drill it to the length of the body brass tube (2.36" for this project). Drill a second hole 2.6" deep, using a #N drill bit, or 5/16" if you don't have letter bits. The holes should be concentric, so drill the second hole before removing the blank from the drill jig. This secondary hole allows a spare cartridge to be stored or accommodates a conversion pump.

In the steps shown here, I do not use a tailstock. The Beall chuck eliminates the chance that the mandrel will come out of the headstock. If you use a drill chuck to hold the mandrel, you need to bring up a live center to prevent the chuck from coming out of the spindle.

Coat the mandrel with wax; this will prevent the blank from sticking to the mandrel if you use

This pen project requires 1½ pen blanks and just the Gentlemen's parts shown *above*. Discard extra parts from the pen kit.

With a 1/2" spindle gouge or 1" skew, turn the pen barrel with a rounded end.

cyanoacrylate (CA) glue for a finish. It is not necessary to use a pen mill to square the blank; we'll do that later on the mandrel.

Measure the trim ring that butts up against the open end; this one measured 0.598". It's best to measure each ring. Be sure to use the same calipers on the pen barrel. Using a ½" spindle gouge or a 1" skew, turn to whatever shape pleases you *(Photo 1)*. For a large pen, I prefer a rounded shape. The safest way to round over the end is with a diamond-point tool, but a spindle gouge or a skew works fine.

Make sure there is enough wall strength where the body brass tube ends. I aim for 0.050". The brass tube diameter is 0.450", so you want to measure at least 0.550" at that point. This still allows you to give the pen a

nice shape with a slight taper in the upper part. Use calipers to bring the headstock end of the barrel to about 0.592"–0.595", slightly smaller than the 0.598" trim ring. Remember that the CA finish will build up a few thousandths. Square the open (left) end with a parting tool.

Apply the finish

For finish, apply the first coat of thin CA with 400-grit sandpaper. (Because CA is an irritant, I prefer low-odor CA.) While the lathe is running, work the CA into the grain, which creates a slurry that seals the wood and fills small holes or torn grain. When the finish dries, sand down the CA completely to bare wood, which removes any cloudy film sitting on the surface.

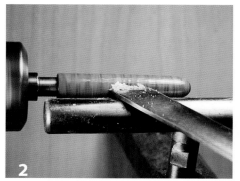

With an old skew gently scrape cured cyanoacrylate (CA) from the body.

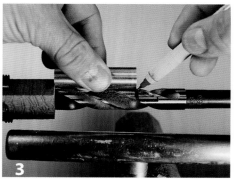

Use the cap brass tube to precisely mark the drilling depth.

With the cap mounted between bushings, turn the stock to a 0.650" diameter.

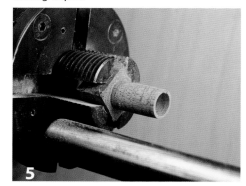

Reduce the diameter to 7/8", which will slip into the cap brass tube.

Part off the finial cap, leaving a 1/2"-long tenon.

With the lathe running at a low speed, drizzle CA on the blank, and spread with your finger wrapped on a polyethylene bag. Repeat this process to build three or four coats of finish.

Scrape and polish

By the time you've applied three or four coats, the surface should be a little bumpy. If you start sanding this, there is a good chance that you'll sand through some of the low spots before removing all of the high spots. With a skew, gently scrape the CA, taking off fine shavings (Photo 2). You want to remove all the high spots; generally 60–80 percent of the surface will be dull. Then return to 400-grit sandpaper and remove all the shiny spots. Do not wrap the sand paper around the body; you have to allow dust to fall off.

Here's the sanding technique that works well for me: While I hold the sandpaper in my right hand, my left index finger rides the blank to feel for bumps and monitor the temperature. At this step, the surface needs to be completely dull; any shiny spots are low and will show up later.

Finish up by sanding the barrel lengthwise with the lathe stopped; turn the spindle by hand. Now step through Micro-mesh 1500, 1800, 2400, 3200, and 4000 finishes. At each step, polish out the lengthwise scratches from the previous step on

the running lathe, and then finish up with new lengthwise strokes before switching to the next finer size. Concentrate on the end of the barrel throughout the polishing; it spins slower than the rest of the pen and it's easy to end up with a duller finish there.

Finally, remove the collet chuck from the lathe and buff on a buffing wheel charged with white diamond. (The collet chuck makes a convenient handle.) For most projects, white-diamond compound is all that's needed to bring up the luster. If a defect appears, go back to a Tripoli polishing bar, and then repeat with the white diamond.

Finally, retrim the open end to produce a square shoulder (usually a little CA needs to be removed).

Turn the cap

Prepare the cap barrel blank in the conventional way. Cut to the brass tube length (2.05") plus ¼" and

drill a 37/64" hole. With the drill bit shoulder flush with the blank, use the brass tube to mark the drilling depth (Photo 3). You can drill this hole at the lathe or with a drill press. Take care to avoid exiting the cap.

Cut the drilled blank to the brass-tube length. Glue in the brass tube using 5-minute epoxy. Square the ends using a pen mill or a disk/belt sander with a squaring jig. Turn between bushings to final diameter 0.650" (Photo 4). Apply a CA finish following the step-by-step process described earlier.

Make the cap finial

The cap finial is turned from a 1" to 1½" pen blank. The exposed finial is about 3/8" high, and you'll need a 3/8" to ½" tenon inside the cap. There are plenty of techniques for this key detail, but I prefer holding this small cap in a 4-jaw scroll chuck.

Drill a 13/32" hole to a depth of 1", measured at the shoulder of

---

7 With a scraper or parting tool, reduce the centerband fitting for a slip-fit.

8 To knock out the threads from the grip, use a 19/64" punch and block with a 10mm hole.

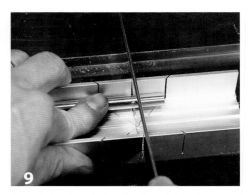

9 A model railroader's miter box is ideal to cut brass tubes to length.

the drill bit. Using a spare tube or the pen barrel to check the fit, turn a tenon that slips into the tube with a 7/8" length. It's OK to be a little undersized at the open end, but you need a precise fit at the shoulder to ensure proper centering of the clip attachment ring *(Photo 5)*.

Switch to the Beall collet chuck and appropriate collet, and reverse the finial. The wall thickness of the tenon tube is about 0.06". Turn the finial to the desired shape; I like a ⅜" height for the finial. (The dome diameter needs to match the pen barrel, i.e. 0.650". Beyond that, the shape is arbitrary.)

Finish with thin CA as described above. Then resquare the shoulder, taking care to remove any CA that oozed around during the finishing step. Part off the cap finial, leaving about ½" of the tenon. *(Photo 6)*.

Before assembly, turn down the centerband fitting for a slip-fit. I chuck up a center coupling in the appropriate collet and screw the centerband fitting onto that. A scraper easily turns down the black plastic and the metal part *(Photo 7)*.

Assemble the cap by epoxying in the centerband fitting, finial, and clip. Be sure to get some epoxy under the clip ring to prevent it from rotating later.

Make the grip

Unscrew the nib from the grip section (it comes out as one assembly). Use a 19/64" punch (a transfer punch set in 64ths is a great tool to acquire for general pen disassembly) plus a hardwood block with a 10mm (25/64") drilled hole to carefully knock out the threads from the stock grip section *(Photo 8)*. Tap lightly or you may damage the internal threads of the piece you are removing.

After removing the threaded piece, screw the nib assembly into the threads to check the fit. Since the grip section needs to pass through the cap threads, you need to measure the ID of the cap threads, or measure the front of the original metal grip. On the Gentlemen's kit, this is .440": This is the maximum diameter you can allow for the wood grip.

Cut a 3/4" section off a spare tube for a Broker pen. These tubes are available from Craft Supplies USA or Woodcraft as spares for the original Wall Street pen. A small miter box *(Photo 9)* is the best tool I found to cut brass tubes. Exacto's razor-saw and miter gauge (about $14), used by model railroaders, are available at many hobby stores.

Cut a 3/4" long section of wood, and drill with #U (0.368") bit. It is important to get an excellent glue joint here, so take all the precautionary steps: Sand the brass tube slightly, cover the brass tube

with glue, cover the inside of the drilled hole with glue, and insert with a twisting motion. Unlike most other pen parts, this glued tube has an unbalanced load on it, and must be perfect to not come loose in time.

After the glue dries, scrape glue residue from the inside of the brass tube using a round file or the small blade of a pocketknife. Square the ends down to the brass tube.

Now comes another critical step: Because you will insert the end in ink while filling from a bottle, it must be sealed well. I do this by running a small bead of thin CA around the brass tube *(Photo 10)*. Once it dries, resquare using the pen mill, being careful to leave a continuous film of CA.

Now turn the barrel. Use the 0.425" bushings from a Broker pen. Check the sizing frequently with calipers; turn to 0.44" or slightly under. It's actually better to turn slightly under 0.44" and build back up with CA; that way, you can be sure you have a good seal all around. Avoid gluing the grip section to the bushings by coating the bushings with wax before you start. This is especially important with a small piece like the grip section. The final diameter of 0.44" is critical. If you go above that, the grip may not pass through the cap threads. If you reduce the diameter too much, the thread pre-alignment suffers, it's

Square the end

Soak the end with CA

Resquare the bead

10

To prevent ink from entering the grip section when reloading the fountain pen, follow the 3-step process: square, soak with CA and leave bead, and resquare the bead.

11

Turn the grip between centers and finish with thin CA glue.

12

Screw the nib housing into the threaded fitting knocked out from the original grip.

13

Hold the nib housing in a Beall collet chuck and reduce the tenon to 0.336".

14

When reassembled, the new parts are ready to thread into the body.

harder to start the thread, or easier to cross-thread the pen.

Turn a slight hourglass shape to the grip (*Photo 11*). The drilled hole was nominally 0.368" so you can turn down to just above that. (I routinely go down to 0.385".) Finish with CA as described earlier.

Adapt the nib

First remove the nib. By squeezing the two wings of the nib and rocking back and forth, you can remove the nib and feed (the feathery part), leaving the nib housing (*Photo 12*).

The nib housing has three diameters—the main barrel is about 0.295", a short section that tenons into the original metal grip section is 0.375", and a slightly larger disk you won't need to change. Turn down the tenon to fit into the grip made earlier. The Beall collet chuck with a 5⁄16" collet provides the simplest way to hold the nib housing (*Photo 13*).

Use a parting tool to trim the short tenon to 0.336". Remove the nib housing from the collet to check the fit into the Broker brass tube (it remounts in the collet with sufficient accuracy) or measure the tenon.

Assemble the pen

Reinsert the nib and feed. Notice there is a flat inside the housing. The feed can only go in one position. The nib and feed should be fully seated.

Dry-assemble the parts. The threads removed from the original grip should screw into the nib assembly smoothly. Be careful when threading. The nib assembly is soft plastic, and the threads are fine. You'll notice the threaded piece is slightly loose in the brass tube— that's OK. Use 5-minute epoxy inside both ends of the turned section and screw the pieces together (*Photo 14*). You can still remove the nib itself and swap to a different size or a 14k nib by removing it and the feed.

When you glue up the grip section, orient it to show the nicest grain lined up with the nib. With a closed-end pen, you can easily damage the closed end during assembly, so make sure the anvil of your press has a soft liner. (I like turning down the metal tenon of the center coupling for a slip-fit and gluing it in place.)

Use epoxy to glue the center coupling into the pen body. Screw the grip section into the center coupling first, then glue the center coupling into the body. Select the best grain to line up with the nib.

That's it! This lightweight, large fountain pen shows off wood like no other. It weighs about half as much as a standard kit Gentlemen's pen.

Richard Kleinhenz, pen turner, instructor, and author of The Pen Turner's Bible, *is the founder of the Penmaker's Guild and owner of Wappingers Woodworkers in NY. Visit Richard at www.beautifulhandmadepens.com.*

Modifying the El Grande for a wood grip

A similar grip modification is possible on the El Grande family of pens (El Grande, Churchill, Ligero), and perhaps other kits. On those models, there is little or no weight-saving since the grip section is plastic, but the modification shows more wood.

Remove the nib and feed by squeezing on the wings of the nib and rocking the nib and feed out as described for Gentlemen's pen. Your goal is to turn down the plastic grip to slip a Broker tube over it, which has a turned and shaped grip section as above.

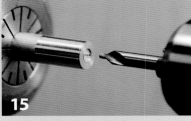

15

A centering drill is ideal for drilling aluminum rod.

The outer diameter of the grip section should be 0.433" to clear the cap threads and ensure thread prealignment. The Beall collet chuck comes in handy because it grips the extension just behind the threads.

To avoid damaging or collapsing the section, I turn a small insert (you can use hardwood, brass, or aluminum). You cannot use a live center directly in the other end of the section because an internal flat (there to align the feed section) will push the point off-center and it will not run true.

16

Turn a 0.335" tenon about 0.020" wide in the insert.

Note that there is a small recess that is circular and concentric; I missed this detail until fellow penturner Perry Copus pointed it out to me recently. This recess is enough to make a centering disc. For this step, I used ⅜" aluminum rod. Use a centering drill with 60-degree countersink. (A centering drill is a short specialty drill that is used widely in metalworking and is available in machine-shop supply stores.) If started a bit off-center, the bit will pull itself into the center *(Photo 15)*.

17

Grip the El Grande section in a collet, add the little support disk, and use a live center in the dimple. Turn away the contoured grip to a .335" diameter for a slip-fit Broker tube.

Drill deep enough to create a conical surface. Now part off about a ¼" disc. Reverse it in the collet. With a parting tool, turn a small 0.335"-diameter tenon about 0.020" wide. *(Photo 16)*.

This 0.335" diameter is the ID of the Broker kit brass tube *(Photo 17)* that will support the turned wood section You can use the original plastic section for test fits.

This little disc will now be the outboard support. Now you can turn the section down for a slip-fit of the Broker brass tube, and epoxy it in place.

Within the El Grande family, the Ligero is actually the most suitable for this modification because there is no load on the turned wood.

—*Rich Kleinhenz*

Christmas Tree Topper

Show off your turning skills this holiday season

If you are a woodturner who turns holiday tree ornaments, the fall and early winter months are busy times. Over the years, I have turned a lot of tree ornaments, birdhouse ornaments, acorn birdhouse ornaments, teacher's bell ornaments. You name it; I've probably turned it for the holiday tree.

I wish I had a dollar for every time my wife, Susan, has asked me to come up with a design for a Christmas tree topper. But I just hadn't found a style of tree topper that I liked.

Then I remembered listening to someone critiquing hollow forms. That person (David Ellsworth, I recall) said that one of the characteristics of a good turned piece is that the form looks pleasing even if you turn it upside down. I turned one of my standard Christmas ornaments upside down and had my tree topper design right in front of me!

The major difference between the tree topper and the Christmas tree ornament that I turn—besides being upside-down—is that it's a bit larger, so that it noticeably crowns the top of a tree. And, this design has what I call a funnel on the bottom so it can fit securely on top of the tree.

The diameter of my Christmas tree ornaments is about 2¼". The tree topper globes are generally 2½" or larger in diameter. The important thing is that the finial and funnel are all in proportion to the size of the globe.

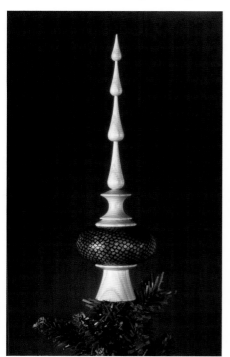

AW 20:3, p28

Get started

The finial requires a small roughing-out gouge. A ¾" roughing-out gouge works fine, but if you like turning pieces like this, a ½" roughing-out gouge is a big help.

You also will need some good bent-angle tools for hollowing the globe and a small round skew as shown. Other than that, standard turning tools should suffice: ⅜" spindle gouge, ½" spindle gouge (optional), small squarenose scraper, ¼" roundnose scraper, small skew, and parting tools.

You will need a sturdy chuck with #2 jaws for turning the globe. A set of spigot jaws is almost indispensable for turning the finial, but you can manage without them—the process is just a bit slower. If you don't have spigot jaws, use a faceplate with an attached waste block. Drill a 1" hole in the waste block, then turn a 1" tenon.

In my work, I make extensive use of glue blocks. These allow me to use smaller pieces of precious wood and to get the wood away from the spinning jaws so that I can turn it safely. Don't allow the waste blocks to be too long, or you will have a chatter problem.

You will need a piece of burl about 2¾×2½" for the tree-topper globe. If you have other nicely figured wood such as ambrosia maple, incorporate that.

You also will need a piece of straight-grained wood for the finial and a piece of similar wood for the funnel. For the toppers featured in this article, the finial material is about 1⅜×8" and the funnel material about 1⅜×4".

Turn the globe

Using a spindle gouge, true the globe stock to about 2½" diameter and begin shaping the globe. (I prefer an oblong shape to a spherical globe.) Regardless of the

After truing up the globe stock, use calipers to check the diameter of the material. The globe should be about 2½" in diameter.

shape you select, make sure that you leave about 1½" of material at the top of the globe to allow you to hollow. If you remove too much material, you will get a lot of chatter when you attempt to hollow, and the piece may fly off the lathe.

After shaping the globe, mark the opening of the bottom of the tree topper. This will be the end toward the tailstock. Using a set of vernier calipers or a compass, mark about a 1" opening, then drill a ½" hole all the way through the globe. This hole will center the top and bottom of the globe.

Open the interior of the globe with a small squarenose scraper. This tool isn't a heavy tool, so when it starts to chatter, do not cut any deeper with it or you may have a nasty catch. Once

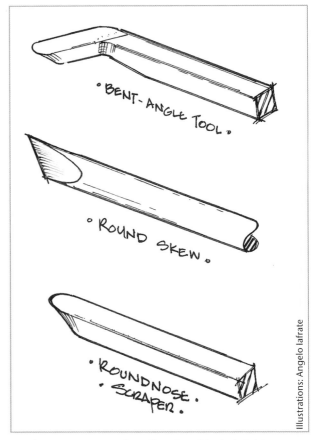

BENT-ANGLE TOOL

ROUND SKEW

ROUNDNOSE SCRAPER

For this project, a set of small tools will be helpful. You may find use for as many as three bent-angle tools of various sizes to remove stock.

you remove all the material you can with the squarenose scraper, switch to the small roundnose scraper and remove more material from the interior. Be sure to use compressed air often to remove chips from the interior.

Now, switch to bent-angle tools to thin down the wall. To hollow something small, I rely on three bent-angle tools—a long, medium, and short—although you can generally get by with two, a long one and a short one. The short tool allows you to get around the initial opening, while the longer tools allow you to go deeper into the turning. The bent-angle tools I use are homemade. The shafts of the tools are ¼" mild steel, and the tips are ³⁄₁₆" high-speed steel. I weld the tips at about a 42-degree angle using Euctectic silver solder. (No. 1630XFC available from Euctectic; 800-323-4845.)

When hollowing the globe section of the tree topper, I actually alternate between using the bent-angle tools and the roundnose scraper. After using the bent-angle tools to get "around the corners" of the globe, I switch to a straight roundnose scraper.

The scraper is easier to control when hollowing the final one-third of the globe. Once I have the piece hollowed to about ⅛" thick, I refine the top, reducing the area that allowed me to hollow without a lot of chatter.

When you're pleased with the wall thickness, sand the piece and part it from the lathe.

At this point, the globe may be considered finished. As alternate designs, you can paint it, carve it, burn it, or dye it. Two variations are shown.

A bent-angle tool is essential in removing stock from inside the globe.

When turning the finial, always leave adequate mass at the base to dampen vibration. A small round skew and ½" roughing-out gouge are ideal for this task.

Switch to a small parting tool to turn the tenon that will fit into the globe.

Turn the finial

Turn the finial from straight-grained stock about 1⅜×8" long. Mount the piece in a chuck with spigot jaws. The spigot jaws extend out about 1½", producing the solid grip required for turning without tailcenter support.

With the finial stock held in the spigot jaws and the tailcenter in place, use the roughing-out gouge to turn a taper on what will become the top of the finial. Turn the roughing-out gouge on its side using the flat area of the tool.

Now, remove the tailcenter and use the skew to refine the top segment of the finial. I use the small spindle gouge to round over each segment on the finial. Sand each segment and apply sanding sealer before proceeding to the next one. The finial will be too delicate to sand after turning all the segments.

The first segment dictates the length and size of the rest of the segments. Once you establish the first segment, each successive segment needs to be a little bit larger and a little bit longer. Turn segments 2, 3, and 4 using a roughing-out gouge on its side, followed by the skew and finally the spindle gouge.

Once the four segments are complete, use a spindle gouge to turn a cove and decorative steps at the base of the finial. After sanding and finishing this section, cut a tenon to fit into the ½" hole in the top of the globe. Undercut the tenon so it fits on the globe with no gaps. Finally, part the finial from the lathe and glue the finial into the globe.

Turn the funnel

At this point, you should have a completed globe with an attached finial. Now you need some attractive way to have the tree topper sit on the top of the tree.

Hold the funnel stock (about 1⅜×4") in the spigot jaws and turn

To speed up hollowing of the funnel, remove stock with a ½" drill bit.

With a spindle gouge, enlarge the opening of the funnel. When completed, the tree leader (top) will fit into this opening.

it into a cylindrical shape. Estimate the finished length of your funnel, then cut a tenon that will fit into the bottom of the tree-topper globe.

Using a spindle gouge and skew, shape the funnel, then drill a ½" hole through the bottom of the funnel. With a small spindle gouge, open the interior of the funnel. Sand the funnel, apply sanding sealer, part from the lathe, and glue in place.

Apply the finish

All that remains is to apply a finish. Spray the completed tree topper with satin lacquer, then carefully buff with 0000 steel wool before applying a second coat.

If you prefer an oil finish, carefully apply oil to the pieces separately prior to assembly.

*A previous member of the AAW Board of Directors, **Robert Rosand** is an instructor and frequent contributor to* American Woodturner. *Visit Robert at www.rrosand.com.*

Colorful Christmas Lights

A clever design for spreading holiday cheer

Photos: Judy Chesnut and Vickie McClain

AW 19:3, p39

This past Christmas, I gave more than 60 Christmas bulbs as gifts—and not one required an electrical outlet.

You can turn these light bulbs in a variety of sizes for different uses. I have made them for Christmas tree ornaments, decorations for holiday wraps, and turned smaller versions for necklaces and earrings.

For this project, my favorite wood is Dymondwood. Although the laminations are slightly more difficult to turn, it does make an attractive bulb like the examples shown here.

Once you get started, it is easy to turn these in multiple quantities because it doesn't take much more time to make six than it does to make one.

I've collected Christmas ornaments since 1970. This design was partially inspired by an ornament Chip Siskey brought to one of our Kansas City-area AAW chapter holiday parties.

Select stock and tools

I recommend the first time you make these, choose a wood that is easy to turn. Padauk (for the bulb) and yellowheart (for the threads) work well. You'll also need a 1/4" birch dowel.

I suggest you use whatever tools you are most comfortable with and happen to own. I turn my Christmas bulbs with micro (also called mini or

detail) tools. If you turn these bulbs with larger tools, use a light touch.

Cut the blanks

The padauk blank is 1" square and 1-3/4" long. The yellowheart is 3/4" square by 5/8" long. For this part, I slice pen blanks up in 5/8" lengths. Cut the 1/4" birch dowel 2-1/4" long.

I mount my stock in a Beall collet chuck with a 1/4" collet. If you do not have a collet chuck, a set of spigot jaws will work. Just cut the

yellowheart blank long enough to mount in the chuck and eliminate the 1/4" dowel.

For me, the dowel serves a dual purpose. The dowel makes it quick and easy to mount and turn multiple bulbs. In addition, I leave enough dowel on the bulb to serve as the filament contact portion when I part off the bulb from the headstock.

Drill the blanks and glue the parts

Mark the centers on the yellow-heart and padauk. I drill with a size F bit so that the hole is slightly larger than 1/4". This produces a snug fit, but not so tight that it splits the blanks. If you don't have a size F drill bit, you can lightly sand the dowel so it doesn't fit in the hole too tightly.

Using a vise or clamp to hold the stock, drill a hole 5/8" deep in the end of the padauk. Drill completely through the yellow-heart as shown in *Photo A*.

Assemble the three pieces with cyanoacrylate (CA) glue.

Mount the bulb stock

Mount the blank on the lathe as shown in *Photo B*. I like to leave just enough dowel exposed to safely part it off with a small skew when finished. This reduces the chance of vibration or of the dowel breaking.

Snug the tailstock, then begin turning

It is important to bring up the tailstock and check it often to be sure it remains snug. If you try to turn this without the tailstock, the dowel will twist and break.

Using a light touch, turn the bulb to a cylinder. Check your tailstock again and be sure it is snug, but not too tight. Begin shaping the bulb with a 3/8" spindle gouge, taking light cuts.

Turn the bulb shape

For reference while turning, it is helpful to have a real Christmas bulb in front of you. At this point, I suggest holding a dark-colored bulb up to the stock and lightly touch the bulb to the padauk while the lathe is turning. This leaves a line around the wood, which marks the widest part of the bulb as shown in *Photo C*. I cut downhill from that line, which simplifies shaping.

Beads sub for threads

Instead of threads, I turn three beads on the yellowheart. This gives the appearance of threads and they are much easier to turn.

Refine the shape

After cutting the beads, refine the shape of the bulb. leaving just enough at the tailstock end to keep the bulb stable. I do most of my sanding at this point, beginning at 220 grit and working through 600 grit.

With a small skew or gouge, gently part off the bulb at the tailstock end as shown in *Photo D*. Finish-sand as necessary.

Apply finish

Apply the finish while the bulb is still mounted in the chuck. I've had good luck applying a sanding sealer and then friction polish. With the lathe running at a slow speed (500 rpm), buff with a soft paper towel.

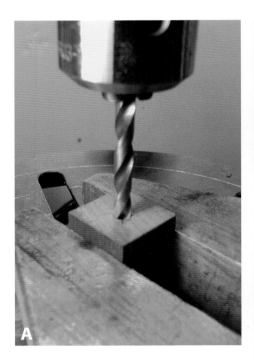

Getting Started in Woodturning

Don't use too much muscle on this step as the dowel can easily twist off.

With a marker, add detail

Stop the lathe and add a black line around the dowel next to the beads as shown in *Photo E*. Rotate the lathe by hand and support the marker on the tool rest. I prefer a flat-tip calligraphy pen, because it makes a neater line than a round tip. These pens are available at office-supply or art stores.

Parting off from lathe

With a small skew, part off the dowel at the edge of the black line, leaving about 1/8" of dowel on the bulb as shown in *Photo F*.

Final touches

Using a #60 drill bit, drill a small hole in the center of the dowel about 1/2" deep as shown in *Photo G*. I have not found a screweye small enough for this ornament, so I use the eye from a #202 brass fishing hook.

Before gluing the shank into the bulb, paint the end of the dowel with a silver Sharpie pen (available at office-supply stores) as shown in *Photo H*.

Finally, adhere the shank of the fishing hook into the bulb with CA glue as shown in *Photo I*.

*Woodturner, writer, and instructor **Judy Chestnut** is vice president of the Kansas City Woodturners Club.*

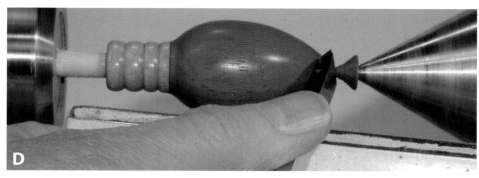

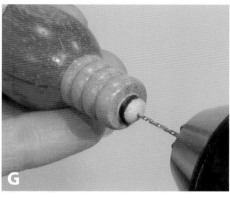

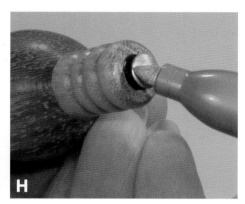

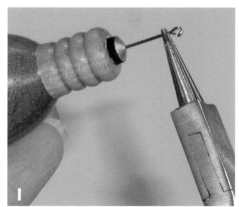

Two-Part Goblet: Tenon Connects Bowl to Stem

Simple solutions for a challenging turning technique

About a year ago, we were invited to attend the bat mitzvah of a friend's daughter. Unfortunately, we were unable to attend because of prior commitments, but we wanted to send a meaningful gift.

The gift we came up with was a kiddush cup. Kiddush is a ceremony held at the beginning of many Jewish holy days, including the bat mitzvah (females) and bar mitzvah (males). The kiddush cup or wine goblet is used during that ceremony.

Traditionally, kiddush cups are made of gold or silver and many are etched with images of grapes to represent wine. They may include images of birds or animals, people's names, or Old Testament verses.

As a woodturner, I turned the kiddush cup from wood. Using pyrography tools, I burned Mimi's name on the goblet in Hebrew. My wife, Susan, painted the stem portion of the goblet.

If you turn a goblet, it may be made out of a single piece of wood. Or you may turn the goblet in two sections—bowl and stem/foot—as I did. For this project, the bowl section was turned from maple burl and the stem was turned from cherry.

Get started

For tools, you'll need a ⅜" bowl gouge or ⅜" spindle gouge, ½" or ¾" roundnose scraper, ½" skew, roughing-out gouge, and parting tool. You'll also need a 4-jaw self-centering scroll chuck.

Photos: Bob Rosand   Illustration: Roxanne LeMoine

AW 20:3, p42

Getting Started in Woodturning

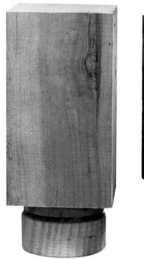 

The cherry stem, left, and maple bowl, right, are shown mounted to waste blocks. Be sure to choose straight-grained stock.

GOBLET FULL-SIZE PATTERN

3¹⁄₈"

3³⁄₄"

³⁄₈"-diameter

3⁵⁄₈"

2³⁄₈"

The illustration above provides rough dimensions for a goblet.

For the bowl, I chose a piece of 3¼×4" maple burl. For the stem, I selected a piece of 2½×4½" cherry. You'll simplify your lathe work on the stem by choosing straight-grained turning stock.

Turn the bowl

When you turn the bowl section of the goblet, think of the project as just a bowl. The walls are steeper and thinner, and, in this case, you need to turn a tenon on the bottom to fit into the stem. But nonetheless, it's still a bowl.

Using a ³⁄₈" bowl gouge or ³⁄₈" spindle gouge, true up the sides of the bowl, then true up what will become the top. (If you don't true the blank, you will get a fair amount of vibration.)

Begin to define the shape of the bowl section with the gouge. You need to leave enough material at what will become the base of the bowl so that you can hollow it without getting a lot of vibration.

Once you can see the shape of the bowl emerging, begin hollowing the interior. After you true up the

top, bore a 1½" Forstner bit almost to the bottom of the bowl section. The more material you remove with the drill bit, the less you have to remove with the gouge.

Begin hollowing with the small bowl gouge. Don't hollow too deep. Why? As you go deeper, the wall becomes flexible and chatter develops. After you get a finish cut on that top third, proceed with the middle third.

Once you have hollowed the vessel about two-thirds of the way down, return to the outside and continue refining the bottom section of the goblet. When you're satisfied with the shape, remove more material from the inside. You may need to do this two or three times until the wall thickness is consistent and you have hollowed as deep as necessary.

As you get near the bottom of the interior of the bowl section, you will no longer get a smooth cut because you can no longer rub the bevel of the gouge. When this happens, switch to a roundnose scraper to finish the bottom of the interior of the goblet.

When you are satisfied with the depth and wall thickness of the goblet section, sand the inside and outside of the bowl. To prevent the bowl section from popping off the waste block, support the piece with

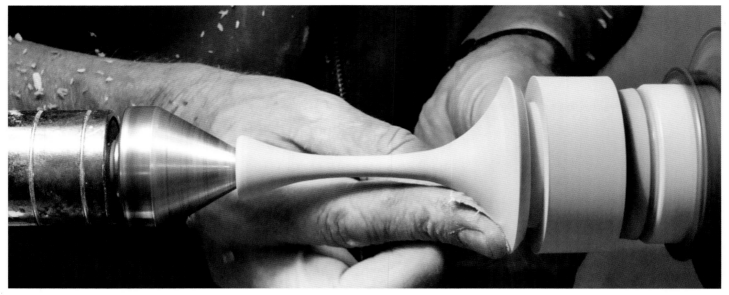

After turning the stem (still supported by the tailcenter), sand the piece smooth with progressive grits of 150-, 180-, and 220-grit papers.

After sanding the stem, begin hogging off stock with a spindle gouge to prepare the base of the stem.

your hand while sanding. With the spindle gouge, refine the base a bit more and turn a ⅜" tenon about ½" long. This tenon will fit into the stem and base.

Turn the stem and foot

Turn the stem of the goblet from a piece of straight-grained cherry. Glue this turning stock to a waste block, then mount in a self-centering scroll chuck. To be safe, bring up the tailcenter, then use the roughing-out gouge to turn the stem to a cylinder.

Remove the tailcenter and true up what will be the top of the stem. Using a small spindle gouge, turn a recess for the bowl base. Then drill a ⅜" hole ½" deep for the bowl tenon. Check the fit.

If the recess isn't deep enough, use the spindle gouge to make it

deeper. When you are satisfied with the fit, bring up the tailcenter again for support.

Use the parting tool to define what will be the base of the goblet stem (for this goblet, 3¾"). The finished width of the base will be about 2⅜". Using a combination of the roughing-out gouge and spindle gouge, turn the stem of the goblet. The finished diameter of the stem should be about ⁵⁄₁₆", depending on esthetics and your skill level. After you sand the goblet, part the goblet stem from the waste block.

You could use a parting tool to separate the stem and base from the waste block, but that would leave an unfinished base. Attempting to sand the base flat on a belt sander—which is what I used to do—won't guarantee that the finished goblet will sit level.

The method I prefer is to remove waste from below the foot of the stem with a spindle gouge. This gives me enough clearance to use the spindle gouge to undercut the foot slightly. When I've reduced the tenon to about ¼", I use the long point of a skew to carefully cut away the remaining tenon.

After parting off the stem, sand the bottom with a sanding disc as shown.

Apply the finish

For most of my turned pieces, I apply three or four coats of a penetrating finish. I generally dip a wad of 0000 steel wool into Waterlox, then rub the piece and wipe it dry with an old T-shirt.

There are other finish options. In my opinion, the one drawback to salad-bowl finish is the gloss finish, but you can soften this with steel wool. You might also try "Good Stuff" made by Bally Block and Michigan Maple Block Co. I found this gel urethane at my local lumberyard as well as at Grizzly Imports. I really like the feel of the finished wood after using this product.

If you are concerned about liquid penetrating the bowl section, consider purchasing the glass-bowl sections of the goblet from turning supply companies. Then, you can focus your attention on turning stems.

After applying finish and buffing, epoxy the two parts with cyanoacrylate (CA) glue or 5-minute epoxy.

A previous member of the AAW Board of Directors, **Robert Rosand** is an instructor and frequent contributor to American Woodturner. Visit Robert at www.rrosand.com.

Use a spindle gouge to eliminate waste wood between the foot and your chuck. After doing this, you can undercut the foot to create a pleasing, stable base.

To sand the base of the foot, chuck a small sanding disc into your 4-jaw chuck.

Door Knob Upgrade

This handsome handmade touch sets your entryway apart

Woodturning provides a never-ending opportunity to make emotional connections with our daily lives. I personally enjoy the challenge of making things that get used around our home, and turned wood doorknobs fit this description to a tee.

In addition to adding beauty to interior doors, a well-designed doorknob highlights the natural beauty of wood and feels warm to the touch.

Get started

Finding the right hardware is the key to this project. You'll need hardware that allows you to easily attach the wood knob to a functioning door latch. I examined several interior doorknob sets and chose a model on line with a porcelain knob.

Remove the retaining ring that holds the knob to the back plate, and set the back plate and retaining ring aside. Break the knob and salvage the spindle socket shown *at right*.

At the lathe you'll need a 3/4" to 1-1/4" spindle roughing gouge, 3/8" spindle gouge, parting tool, 3/4" or 1/2" skew chisel, and a 4-jaw chuck.

For turning stock you'll need a 2-1/2×2-1/2×5" stable and dry turning square.

Turn the knob

Mount the turning square between centers. With a spindle roughing gouge, turn the square to a 2-3/8"-diameter cylinder. Then use a parting tool to turn a tenon to fit

the jaws of your 4-jaw chuck on one end *(Photo 1)*. Grip the tenon with the 4-jaw chuck, and mount a drill chuck in the tailstock quill. Install a 1/4" drill bit in the chuck. With the lathe running, advance the quill and drill a 1"-deep hole in the end of the cylinder *(Photo 2)*.

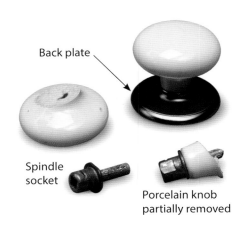

Back plate

Spindle socket

Porcelain knob partially removed

Remove the porcelain knob from the back plate, break the knob with a hammer, and salvage the spindle socket.

Replace the drill chuck with a cone live center, and support the end of the cylinder by inserting the cone center into the 1/4" hole. Next turn a 3/4"-diameter tenon 1/8" long on the end of the cylinder *(Photo 3)*. Check the fit of this tenon into the knob back plate *(Photo 4)*. Now shape the knob using a spindle gouge *(Photo 5)* and skew chisel. The finished knob should be about 1-3/4" long and 2-1/4" in diameter. Install the back plate to check the size and fit *(Photo 6)*.

Look at existing doorknobs and the knob gallery for design ideas. Add interest with carving or chatter work or by incorporating metal accents.

Sand the knob to 220 grit, and use the skew chisel (toe pointed down) to part it from the block *(Photo 7)*.

Finished photos: Paige DeWess How-to photos: Alan Lacer

AW 23:3, p48

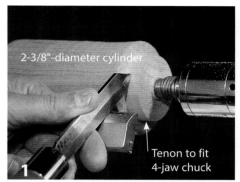

1 With the turning square rough-turned to a 2-3/8"-diameter cylinder, use a parting tool to form a tenon on the end.

2-3/8"-diameter cylinder

Tenon to fit 4-jaw chuck

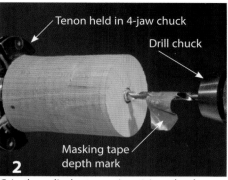

2 Grip the cylinder tenon in a 4-jaw chuck, install a drill chuck in the tailstock, and drill a 1/4" hole 1" deep.

Tenon held in 4-jaw chuck

Drill chuck

Masking tape depth mark

3 Support the cylinder with a cone center, measure the hole in the back plate with calipers, and turn a 1/8"-long tenon.

1/8" long tenon

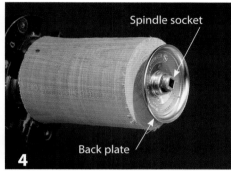

4 Dry-fit the spindle socket into the 1/4" hole in the cylinder, and check the fit of the 1/8" tenon into the back plate.

Spindle socket

Back plate

5 Support the workpiece with the tailstock cone center, and use a spindle gouge to shape the knob profile.

6 Before parting off the turning stock, check the fit of the back plate with the 1-3/4"-long, 2-1/4"-diameter knob.

Dry-fit back plate

7 With the knob finish-sanded, use a skew chisel to reduce the tenon.

Apply a finish

Because doorknobs are constantly being handled, they need special finishing considerations. A coat of oil really brings out the wood grain. Natural skin oil will renew the finish during use.

Burnishing is another option. To do this, sand the knob to 400 grit, then rub it with your hand. The natural oil and mild abrasiveness of your hand will start the finishing process. Over time the knob will develop a patina.

Mount the knob

Mount the finished knob onto the spindle socket with a slow-curing epoxy. After the epoxy cures, reconnect the socket to the back plate with the retaining ring. Follow the manufacturer's directions to install the hardware in the door.

Tim Heil *(tim@heiltruckbrokerage.com) is a member of the Minnesota Woodturners Association. He lives in Gem Lake, MN.*

Index

American Woodturner journal is the leading publication on the art and craft of woodturning in the world. A wellspring of practical information, inspiration, and resources, the *American Woodturner* is published six times each year by the AAW and is one of the premier benefits of membership. To learn more, visit www.woodturner.org.

The American Association of Woodturners (AAW) is a nonprofit organization head-quartered in Saint Paul, Minnesota, dedicated to advancing the art and craft of woodturning worldwide. The AAW provides opportunities for education, information, and organization to those interested in turning wood and is focused on establishing lathe-turned work as a major element in the craft world. Established in 1986, AAW has thousands of members and a network of local chapters globally, representing professionals, amateurs, gallery owners, collectors, and wood/tool suppliers. To learn more, visit www.woodturner.org.

222 Landmark Center
75 5th St. W
St. Paul, MN 55102-7704
www.woodturner.org